REPUBLIC OF
RELIGION

REPUBLIC OF
RELIGION

The Rise
and Fall *of*
Colonial
Secularism
in India

ABHINAV CHANDRACHUD

PENGUIN
VIKING
An imprint of Penguin Random House

VIKING

USA | Canada | UK | Ireland | Australia
New Zealand | India | South Africa | China | Singapore

Viking is part of the Penguin Random House group of companies
whose addresses can be found at global.penguinrandomhouse.com

Published by Penguin Random House India Pvt. Ltd
4th Floor, Capital Tower 1, MG Road,
Gurugram 122 002, Haryana, India

First published in Viking by Penguin Random House India 2020

10 9 8 7 6 5 4 3 2

ISBN 9780670092451

Typeset in Adobe Garamond Pro by Manipal Technologies Limited, Manipal
Printed at Replika Press Pvt. Ltd, India

www.penguin.co.in

To Radha
I am not me without you

Contents

Introduction

How did India aspire to become a secular country? Given our colonial past, we derive scores of our laws and institutions from England. Many provisions in our statutes like the nineteenth-century Indian Contract Act and Indian Evidence Act are based on the English common law. We have a parliamentary democracy with a Westminster model of government. Our courts routinely use catchphrases like 'rule of law' or 'natural justice' that have their roots in London. However, in more ways than one, during the period of colonial rule in India and even thereafter, England was not a 'secular' country, in the sense in which we might understand that word today. For instance, for much of the nineteenth century,[1] a person who merely denied 'the truth of Christianity in general, or of the existence of God' in England could find himself behind bars for committing 'blasphemy'. Until the mid-1850s, students at the universities of Oxford and Cambridge had to take an oath subscribing to the thirty-nine articles of the Church of England.[2] Until as late as 2015,[3] a member of the royal family could be disqualified from succeeding to the Crown upon merely marrying a Roman Catholic.

Even today, there are many things about England which make it formally look like anything but a secular state.[4] The king or queen of England must mandatorily be a Protestant Christian and is considered to be the 'Defender of the Faith' and the 'Supreme Governor of the Church of England'.[5] High-level ecclesiastical officials like the Archbishop of Canterbury are appointed by the government, and new monarchs are crowned by a senior member of the clergy. Senior bishops sit, by virtue of their office, in the House of Lords. The House of Lords consists of the 'Lords Spiritual and Temporal'—the 'Lords Spiritual' are senior members of the clergy like the Archbishops of Canterbury and York.[6]

Though scholars disagree on the meaning of secularism, broadly speaking, two factors go into making a secular state: no religion should be established by law as the official state religion and all citizens should have the freedom to practise their own religious beliefs.[7] Unlike the US, England has an established religion. If India derives so many of her laws and institutions from England, how is it that there is no established religion in India?

In the coming pages, we will see that secularism was artificially imposed by the British colonial government in India even though it did not fully exist in England. The law in England assumed only Christianity to be the one true religion, and Indian religions like Hinduism and Islam were considered to be 'heathen'. Therefore, though England had an established religion—Christianity through the Church of England—it could not declare an Indian religion, like Hinduism or Islam, as the official religion of India. It could not force Christianity on India probably due to the fact that this would have made the colony ungovernable.[8] Instead, it decided to separate religion and the state in India. Though government officials in England were entangled with the administration of churches there, colonial officials felt uncomfortable associating with 'false' Indian houses of worship like temples and mosques and therefore assigned them to the administration of Indian trustees.

British officials adopted a policy of secularism in India—in contrast to England—which will be referred to here as 'colonial secularism'. Though 'secularism' is itself a relatively new[9] word and one of imprecision,[10] broadly speaking, colonial secularism in

British India meant that the government did three things. Firstly, the colonial state would not endorse or get itself entangled in the administration of any local religions. So it disentangled itself from the management of temples—a function which was historically performed by Indian rulers—and handed temple administration over to trustees. This was despite the fact that a parallel nineteenth-century campaign to disestablish the Church of England failed in the metropole.[11] Further, before taking up office, public officials in India were made to solemnly swear or affirm their oaths, though they might have had no conscientious objection to swearing in the name of God, Vishnu or Allah. In other words, any mention of the word 'God' was removed from the oaths administered to public officials in India—an accommodation which was only available to Quakers and some others in England. Secondly, the colonial state provided heightened protection to religious minorities, often feeding into a sense of paranoia that they would be left helpless without its imperial intervention. So the personal laws of different religious groups were, in theory,[12] left alone,[13] though England did not have a separate set of 'personal' laws for its religious minorities like Catholics and Jews. Adopting the old Roman strategy of retaining the laws of conquered territories in order to make them more easily governable, colonial officials decided against adopting a uniform civil code in family law matters. Cow slaughter, though reviled by much of India's majority Hindu populace, was permitted to be carried out by Muslims during the festival of Bakr Id and Hindus who objected to it were considered 'hypersensitive'. Seats on legislative bodies were filled by voters on the basis of separate electorates. Thirdly, the government tacitly, though nervously, encouraged Christian missionaries to preach Christianity and obtain converts though a Hindu or Muslim preacher who might have tried to do the same in England would have put himself at risk for criminal prosecution.

In 1835, Thomas Babington Macaulay wrote in his infamous minute[14] that English education ought to be introduced in India because teaching Indians in languages like Arabic and Sanskrit would mean teaching them 'false history, false astronomy [and] false medicine' that kept company with a 'false religion'[15] and an 'absurd theology'.[16] Macaulay's father, Zachary, was an evangelical, who had lobbied colonial officials to open British India up to Christian missionaries.[17] Macaulay and others like him believed that English education in India would destroy Hinduism.[18] Thereafter, Charles Wood's[19] dispatch of 1854 declared that the education provided in government institutions would be 'exclusively secular',[20] even though there was no secular public education for schoolchildren in England at that time.[21] The idea behind this was that secular education would pave the way for the introduction of Christianity into India.[22]

In the middle of the nineteenth century, Austrian-born Aloys Sprenger was appointed the principal of the colonial government's madrasa in Calcutta. Sprenger thereafter wrote a book in which he condemned Islam as a false religion and banned students from attending religious ceremonies during class hours.[23] Secularism in British India was born out of a sense of revulsion towards 'heathen' Indian religions. The word for 'Hindu' during the early period of European colonialism in India was *Gentoo*, which can be equated with 'gentile' (Latin: gentilis). Christian writers often referred to the heathen as 'gentiles'.[24]

Since 1854, the colonial government's policy was that education at government institutions had to be secular,[25] though grants-in-aid could be handed out by the government to private educational institutions at which both secular and religious instruction were provided.[26] However, this changed in 1915, when the imperial legislative council enacted a law that established Banaras Hindu University. This was unprecedented because 'religious instruction and examination in [the] Hindu religion'[27] was to be provided there, despite the fact that the university, established by statute, had the Governor-General as its 'Lord Rector'[28] and Lieutenant-Governor of the United Provinces as its 'Visitor'.[29] This was followed by the establishment of Aligarh Muslim University in 1920 at which Muslim theology was to be taught.[30]

There is some evidence to suggest that the government reversed its secular education policy because it believed that students who were given religious instruction would be more loyal to the government and less seditious.[31] When the bill to establish Banaras Hindu University was introduced into the Imperial Legislative Council,[32] many legislators made speeches in which they said exactly that.[33] For instance, Madan Mohan Malaviya said that 'instruction in the truths of religion . . . whether it be imparted to the students of the Benares Hindu University or of the Aligarh Moslem University, will tend to produce men who . . . will be true to their God, their King and their country'.[34] Another member of the council opined that 'one of the cardinal principles of the Hindu religion is absolute obedience and respect to the Sovereign who is regarded as a part of Divinity'.[35] On the other hand, a few of the council's members accused the government of creating sectarian institutions where Hindu and Muslim students would not mingle with one another and which would deepen the religious schism in the country.[36] So when it came to educational policy, secularism was first brought in by the colonial government in order to pave the way for the introduction of Christianity in India, and later abandoned in order to make India less disloyal to Britain and possibly more deeply divided within itself.[37]

Though the British did not invent Hindu or Muslim identities,[38] they helped sharpen the divide between hazy communal categories. While conducting the census in India, for instance, colonial officials asked participants what religion they belonged to. Often, the answer to this question was not so straightforward. Hinduism, in particular, was 'a loosely integrated collection of sects'.[39] A Hindu may have viewed himself as belonging more to a religious sect or a caste.

So how would the government identify whether a person was a Hindu?[40] In 1881, a census official in Punjab remarked that whenever an Indian was unable to identify his religion, or said he belonged to a religion that was not recognized, he was classified as a Hindu.[41] In the census in Gujarat in 1911, some 2,00,000 people described themselves as 'Mohammedan Hindus'.[42] Molesalam Girasia Rajputs had two names, a Hindu one and a Muslim one.[43] In identifying India's populace as being Hindu, Muslim, Christian or Parsi, etc., colonial officials made Indians look at themselves through the lens of these mutually separate religious categories.[44] This was despite the fact that the census in Britain almost never contained any data relating to religion.[45] In colonial India, the binary categories, of 'Hindu' and 'Muslim' were reinforced through tools like the census, through which distinct and mutually exclusive religious identities were reiterated. In pre-colonial times, some Hindus followed norms of Muslim law.[46] However, colonial administrators ensured that the religious 'personal laws' of Muslims would only apply to Muslims and of Hindus only to Hindus.[47] Once religious identities were reduced to watertight binaries in India, the British justified their rule by promising that they would protect religious minorities through their secular policy of non-interference.

Though correlation is not causation, and though inter-religious conflict occurred even in pre-colonial India,[48] it is hard to ignore that there was a marked increase in sectarian riots with the advent of the British in India.[49] Between 1800 and 1850, there was one major Hindu–Muslim riot every five years. From 1870 to 1920, one such riot occurred every two years. However, in only a ten-year period thereafter, between 1920 and 1930, about fifteen Hindu–Muslim riots took place every year.[50] When the Arya Samaj started a cow protection movement in north India in the late nineteenth century, one colonial official found a 'measure of safety' in the fact that this would throw Muslims 'into the arms of the British Government'.[51] In 1887, the viceroy,[52] Lord Dufferin, denied that the British were consciously pursuing a divide and rule regime in India, but remarked: '[t]he diversity of races in India, and the presence of a powerful Mohamedan community, are undoubtedly circumstances favourable to the maintenance of our rule'.[53]

In the guise of protecting religious minorities in British India, the colonial government sometimes appeared to use secularism as a device to pursue a policy of divide and rule.[54] Nothing illustrates this better than the system of separate electorates. When elections took place to the House of Commons in England, voters were not segregated on the basis of their religious beliefs. However, from 1909 onwards, when elections were introduced to legislative bodies in India, voters were divided on the basis of their religion—Hindu voters would only vote for Hindus, Muslim voters only for Muslims, and so on. Further, Muslims were given a weightage of seats in legislative bodies which far exceeded their numbers in the population. For instance, in 1919, Muslims constituted only 14.3 per cent of the population of the United Provinces, but they received a share of 26 per cent of the seats in the provincial legislative council. None of this was prevalent in England, on the other hand, where religious minorities like Catholics and Jews were not given separate electorates.

This system in British India encouraged radical electoral candidates to contest elections. For instance, candidates fielded by the Muslim League could demand the creation of Pakistan knowing that their electoral success depended only on the votes of the Muslim electorate, and that they did not have to care about Hindu voters. Even a scholar who disagrees that the British consciously pursued a policy of divide and rule in India argues that the colonial government's policies hugely contributed to Muslim separatism in India.[55]

In other words, colonial secularism in British India was imperial hypocrisy, an example of colonial difference, an instance of how Britain did one thing at home and another in the colonies, a device used to justify and sustain Britain's hold over India. In fact, the colonial government's decision to secularize laws and institutions and offer English education to Indians was, at some level, designed to pave the way for the spread of Christianity in India, by reducing the dependence of Indians on their own indigenous religious customs and institutions.[56]

Therefore, given its dubious origins, the disintegration of the secular state in India began much before the rise of the Hindu right, the Bharatiya Janata Party (BJP) and the Rashtriya Swayamsevak Sangh (RSS). When Indian leaders came to power, both before and after Independence, they rejected the enforced notion of colonial secularism—a secularism which was born out of a Christian evangelical sense of revulsion towards Indian religions. Instead, they adopted a version of secularism which is described here as 'soft secularism'. God was introduced into the Constitution through the oaths that public officials were required to take prior to assuming office. Governments began entangling themselves in the administration of Hindu temples with a view to preventing corruption.[57] Abandoning Queen Victoria's proclamation which, since 1858, had asked the government to stay aloof from religion and refrain from interfering with religious beliefs, Indian leaders started overtly reforming their own religious laws. The statute which established Banaras Hindu University in 1915, reversing the colonial government's 1854 policy of secularism in education, originated as a private member bill drawn up by Indian legislators and then sponsored by the government for its own reasons.[58] The 1937 Muslim Personal Law (Shariat) Application Act, which made the Shariat applicable to all Muslims in some matters, was introduced into the central legislature by a member of the All-India Muslim League. As part of the colonial policy of religious non-intervention,[59] British Indian courts had issued injunctions restraining members of the lower castes from entering Hindu temples, awarded damages when they had done so, and held the entry of lower castes into Hindu temples to be a criminal offence under Section 295 of the Indian Penal Code.[60] However, from 1938 onwards, Indian legislators in the provinces reformed Hinduism by removing social disabilities faced by 'untouchables',[61] a process which was continued with the enactment of the Constitution in independent India, by which untouchability was abolished, public places were thrown open to all, and the government was permitted to enact temple-entry laws.[62] The Hindu Code reformed Hinduism even further, especially by allowing inter-caste marriages and inter-caste adoptions for the first time.[63] Unlike the wall of separation between church and state in the US, soft secularism in India involves the reform of religion through legislative and judicial interference.[64]

At the same time, laws were enacted in independent India to make leaving Hinduism more difficult and to preserve its sacred symbols. In 1950, India's president, a Congress leader, issued an order which deprived Scheduled Castes of some benefits if they left Hinduism and converted to other religions. Between 1955 and 1956, India's Parliament, under Prime Minister Nehru, enacted the Hindu Code which contained many provisions that disincentivized Hindu conversion to other faiths. Against the better instincts of secular leaders like Nehru and Gandhi, provincial Congress governments started enacting laws banning the slaughter of cows, regardless of how useful cows actually might have been to India's agrarian economy. Many of these laws were upheld by the Supreme Court on the grounds that it is only optional for Muslims to slaughter cows during Bakr Id. Though India's Constitution gives everyone, not just citizens, the right to 'propagate' religion, state governments enacted anti-conversion laws, making it hard for Christian missionaries to proselytize and convert, and those laws were upheld by the Supreme Court as well. In 2011, the Gujarat High Court held that the performance of a Hindu ceremony known as 'bhoomi pujan' to mark the laying of the foundation stone for the court's new building, at which Brahmin priests recited Sanskrit slokas, did not conflict with India's secular Constitution.[65]

Many nationalist leaders considered separate electorates to be almost single-handedly responsible for the eventual partition of India. However, in the colonial period, the Congress had wanted to replace separate electorates and weightage with a system under which a certain number of seats would be reserved on legislative bodies for religious minorities, commensurate with their share of the population. Reservation of seats in a joint electorate and without weightage would not be evil, they argued, because candidates contesting reserved seats would have to satisfy all voters, regardless of their religion, in order to get elected.

However, when India became independent, not merely did the Constituent Assembly abolish separate electorates but, in a mysterious meeting, one of its subcommittees also did away with reservations for religious minorities, reversing decades-old Congress policy. This was done because it was thought that reservations would encourage separatist tendencies—but this does not then explain why reservations were retained for members of the Scheduled Castes and Scheduled Tribes. Consequently, religious minorities like Muslims have had a share of seats in Parliament which falls substantially short of their numbers in the population.

In the chapters that follow, this book makes the argument that the secular structure of the colonial state was imposed by a colonial power on a conquered people. It was an unnatural foreign imposition, perhaps one which was bound, in some measure, to come apart once colonialism ended.[66] Importantly, colonial secularism in India did not end with the rise of the Hindu right—its decline pre-dated the ascendance of the BJP and RSS. The insertion of God into constitutional oaths, government entanglement in temple administration, the ban on cow slaughter, legislative reform of Hinduism, the abolition of reservations for religious minorities on legislatures, even a statute that banned inter-faith conversions in the Central Provinces and Berar—all this happened in the early years of the republic with Congress governments at the helm. Though the Constitution of independent India sought to entrench much of the colonial status quo (e.g., the laws governing speech and expression[67]), it sought to break away from the traditions of the colonial secular past.

Much literature has been written on defining the meaning of a secular state and whether India can be considered secular.[68] I am not directly, here, concerned with that question. It could be argued that a state which administers temples, bans the slaughter of cows, reforms Hinduism, and makes conversion to Christianity harder is, in some accommodative sense, despite all of this, still secular.[69] This is especially so when one compares India with its neighbours like Pakistan, which prescribes the death penalty for blasphemy[70] and whose Constitution requires the President to solemnly swear that he is a Muslim and that he believes 'in the Unity and Oneness of Almighty Allah', etc.[71] Nor is it sought to be argued here that the secularism espoused by India's Constitution is normatively wrong— the idea that people of all faiths must peacefully coexist is central to human existence itself. The destruction of the Babri Masjid in 1992[72] and cow vigilantism[73] in more recent memory constitute a shameful blot on the secular fabric of the republic.

However, this book essentially makes three claims. Firstly, the British state in India introduced a version of secularism that did not exist in the metropole. This book investigates the origins of colonial secularism in India and its roots in the notion of colonial difference. Secondly, the secularism which was pursued by the colonial state[74] in British India was softened once India became independent. The transfer of power from British to Indian hands and the enactment of the Constitution represented a shift from colonial secularism to soft secularism. The older generation of scholars believed in a 'secularization thesis',[75] that with time, India would become more, not less, secular, and remake itself in the image of Western countries.[76] Instead, in a sense, we are less secular today than we were back then. Thirdly, the fall of colonial secularism pre-dated the rise of India's Hindu right.

Chapter Overview

In Chapter 1, we will see that cow slaughter was permitted in British India despite a provision in the Indian Penal Code that prohibited the destruction of sacred 'objects', thanks to a judgment of the Allahabad High Court delivered in 1887 which held that cows are not inanimate objects. Thereafter, though cow slaughter was a constant source of communal conflict in the colonial period (giving rise to especially large-scale rioting in 1893), Muslims were permitted to slaughter cows during the festival of Bakr Id so long as this was done discreetly and without much fanfare. Justice Sen of the Allahabad High Court referred to Hindus who objected to cow slaughter as 'hypersensitive'.

Leaders like Gandhi and Nehru were against an outright legislative ban on cow slaughter. In 1938, Nehru even assured Jinnah that cow slaughter would not be barred in independent India. Later, Nehru threatened to resign as Prime Minister if a nation-wide ban on cow slaughter were to be enacted.

However, despite Nehru and Gandhi, after Indian Independence, colonial secularism was rejected by the framers of the Constitution when Article 48 was enacted as a directive principle of state policy—a provision which calls upon the state to take steps to prohibit the slaughter of cows, calves, milch and draught cattle. Congress governments in several states enacted laws prohibiting cow slaughter. In 1958, the Supreme Court permitted a ban on the slaughter of all cows, calves and of all 'useful' bulls, bullocks and buffaloes. It did so by holding that cow slaughter is not obligatory in Islam, though the free exercise of religion is often not about what is mandatory. Further, in 2005, the Supreme Court essentially held that all bulls and bullocks were 'useful' because they produce dung, which can be used in biogas. A complete ban on the slaughter of all cattle is therefore now permissible in India.

In Chapter 2, we will see how the colonial government nervously encouraged the activities of Christian missionaries in British India. Though merely denying the truth of Christianity was a crime in England for much of the nineteenth century, denying the truth of Hinduism or Islam was never punishable under the Indian Penal Code absent a deliberate intent to wound religious feelings. This was designed to encourage proselytism by Christian missionaries in British India. A law enacted in 1850 ensured that a person who converted to Christianity (or, for that matter, any other religion) in India would not lose his right to inherit family property. Thereafter, the Constitution of independent India gave everyone, including Christian missionaries, the right to 'propagate' their religion. However, despite what the Constitution said, and despite the generally liberal and benevolent attitude of Prime Minister Nehru towards Christian missionaries, Indian state governments started enacting statutes that made it difficult for Hindus to convert to Christianity. These statutes were broad enough to include not merely conversions that were obtained by force or fraud, but even possibly voluntary conversions. Laws of this nature were then upheld by the Supreme Court on the questionable principle that the right to 'propagate' one's religion, conferred by the Constitution, did not include the right to convert someone to another religion. Similarly, an order passed by the President of India in 1950 made members of the Scheduled Castes lose some of their constitutional benefits if they converted to other religions. The Hindu Code disincentivized Hindu conversion to other religions. Therefore, though the Constitution of independent India gives everyone the right to profess, practise and 'propagate' religion in theory, in practice, there has been a change in the nature of the secular state in India from colonial times to present day. Colonial secularism, marked by the British government's tacit encouragement of Christian missionaries in India, has been replaced by soft secularism in independent India, designed to keep Hindus within the fold.

In Chapter 3, we will see how in 1909, Viceroy Minto's regime introduced separate electorates for Muslims in India, though no such practice existed in England, in order to prevent Muslims from joining the Congress. Under this system, voters were segregated on the basis of their religion in elections to legislative councils. The result was that a Hindu could not vote for Jinnah even if he wanted to, since Jinnah was a Muslim. Muslims were also given a weightage of seats far in excess of their proportion of the population. Thereafter, though the colonial government recognized that separate electorates were harmful to India because they created a 'divided allegiance' in the population, the system of separate electorates was retained and even extended to other communities by the colonial government. It was therefore no surprise that the Constituent Assembly of independent India abolished separate electorates.

However, in this chapter we will also see that in a mysterious meeting held in May 1949, the Advisory Committee of the

Constituent Assembly also resolved to abolish reservations for Muslims in legislative bodies in India, thereby reversing the decades-old promise of the Congress to abolish separate electorates but retain reservations. Consequently, in independent India, Muslims have generally had a share of seats in Parliament which falls substantially below their numbers in the population. In short, colonial secularism in the form of separate electorates was possibly a tool used by the British to divide and rule India. The fall of colonial secularism, marked by the abolition not merely of separate electorates but of reservations for religious minorities in legislative bodies, began much before the rise of India's Hindu right.

Chapter 4 examines how the East India Company initially took over the administration of Hindu temples once it came to power just as indigenous rulers had done in pre-colonial India. However, under pressure from Christian missionaries who objected to government entanglement in 'heathen' and 'false' religions like Hinduism and Islam, the government distanced itself, between 1833 and 1863, from the management of religious institutions in India, handing them over to Indian trustees instead. When Indian legislators came to power in the twentieth century, they abandoned this form of colonial secularism by enacting the Madras Hindu Religious Endowments Act, 1926, under which the government could heavily regulate and administer Hindu temples. While the Constitution of independent India was being debated, the 'establishment clause' in Ambedkar's draft was mysteriously deleted, possibly to protect the Madras law. Consequently, over the years, the Supreme Court of India has permitted governments to vastly interfere with the administration of Hindu temples and other religious institutions, especially by holding that the management of temples is a secular function, unessential to Hinduism. Further, the Constitution itself allows the government to interfere with and reform religious practices.

Chapter 5 makes the following arguments. Firstly, the British had a uniform civil code for its citizens back home, but a regime of separate 'personal laws' for different religious communities in

India. Secondly, in theoretically retaining personal laws in British India, the colonial government was following a policy pursued by the Roman Empire, of retaining the religious laws and institutions of conquered territories in order to minimize opposition to foreign rule. It is interesting that the government in India today, in failing to enact a uniform civil code even now, is still informally perpetuating this policy, though Article 44 of the Constitution, in calling for a uniform civil code, has formally abandoned it. Thirdly, the uniform civil code debate has, in reality, little to do with religion and more to do with the family. In British India, the colonial government repeatedly legislated on religious subjects in the public sphere, replacing the Hindu and Muslim law of contract, evidence and crime with secular codes in the nineteenth century. However, this hardly generated any opposition among orthodox religious conservatives in India. On the other hand, when the colonial government tried to reform Hindu law by abolishing sati, permitting Hindu widows to remarry, or raising the age of consent for sexual intercourse, it was met with a volley of opposition among conservative Hindus who argued that the government should not interfere in religious matters. This contradiction suggests that the opposition to the uniform civil code has less to do with religion and more to do with the fact that it concerns the private (as opposed to public) sphere. Fourthly, when Indian legislators came to power in colonial India, they rejected colonial secularism by reforming their own personal laws, a process which was continued with the enactment of the Hindu Code in independent India. Further, Article 44 of the Constitution formally repudiated colonial secularism by abandoning the policy of religious non-interference which had been in place since the time of Warren Hastings in 1772. Fifthly, in seeking to reform regressive religious practices, colonial legislators started investigating whether those practices were essential to the religion in question or not—a test which has now been adopted by the Supreme Court of independent India. In supporting laws that reformed Hinduism—laws banning sati, permitting Hindu widow remarriage, or raising the age of consent for sexual intercourse—colonial legislators argued that sati, the bar on Hindu widow remarriage and sexual intercourse with an immature girl were not considered essential to Hinduism. This was quite possibly the origin of the 'essential to religion' test which is now applied by the Supreme Court.

Chapter 6 examines how the colonial state removed God from the public sphere by requiring public officials in British India to swear their oaths of office without any mention of the word 'God' in them. The Constituent Assembly rejected this form of colonial secularism by inserting the word 'God' into the Constitution—public officials are now given the option of swearing their oaths of office either in the name of God or on the basis of a solemn affirmation. Disavowing colonial secularism, the framers of India's Constitution believed that secularism did not imply a Godless state. Further, in the colonial period, it was presumed that Hindu and Muslim witnesses had a conscientious objection to swearing religious oaths prior to giving their testimony. Hindu and Muslim witnesses were therefore forced to swear oaths like Quakers in England. This is no longer true in independent India. However, in this chapter we will also see that both in colonial India and in independent India, there are no religious tests for holding public office or deposing as a witness.

1

Holy Cow

This chapter examines how independent India became less secular than British India by permitting laws that banned cow slaughter.

In British India, Muslims were allowed to sacrifice cows during the festival of Bakr Id[1] (the word *bakr* is Arabic for cow[2]), though Hindus worshipped cows. This changed shortly after India became independent, when laws banning cow slaughter were enacted in many states. This was despite the fact that leaders like Gandhi and Nehru strongly opposed such legislation. Though Gandhi considered it his duty, as a Hindu, to protect cows, he believed that he had to persuade Muslims to voluntarily give up beef. Nehru did not think much of the cow protection movement and once even promised Jinnah that his government would not ban the slaughter of cows. However, after Independence, cow protectionists succeeded in making the ban on cow slaughter a directive principle of state policy by arguing that there were advantages, to India's predominantly agricultural economy, in keeping cows, bulls and bullocks alive so that they may yield milk, work as draught animals, breed and produce manure. These arguments were then used by the Supreme Court to uphold the validity of cow protection laws.

Though the economic arguments in favour of cow protection are sometimes tenuous, and though there are obvious religious motivations in favour of the ban on cow slaughter, soft secularism in independent India means that cow protectionists have to mask their religious arguments with economic ones. Indian Muslims can now be prevented from sacrificing cows on the grounds that Islam does not make cow slaughter mandatory, though matters of faith are often not about what is mandatory.

Cow Slaughter in British India

Hindus regard cows to be sacred and consider cow slaughter to be a sin. This principle is of relatively recent vintage in Hinduism and dates not to the Rig Veda (around 1500 BC[3]) but to the Gupta dynasty (around 319 AD[4]).[5] Muslims, by contrast, used to slaughter cows during the festival of Bakr Id.[6] In the colonial period, this was a constant cause of communal tensions. Clashes and rioting took place between Hindus and Muslims because of the slaughter of cows by Muslims.[7] Broadly speaking, there was no blanket prohibition in British India against the slaughter of cows.[8] The East India Company temporarily included a ban on cow slaughter in their treaties with some Indian rulers.[9] Cow slaughter may have been regulated by some municipal governments since the 1920s or earlier.[10] Colonial-era laws placed restrictions on how and where cows could be slaughtered. For instance, a law in 1662 in Bombay said that there could be 'no cow killing in Hindu quarters'.[11] During the colonial period, Muslims were told by the law that they could slaughter cows provided that they did so in a walled enclosure, away from the gaze of Hindus, and discreetly, without much fanfare.[12] Hindus who objected to such sacrifices were considered to be 'hypersensitive'.

Enacted in 1860, Section 295 of the Indian Penal Code made it a crime for any person to destroy 'any object held sacred by any class of persons' or defile 'any place of worship', knowing that this would be considered an insult to their religion.[13] This provision was originally intended to prohibit cow slaughter in a sacred place. In an explanatory note, the framers of the Indian Penal Code wrote that they were moved to draft this provision, among other reasons, because the 'slaughter of a cow in a sacred place at Benares in 1809 caused violent tumult, attended with considerable loss of life'.[14] Two Muslims were then convicted by a magistrate in the United Provinces under Section 295 for slaughtering cows. Setting aside the conviction, however, the Allahabad High Court, in a hugely controversial decision in 1887, held that a cow—a living creature—could not be considered an inanimate object and Section 295 only spoke of the destruction of 'objects'.[15] The judgment of the Allahabad High Court heightened communal tensions between Hindus and Muslims in north India. Indian Muslims thereafter began to carry out cow slaughter in greater numbers, a higher proportion of cows were slaughtered in the 1890s, and prominent Hindus like the Maharaja of Darbhanga[16] lent their support to the cause of cow protection.[17]

Around 1882, the Calcutta High Court allowed Muslims to slaughter cows because the 'animals were sacrificed within a walled enclosure, no one could see the process from the outside' and the sacrifices did not result in 'noisy or riotous demonstration[s]' that could disturb the neighbours. Hindus, it was held, could not object to cow slaughter because theirs was 'simply and solely a matter of religious feeling'.[18] Thereafter, several cases were decided by the high courts of British India, especially the Allahabad High Court, in which Muslims were permitted to slaughter cows.

In another case decided in 1908, a district magistrate banned the slaughter of cows by Muslims in a village called Behta Gushain in north India. The Allahabad High Court set aside the order.[19] The court began by saying that it would be 'in the highest degree desirable' for 'members of the different religious persuasions' in India to 'show respect for the feelings and sentiments' of other religions while observing their religious ceremonies.[20] However, it held that cow slaughter by Muslims was not illegal and that it was the 'legal right of every person to make such use of his own property as he may think fit', even if, in doing so, he hurts the 'susceptibilities of others'.[21] Muslims were allowed to slaughter cows in the village, so long as they did not create a nuisance.[22]

In 1928, the Allahabad High Court allowed a Muslim to sacrifice a cow in his 'residential house' and 'in any place which is not exposed to the public view'.[23] Thereafter, in 1930, an Indian judge of that court, Justice Sen, allowed Muslims to slaughter cows over the protests of Hindus. He said that if the sacrifice took place 'within walled enclosures, so that no one could see the process from outside', or if it took place quietly, with decency, and 'unattended with noisy or riotous demonstration', then no Hindu could object. He added that if such sacrifices offended 'the Hindus individually or collectively, the act cannot be branded as a public nuisance for the law makes no allowance for the susceptibilities of the hypersensitive'.[24]

On the other hand, a Muslim who deliberately tried to slaughter cows in a manner that would be visible to Hindus was considered to have violated the law.[25] For instance, a Muslim who slaughtered a cow in front of a Kali temple was put through a trial and convicted.[26]

However, cows were not only slaughtered or consumed by Muslims in British India. As Gandhi repeatedly wrote, there were slaughter-houses in 'all the big cities of India' where '[t]housands of cows and bullocks' were slaughtered, for supplying beef to the British.[27] 'We say nothing to the English in India for whose sake hundreds of cows are slaughtered daily', he wrote. 'Our rajas do not hesitate to provide beef for their English guests', he said. 'Our protection of the cow, therefore, extends to rescuing her from Mussulman hands.'[28] Nehru too believed that cows were frequently slaughtered in British India in order to supply beef to the British army.[29] Even Hindus were partially responsible for cow slaughter in British India. As Gandhi wrote, 'The cows find their neck under the butcher's knife because Hindus sell them.'[30] 'To blame the butcher', he wrote, 'is like blaming the doctor for your fever.'[31] He also noted that cows were exported to Australia, often from Gujarat and Kathiawar, for producing beef that was 'worth crores of rupees'.

'Even our Muslim brethren', he wrote, 'do not carry out so much slaughter on Bakr Id day'. 'We [i.e. Hindus] thus commit this sin directly', he added.[32] Livestock census results for 1935 showed that while 80 per cent of cows in India died naturally, 20 per cent were slaughtered.[33]

It was not merely the British and Muslims who consumed beef. As Ambedkar wrote, census results showed that 'the meat of the dead cow' was the '[c]hief item of food consumed by communities which are generally classified as untouchable communities'.[34] Though members of 'lower' castes did not slaughter cows, Gandhi wrote of how they ate carrion 'with the greatest relish'.[35] Even upper-caste Hindus sometimes consumed beef. Gandhi spoke, on more than one occasion, of his 'Vaishnava friend who had beef tea saying he had to take it because his doctor said that he would not survive without it'.[36]

Gandhi frequently argued that cows should not be slaughtered in British India. In supporting this argument he appealed both to religion and to economics. Thus, on the one hand, he wrote that the cow was 'the protector of India' because India was an 'agricultural country . . . dependent on the cow' and the cow was 'a most useful animal in hundreds of ways'[37]—an argument founded in economics and the importance of the cow to India's agricultural economy.[38] On the other hand, he would say: 'If someone were to ask me what the most important outward manifestation of Hinduism was, I would suggest that it was the idea of cow protection'[39]—a plainly religious argument. The 'worship of the cow', thought Gandhi, was Hinduism's 'unique contribution to the evolution of humanitarianism'.[40] 'Cow-preservation is an article of faith in Hinduism', he wrote.[41] He even encouraged his followers to give up 'buffalo milk and ghee'.[42] 'Cow's butter (and ghee)', he said, 'has a naturally yellowish colour which indicates its superiority to buffalo's butter (and ghee) in carotene'. India's 'prejudice in favour of buffalo's milk and ghee', he felt, was making the cow extinct.[43] Gandhi was of the view that cow worship was 'largely confined to Gujarat, Marwar, the United Provinces and Bihar'.[44]

However, Gandhi believed that Muslims should not be forced to give up cow slaughter, that they should do so of their own volition. He urged his followers to try to peacefully convince Muslims to avoid slaughtering cows. '[I]t would redound to the credit of Hinduism', he wrote, 'if stopping of cow-slaughter was brought about not by force, but as [a] deliberate voluntary act of self-denial on the part of Mussalmans and others.'[45] He praised Muslim leaders like Maulana Abdul Bari who urged their followers to avoid cow slaughter, and the Ali brothers who stopped beef-eating in their households.[46] He wrote that cow slaughter was optional in Islam, that Muslims were 'not enjoined by the Quran to sacrifice a cow'.[47] He, of course, strongly argued against the use of violence in preventing Muslims from slaughtering cows. However, he also felt that legislation should not be enacted to ban cow slaughter in India. To force a Muslim, by law, to avoid cow slaughter, he believed, would 'amount . . . to converting him to Hinduism by force'.[48] Legislation against cow slaughter, he wrote, should only be enacted with the consent of Muslims, or at least the 'the intelligent majority of the subjects adversely affected by it'.[49] He wrote:

> As a Hindu, a confirmed vegetarian, and a worshipper of the cow whom I regard with the same veneration as I regard my mother . . . I maintain that Muslims should have full freedom to slaughter cows, if they wish, subject of course to hygienic restrictions and in a manner not to wound the susceptibilities of their Hindu neighbours.[50]

However, during the Second World War, there was an 'increased demand for cattle for cultivation, transport, milk and meat', which gave rise to a 'cattle shortage', causing 'considerable anxiety' within the government. Consequently, the Government of India imposed a ban on the slaughter of some useful cattle in military slaughterhouses, i.e. cattle below three years of age, male cattle between three and ten years of age likely to be used as 'working cattle', and cows between three and ten years of age capable of producing milk or bearing offspring.[51] It also asked provincial governments to enact a similar ban in civilian slaughterhouses.[52]

'Satisfied by the Back-door'

Nehru had little sympathy for the cow protection movement. In 1926, he wrote a letter to Devadas Gandhi, Mahatma Gandhi's son,[53] in which he referred, with some contempt, to the 'Cow Conference or the Cow Sabha or whatever it is called'. He said that if cow protectionists from India visited Europe, they would get 'some brighter ideas than keeping enormous *pinjrapoles* for the halt and the lame!' 'I wish however', he added, 'that some other animals— including human beings—might be treated likewise.'[54] Later, in 1938, he wrote a letter to Jinnah, and assured him that cow slaughter would not be banned in India. He told Jinnah:

> As regards cow slaughter there has been a great deal of entirely false and unfounded propaganda against the Congress suggesting that the Congress was going to stop it forcibly by legislation. The Congress does not wish to undertake any legislative action in this matter to restrict the established rights of the Muslims.[55]

Jinnah, on the other hand, told a foreign journalist that Muslims in India had 'no—and I repeat, *no*—sympathies with the Hindu' because '[w]e eat the cow, the Hindu worships it'. 'We cannot live together', he added, 'I tell you, *the Moslems are a nation*.'[56]

In July 1947, a month before Indian independence, Gandhi and other leaders started receiving scores of telegrams and letters advocating a ban on cow slaughter in India. On 19 July 1947, Gandhi made a speech in which he said that he would not convince Nehru or Patel to enact a law prohibiting cow slaughter in India. He repeated that by giving cows little to eat, making bullocks carry heavy loads, and selling cows to slaughter-houses, it was the Hindus themselves who were responsible for cow slaughter. 'No law that Jawaharlal Nehru or Sardar can enact will stop cow-slaughter', he said.[57] In another speech on 25 July 1947, Gandhi said that Rajendra Prasad had informed him that he had received 'some 50,000 postcards, between 25,000 and 30,000 letters and many thousands of telegrams demanding a ban on cow-slaughter'. However, he said, 'In India, no law can be made to ban cow-slaughter.'[58] A law banning cow slaughter, he said, would 'mean coercion against those Indians who are not Hindus'. India did not consist only of Hindus, he said, but also 'Muslims, Parsis, Christians and other religious groups'. 'I shall therefore suggest', he said, 'that the matter should not be pressed in the Constituent Assembly.' 'Pakistan may be said to belong to Muslims', he said, 'but the Indian Union belongs to all.'[59] A few days later, on 30 July 1947, Gandhi once again spoke against any move to ban cow slaughter by legislation. 'We should not assume in our pride that since power has now come into our hands, we can force others to our will through law', he said.[60]

On 7 August 1947, Rajendra Prasad wrote a letter to Nehru in which he said that he had received around 1,64,000 'postcards, letters, packets and telegrams [demanding] that cow slaughter should be stopped by legislation'. The agitation, he said, had 'reached practically all Provinces and very large numbers of people'. 'The Hindu sentiment in favour of cow protection is old, widespread and deep-seated', he wrote. 'I think that the matter does require consideration', he concluded.[61]

Nehru, however, was sceptical about the agitation which Prasad spoke of. In a letter to Prasad that same day,[62] he wrote that while nobody could 'possibly doubt the widespread Hindu sentiment in favour of cow protection', there was 'something slightly spurious about the present agitation'. He believed that Seth Ramakrishna Dalmia, a Hindu industrialist,[63] was behind the agitation. 'Dalmia's money is flowing and Dalmia is not exactly a desirable person', he wrote. Though he agreed that 'for economic reasons certain steps must be taken for stopping the slaughter of milch cows and of trying to improve the breed and condition of cattle', he felt that banning cow slaughter suddenly would stamp the 'better breeds' of Indian cattle 'out of existence'. He also wrote that the question of cow slaughter went to the very heart of whether India should be thought of 'as a composite country or as a Hindu country'. He felt that while cow slaughter could be banned if there were economic justifications for doing so, it could not be done 'purely on grounds of Hindu sentiment'. He wrote to Prasad that Gandhi, though a 'strong . . . advocate of cow protection', did not believe in legislation banning cow slaughter because he felt that India 'must not function as a Hindu State but as a composite State in which Hindus, no doubt, predominate'. He wrote that he felt 'greatly distressed' by the 'Hindu revivalist feeling in the country at the present moment', because it was 'the exact replica of the narrow Muslim communalism which we have tried to combat for so long'. 'I fear', he wrote, 'that this narrow sectarian outlook will do grave injury . . . to the high ideals for which Indian and Hindu culture has stood through the ages.' In a moment of self-doubt, Nehru also wrote that he considered himself 'a poor representative of many of our people today' on account of his views on cow slaughter, and that he 'felt honestly that it might be better for a truer representative to take my place', for that 'would do away with the unnaturalness and artificiality of the present position'.

Thereafter, in February 1948, Pandit Thakur Dass Bhargava[64] and Seth Govind Das,[65] two Hindu members of the Constituent Assembly from north India, suggested that a new article be inserted into the fundamental rights chapter of the draft constitution. The article would call on the state to 'endeavour to organize agriculture and animal husbandry on modern and scientific lines and in particular take steps to preserve, protect and improve useful breeds of cattle and ban the slaughter of the cow and other useful cattle, specially milch cattle and of child-bearing age, young stock and draught cattle'.[66] The draft was possibly inspired by the ban which had been imposed a few years previously, as we have seen, on the slaughter of useful cattle during the Second World War. The constitutional adviser to the assembly, B.N. Rau, recommended that this 'would more appropriately be included in the Part containing the Directive Principles of State Policy', instead of the fundamental rights.[67]

On 24 November 1948, Bhargava then moved an amendment in the Constituent Assembly to make a ban on cow slaughter a part of the unenforceable directive principles of state policy in the Constitution. He spoke in Hindi. Though a member of the assembly from Madras interrupted him and said that 'a large number of South Indians' were unable to follow him, and though the Vice President requested him to speak in English, he continued in Hindi. In supporting his amendment, Bhargava principally made an economic argument. 'Ours is an agricultural country', he said, 'and the cow is "Kam-Dhenu" to us—fulfiller of all our wants.' He referred, in passing, to Lord Krishna who, he said, was known affectionately as 'Makhan Chor' for serving cows devotedly. He said that even during Muslim rule in India, monarchs like Babar, Humayun, Akbar, Jahangir and Aurangzeb banned cow-slaughter, 'not because Muslims regarded it to be bad but because, from the economic point of view, it was unprofitable'. He said that 'cow-breeding' was necessary in the 'present conditions in our country' 'not for milk supply alone, but also for the purposes of draught and transport'. Anticipating an argument that would be accepted by the Supreme Court decades later, he said that even cattle that were regarded as useless were not really useless, 'because we are in great need of manure'. He pointed out that life expectancy among human beings in India was twenty-three years, many children died under one year of age, and that the 'real cause of all this is shortage of milk and deficiency in diet'. He suggested that the cow was worshipped in Hinduism because of its usefulness to the agricultural economy. Further, he said that he was not moving his amendment out of any religious persuasion. 'I do not appeal to you in the name of religion', he said. 'I ask you to consider it in the light of economic requirements of the country.'[68]

Seth Govind Das then stood up to speak and said, also in Hindi, that Bhargava's draft article did not go far enough. Bhargava's version allowed useless cattle to be slaughtered, while Das did not want any cattle, useful or otherwise, to be slaughtered. Das adopted a more overtly religious argument. He said that great importance had been given to the cow in India since the days of Lord Krishna, and that he belonged to a family that worshipped Lord Krishna as an 'Ishtadev'. However, he too argued that cow protection was 'not only a matter of religion' in India, but also 'a cultural and economic question'. He agreed that milk was necessary for preventing infant mortality.[69]

Many members of the assembly, mostly Hindus from north India, then spoke in favour of the new proposed article. Ram Sahai,[70] speaking in Hindi, supported Bhargava's amendment.[71] Shibban Lal Saksena[72] said that cow protection was a part of Hinduism 'because of its economic and other aspects' and that manure made even useless cattle useful.[73] Quoting a Sanskrit sloka, Dr Raghu Vira,[74] later the president of the Bharatiya Jana Sangh, said that the cow in his family was given more importance than the children were.[75] R.V. Dhulekar[76] quoted from the Upanishads and said that in Hindu society, a cow is 'just like our mother. In fact it is more than our mother.'[77]

Some Muslim members of the assembly stood up to oppose Bhargava's amendment while others supported it. Z.H. Lari, a member of the Muslim League who later migrated to Pakistan,[78] asked for certainty, not ambiguity, over the question of whether a cow could be slaughtered by a Muslim during Bakr Id. He said that in his province, a provision in the Criminal Procedure Code[79] was used to prohibit cow slaughter during Bakr Id, which made the law uncertain. He said that the ban on cow slaughter should be included in the fundamental rights chapter of the Constitution so that there would be no doubt that it was prohibited. He admitted that slaughtering cows was not necessary in Islam, though it was permitted.[80] However, Syed Muhammad Saadulla,[81] a Muslim Leaguer from Assam, then rose and said that the economic argument in favour of cow slaughter was a veil to mask the religious viewpoint of Hindus. '[T]hose who put [the ban on cow slaughter] on the economic front . . . do create a suspicion in the minds of many that the ingrained Hindu feeling against cow slaughter is being satisfied by the back-door', he said. He added that Muslims 'are a meat-eating people', that the 'price of mutton is so high that many poor people cannot buy it', and that 'on rare occasions', poor Muslims have to 'use the flesh of the cow'. He said that as far as he knew, 'it is only the barren cows that go to the butcher'. He also said that beef was consumed by non-Muslims—it was consumed by 'the hill people' in Assam, and there was 'only one Muslim butcher against seventy from the hill people' in the town of Shillong.[82]

Mysteriously, Ambedkar, who had written a treatise on how cow flesh was consumed by members of the 'lower' castes, and how cow slaughter was not originally considered to be prohibited in Hinduism, rose and supported the amendment with the solitary line: 'I accept the amendment of Pandit Thakur Dass Bhargava.'[83] Bhargava's motion to amend the draft Constitution was accordingly adopted, and banning cow slaughter became a part of the directive principles of state policy (eventually as Article 48 of the Constitution).[84]

Several members of the assembly, many of them Hindus from north India, even thereafter expressed a wish that the ban on cow slaughter ought to have been made absolute or a part of the fundamental rights chapter of the Constitution.[85] However, this was opposed by others. For instance, J.J.M. Nichols Roy, a Christian member of the assembly from the northeast,[86] hoped that the provision would be used to prohibit the slaughter of only 'milch cows and draught cattle, which will be of benefit to people', and not all cows. Otherwise, he said, the provision 'would be a blot' on the Constitution, as it would cause hardship to beef-eaters like the 'Hill people of Assam', Muslims and 'even the Hindu Gurkhas of Assam' who 'sacrifice buffaloes at the time of the Durga Puja'.[87] He said that if useless cattle could not be slaughtered, they would constitute 'a terrible burden on the State', as 'millions of cows' would 'float round the country without any fodder' and '[h]undreds . . . [would] die in the fields without being taken care of'.[88] Similarly, Frank Anthony, an Anglo-Indian who later sat as a member of nearly every Lok Sabha from 1950 to 1984,[89] said that 'fanatics and extremists' had succeeded in 'bringing . . . through the back-door' a provision which they could not introduce 'through the front door'.[90]

Two points are interesting about the debate in the Constituent Assembly on cow slaughter. Firstly, though cow slaughter is against the tenets of Hinduism, the movers of the provision sought to support the directive principle against cow slaughter on an economic argument—that cows were useful to India's agricultural economy. For them, mostly north Indian Hindus, secularism in independent India did not mean that Muslims could continue to slaughter cows on festivals like Bakr Id as they had done in British India. Instead, secularism meant that religious laws had to be given the veneer of economic arguments. Secondly, though leaders like Nehru and Ambedkar did not believe in a ban on cow slaughter (in fact, as we shall presently see, Nehru later staunchly opposed a central law banning cow slaughter), they nonetheless allowed Bhargava's amendment to get into the directive principles chapter of the Constitution without any opposition. This perhaps shows us that they did not take the directive principles of state policy too seriously.

'Futile, Silly, Ridiculous'

In 1949, a law was enacted in the province of Bombay which placed curbs on cow slaughter.[91] It said that a person could not slaughter any bovine animal (bulls, bullocks, cows, calves, male and female buffaloes and buffalo-calves) unless a certificate from a veterinary officer that the animal was fit for slaughter was first obtained.[92] A certificate would not be granted if the animal was (or was likely to have become) useful as a draught animal, for breeding, giving milk, bearing offspring, etc. An animal above the age of fifteen could be slaughtered 'for *bona fide* religious purposes'.[93] In short, cow slaughter was permitted in Bombay so long as the cow was not useful.[94] This was considered by Prime Minister Nehru to be a 'constructive' and model statute.[95]

In July 1951, Prime Minister Nehru made a speech at an All India Congress Committee (AICC) meeting on the draft election manifesto, where he opposed any measure to introduce a central law banning cow slaughter.[96] However, a move was afoot to enact this law. Seth Govind Das, one of the primary proponents of Article 48, prepared an amendment to the Indian Penal Code, which would make cow slaughter a nationwide criminal offence. In September 1951, Nehru wrote a letter to Das and said that the Cabinet had rejected Das's proposal to have his law referred to a parliamentary select committee. He added that many members of the Cabinet believed that Das's law 'was opposed to the letter and spirit of our Constitution'.[97] In a separate letter on the same day, Nehru also conveyed this to Pandit Thakur Dass Bhargava, the author of Article 48.[98]

Not to be outdone, in July 1952, Seth Govind Das introduced a private member bill in the Lok Sabha to ban cow slaughter in India.[99] A debate finally took place on this bill on 2 April 1955. Prime Minister Nehru vehemently opposed the bill on two grounds. Firstly, because the Attorney General of India, M.C. Setalvad, had advised the government (and even addressed the Lok Sabha on this question[100]) that a central law banning cow slaughter was beyond the competence of Parliament.[101] Secondly, he believed that the bill would not achieve its object.[102]

'I wish to make it perfectly clear at the outset', said Nehru, 'that the Government are entirely opposed to this Bill.'[103] He said that everyone hoped to preserve 'the cattle wealth of this country', whether 'for economic reasons' or 'for other substantial reasons'.[104] However, he advocated the more 'constructive' approach which was adopted in Bombay, as against a blanket ban on the slaughter of all cattle.[105] 'I cannot accept', he said, 'that animals are more important than economics and I think human beings are more important than cows.'[106] 'I am prepared to resign from [the] Prime

Ministership but I will not give in', he said.[107] He called the cow
protection agitation 'futile, silly [and] ridiculous', and said that the
government would 'stand or fall on this and not give in because of
agitation of this kind on this point'.[108] During his speech, when
N.C. Chatterjee,[109] a member of the Hindu Mahasabha and a
former judge of the Calcutta High Court,[110] interjected and asked
Nehru if he had heard that the Congress government in Uttar
Pradesh was in favour of a ban on the slaughter of cows, Nehru
said that if this was so, the Uttar Pradesh government was 'taking
a wrong step'. 'Is the hon. Member aware', asked Nehru, 'that the
Bombay Government refuses to take that step?'[111]

The Congress party issued a whip and the bill lost by a vote of
95–13.[112] Two Congressmen, Pandit Thakur Dass Bhargava and
Purushottam Das Tandon[113] ignored the whip and voted in favour
of the bill.[114] Nehru later explained to Tandon that the bill would
also have caused problems for the government in the 'North-East
Frontier Hills and the Tribal Areas', where one of the slogans that
was being raised against the government was that cow slaughter
was going to be prohibited by law. He told Tandon, however,
that he hoped that the slaughter of 'milch cows and their progeny'
would stop.[115]

'Compassion in [Their] Old Age'

Against Prime Minister Nehru's better instincts, Congress
governments in different states enacted laws banning the slaughter
of cows. In 1958, laws enacted by three states—Bihar, Uttar Pradesh
and Madhya Pradesh—were challenged before the Supreme Court
in *Mohd. Hanif Quareshi v. State of Bihar*.[116] The impugned statutes
completely banned the slaughter of cows, bulls, bullocks and calves.[117]
Additionally, the Bihar statute also banned the slaughter of buffaloes
(male, female and calves).[118] The petitioners, Muslim butchers,
argued that the ban on cow slaughter violated their rights to free
exercise of religion and to pursue the occupation of their choice.[119]

Among other advocates, the court heard the arguments of Pandit Thakur Dass Bhargava, author of Article 48 of the Constitution, in support of the ban.[120]

After holding that directive principles could not override fundamental rights,[121] the court first took up the question of whether the impugned statutes violated the petitioners' right to free exercise of religion.[122] The court referred to Charles Hamilton's translation of the *Hedaya*[123] in which Hamilton wrote that '[i]t is the duty of every free Mussulman, arrived at the age of maturity to offer a sacrifice on the Yd Kirban, or festival of the sacrifice'.[124] Hamilton wrote that the 'sacrifice established for one person is a goat; and that for seven, a cow or a camel'.[125] Reading this passage from Hamilton's translation, the court arrived at the conclusion that since Muslims could sacrifice either goats, cows or camels, it was 'optional' for Muslims to slaughter cows. It added that many Muslims do not, in fact, sacrifice cows on Bakr Id day and that many Muslim rulers in India (Babar, Humayun, Akbar, Jehangir, Ahmad Shah and Hyder Ali) prohibited cow slaughter. The court also noted that three members of the enquiry committee in Uttar Pradesh, who concurred in the recommendation to ban cow slaughter there, were Muslims. On this basis, the court held that the statutes banning cow slaughter did not violate the right to free exercise of religion.[126] In fact, the court did not take into account another passage in Hamilton's translation of the *Hedaya* in which Hamilton wrote that buffaloes could also be sacrificed by Muslims on Yd Kirban, since they are 'species of a cow'.[127] Further, the court did not rely on the affidavit of any Muslim theologian before arriving at its conclusions.[128]

The court had a more difficult time dealing with the argument that the statutes violated the rights of Muslim butchers to carry out their occupation under Article 19(1)(g) of the Constitution. In examining this argument, the court began by noting that 'Hindus in general hold the cow in great reverence and the idea of the slaughter of cows for food is repugnant to their notions'. It pointed out that 'this sentiment [had] in the past even led to communal riots', and 'after the recent partition of the country this agitation against the slaughter of cows has been further intensified'. Though the court said that constitutional questions 'cannot be decided on grounds of mere sentiment, however passionate it may be', the court would 'nevertheless . . . [take] into consideration' the reverence of Hindus towards cows 'as one of many elements' in deciding whether the law was reasonable.[129]

The court found that cattle are useful to India's agricultural economy because they provide milk, serve as draught animals, and provide manure.[130] It therefore said that so long as cattle are useful to the economy, a ban on their slaughter is justifiable. It then took into account around five factors in determining whether the ban was valid. Firstly, useless cattle were a 'wasteful drain on the nation's cattle feed', which was limited. Secondly, the presence of useless animals deteriorated the breed of cattle circulating in the country. Thirdly, banning the slaughter of cattle involved a 'serious dislocation, though not a complete stoppage' of the business of butchers. Fourthly, it deprived 'a large section of the people' of their 'staple food' and source of protein. Lastly, it noted that experiments in setting up 'gosadans' (which the court referred to as 'concentration camps') to house useless cattle had failed.[131]

The court held that a ban on the slaughter of bulls, bullocks and buffaloes (male or female) was justified only when they had ceased to be useful—capable of yielding milk, of breeding, or of working as draught animals.[132] Similarly, the court also found that a ban on the slaughter of calves (male and female, whether of cows or she-buffaloes) was justified since they would grow up to be useful animals. However, it upheld a total ban on the slaughter of all cows, whether useful or otherwise. In doing so, it noted that gowalas, or cowherds (who were mostly Hindus), found it uneconomical to maintain a cow during her dry spell (as opposed to a female buffalo), and often maimed cows in order to pass them off as useless so that a certificate could be obtained to slaughter them. In other words, even useful cows were, in practice, being slaughtered on the grounds that they were useless. To put an end to this practice, the court found that a total ban on the slaughter of all cows was justifiable.[133]

Thereafter, some states started enacting laws that made it very difficult for a person to establish that cattle had become useless. For instance, laws in Bihar and Uttar Pradesh said that cattle could not be slaughtered unless they had reached twenty to twenty-five years of age, making it virtually impossible to slaughter them. In *Abdul Hakim Quraishi* v. *State of Bihar*,[134] the court struck these provisions down, and held that once cattle reach the age of fifteen, they generally become useless. The age of usefulness was later increased by the Supreme Court to sixteen.[135]

Article 48 of the Constitution calls on the state to take steps to prohibit the slaughter of cows, calves, and 'other milch and draught cattle'. The Supreme Court had held that while a total ban on the slaughter of cows and calves (belonging to cows and she-buffaloes) was permissible, a ban on the slaughter of bulls, bullocks and buffaloes was only justifiable if the animal had ceased to be useful—to be capable of producing milk, working as a draught animal or being used for breeding. This jurisprudence was altered by the Supreme Court in 2005, in *State of Gujarat* v. *Mirzapur Moti Kureshi*.[136] Apart from barring the slaughter of cows and calves, the government of Gujarat had enacted a total ban on the slaughter of bulls and bullocks regardless of whether these animals were useful or not. This law was challenged.

The Supreme Court held that the directive principles of state policy could be taken into account while determining whether a law was reasonable or not.[137] The court held that bulls, bullocks (and presumably buffaloes[138]) could not, on ceasing to be capable of producing milk or working as draught animals, be pulled out of the category of 'milch and draught cattle' under Article 48 of the Constitution.[139] It held that cattle that have 'served human beings' are entitled to 'compassion in [their] old age when [they have] ceased to be milch or draught' cattle and have become 'useless'.[140] Even otherwise, the court found that these animals do not cease to be 'useful' after the age of 16, since they yield urine and dung which are valuable for biogas and manure.[141]

The court noted that the 'cow and her progeny' (i.e. cows, bulls, bullocks and calves) were considered by the impugned statute to be 'the backbone of Indian agriculture . . . and its economic system'.[142] The government filed affidavits in which it pointed out that due to advances in science, the longevity of cattle in the state of Gujarat had increased;[143] that tractors were not affordable for small farmers, which is why bullocks were used for farming;[144] that the dung or urine of a bull or bullock could fetch Rs 20,000 a year to a farmer (though the affidavit did not say what it cost to maintain a bull or bullock every year).[145] Taking note of these and other arguments, the court upheld the ban on the slaughter of bulls and bullocks. The court rejected the factors that had been taken into account by it in 1958 to invalidate the ban on the slaughter of useless bulls and bullocks.[146]

In 2016, the Bombay High Court upheld similar provisions in a Maharashtra law[147] which imposed a ban on the slaughter of cows, bulls and bullocks.[148] However, the Maharashtra law went beyond the Gujarat law in three respects. Firstly, it prohibited the transportation of a cow outside Maharashtra for the purpose of slaughter.[149] Secondly, it barred the possession of beef, whether the cow was slaughtered within the state or outside.[150] Thirdly, the burden of proof in such cases was on the accused.[151] In other words, contrary to the usual rule of evidence in criminal cases where a person is presumed innocent until proven guilty, the Maharashtra law presumed the guilt of the accused until the accused established his innocence. The court held that the impugned statute could not prohibit the transfer of cattle outside the state for slaughter, nor could it prohibit the possession of beef within the state that was obtained from cattle slaughtered outside the state as this violated a person's right to privacy.[152] The provision which placed the burden of proof on the accused was also struck down.[153]

In 2017, the Central government enacted rules which said that a person could not bring cattle to an animal market unless he provided a written declaration that the cattle were not being brought there for the purpose of slaughter.[154] It also barred those who purchased cattle at an animal market from slaughtering them or sacrificing them for any religious purpose.[155] The rules applied not merely to bulls, bullocks, cows, buffaloes, steers, heifers and calves but also camels.[156] The Madras High Court granted a stay of some of the provisions of the rules, and the government has said that it will be reconsidering the rules altogether.[157]

Where's the Beef?

We have seen in this chapter that independent India is less secular than British India was in the sense that while Muslims were allowed to slaughter cows during Bakr Id in the colonial period, they are now barred from doing so in independent India. Cow slaughter in some form is now banned in a majority of states in India.[158] Faced with a political crisis in 1966–67, Prime Minister Indira Gandhi, Nehru's daughter, instructed states that had not yet enacted cow slaughter bans to remember their constitutional obligations to do so.[159] This was despite the secular ideals of leaders like Mahatma Gandhi and Nehru, who did not believe in enacting legislation against cow slaughter, though they believed in protecting the cow. In 1971, Indira Gandhi's Congress adopted, as its electoral symbol, the image of a cow suckling its calf.[160] Ironically, in 1976, it was her government that inserted the word 'secular' into the preamble to the Constitution.

Arguments in favour of cow protection, whether in the Constituent Assembly or in the Supreme Court, were rooted in economics over religion. The overarching proposition was that cows are useful to India's predominantly agricultural economy, and a law that prohibits their slaughter benefits the country. Bans on cow slaughter were considered not to violate the religious rights of Muslims because cow slaughter was considered to be optional in Islam. However, these arguments are tenuous for the following reasons.[161]

Firstly, should the right to free exercise of religion be determined only on the basis of what is obligatory in a religion? For instance, there may be no written obligation in Hinduism for a Hindu to visit a temple during the festival of Diwali. Many Hindus do not, in fact, visit temples during Diwali. Could a law that bans Hindus from visiting temples during Diwali be sustained on the grounds that visiting temples during Diwali is not mandatory in Hinduism? Religious rituals are often not driven by compulsion as much as they are by faith.[162] As one scholar has noted, 'the sign of the Cross in Holy Baptism and the ring in Holy Matrimony are not enjoined in the Bible', but any attempt to prohibit them would be considered in 'countries of the Christian tradition' as an interference with the freedom of religion.[163] Further, the Supreme Court has not paid much attention to the fact that the restriction on cow slaughter was not observed by many Hindus during the colonial period and earlier—as Gandhi noted, Hindus were themselves responsible for selling cows for slaughter, lower-caste Hindus consumed the flesh of dead cows,[164] and even upper-caste Hindus consumed beef under medical advice. Seen in this light, Hinduism's reverence towards the cow itself appears to be optional.[165] Even in the Constituent Assembly, the demand for Article 48 came primarily from Hindi-speaking north Indian Hindu members of the assembly.

Secondly, the law presumes that cows that are not slaughtered will be used in agriculture—to yield milk, as draught animals, for breeding, or for manure. However, this fails to take into account that cows that are slaughtered in a state might not, if they are not slaughtered, be used in agriculture at all. There is nothing which compels a person to use his cattle for the purposes of agriculture. A cattle owner may decide to abandon his animals once they have become useless (i.e. once their only usefulness is in providing manure) since the cost of maintaining them may exceed the money obtained from the manure produced by them.

Thirdly, most cow protection laws that have been tested before the Supreme Court do not ban the interstate sale of cattle for the purpose of slaughter. In fact, in Maharashtra, where such a ban was sought to be imposed, the Bombay High Court held that the government could not prohibit the sale of a cow from Maharashtra to outside the state for the purpose of slaughter. In other words, if a cow is not slaughtered in Maharashtra, it may still be slaughtered in a state where cow slaughter is permitted, and it will not therefore be used in agriculture at all. Even so, the ban on cow slaughter in Maharashtra was upheld on the grounds that cows are useful for agriculture in Maharashtra.

Fourthly, there are other animals that are useful to India's agricultural economy as well—animals like camels, mules, horses, sheep and goats, which serve as beasts of burden and provide milk and manure. Why is it that despite their usefulness in agriculture these animals are not protected by the law? In short, the sense one gets is that an economic argument is often made in support of banning cow slaughter to lend a respectable secular veneer to an argument that is otherwise religious, i.e. that cow slaughter should be banned in India since cows are sacred to Hinduism.

Fifthly, though the fact that India is primarily an agricultural country is regarded by the Supreme Court as a justification for the ban on cow slaughter, agriculture now contributes around 17.1 per cent to India's GDP, while the services sector contributes 53.9 per cent.[166] Further, according to statistics gathered by the Food and Agriculture Organization of the United Nations, India consistently produces and consumes more beef and buffalo meat than mutton, pork, or poultry.[167] However, agriculture remains a large source of employment in India.[168]

2

Profess, Practise, but Don't Propagate

In colonial India, it was not a crime for a Christian missionary to encourage Hindus, Muslims or others to convert to Christianity. By contrast, in England, it was considered blasphemy, a criminal offence, to deny the truth of Christianity and to thereby encourage Christians to convert to another faith. So, ironically, though England was not secular in this sense, British India was rendered secular in its laws relating to proselytizing and conversion. This was because Christianity was considered by colonial officials to be the one true religion, but it could not be the established religion of the colonial Indian government since the majority of the populace was either Hindu or Muslim. Therefore, unlike in the metropole, it was not a crime for missionaries in colonial India to tell the 'natives' that their religion was false.

When India became independent, it rejected this imperial vision of secularism that had been foisted on it in colonial times. Though the Constitution makes the right to 'propagate' religion and the freedom of conscience a fundamental right, interfaith conversions are legally discouraged here in many ways. An order issued by India's President in 1950 ensured that scheduled-caste Hindus who converted to Christianity would lose some of their constitutional benefits like contesting elections from reserved constituencies. The Hindu Code enacted by India's Parliament in the 1950s discouraged Hindus from converting to other religions. State legislatures passed laws from the 1960s onwards, euphemistically titled Freedom of Religion Acts, which had the laudable motive of seeking to prevent conversions that were made on the basis of force, fraud or material inducements. However, these laws went far beyond their stated objectives. Even offering a copy of a Bible to a Hindu could potentially be considered 'allurement'—a criminal offence under those laws. Enhanced punishments are awarded by the Freedom of Religion Acts for attempts to forcibly convert women instead of men, even if those women are highly educated elites and not members of vulnerable communities. These anti-conversion laws were cursorily upheld by the Supreme Court on the specious argument that the right to propagate religion under the Constitution does not include the right to convert a person to another religion. In doing so, the court failed to draw a distinction between the right of the preacher to propagate his religion and that of the listener to freedom of conscience (which must include the right to convert to another religion). Even the Intelligence Bureau keeps track of religious conversions in India.

At a more fundamental level, all this tells us two things: Firstly, the British colonial origins of secularism in India were dubious. In the colonial period, Indians were given the right to deny the truth of Hinduism and Islam so that Christian missionaries could proselytize in India, though Hindus and Muslims could not deny the truth of Christianity in England. Secondly, colonial secularism was replaced by a different kind of secularism once Indians came to power, a secularism in which a person has the right to profess and practise religion though the state attempts to keep Hindus within the fold.

'The Law Assumes the Truth of Christianity'

The first draft of the Indian Penal Code was drawn up in British India in 1837. The code did not make it a crime for a person to deny the truth of Hinduism or Islam, or to convert a Hindu or Muslim to another religion. However, one of its provisions, which eventually went on to become Section 298 of the code, penalized any person who said something 'with the deliberate intention of wounding the religious feelings of any person'.[1] The draftsmen of the code said that the principle behind this provision was that 'every man should be suffered to profess his own religion, and that no man should be suffered to insult the religion of another'. It was immaterial, they wrote, 'whether that religion [was] true, or false'. In other words, even though a religion like Hinduism or Islam was, according to the draftsmen, false, 'the pain which such insults give to the professors of that religion is real'.[2]

However, thereafter, colonial officials began to worry that this provision would prevent Christian missionaries from proselytizing and from seeking out 'native' converts. In 1846, the Indian law commissioners submitted their second report on the draft Indian Penal Code to the governor general. In it, they recorded several protests against the wounding of religious feelings clause. For instance, judges of the Sudder Court in the North Western Province complained that a Christian missionary might 'use such arguments as are calculated to "wound" the religious feelings of his hearers, without meaning wantonly to insult them'.[3] 'Missionaries of various Protestant Societies' felt uncomfortable with the clause as well.[4] A judge of the Bombay Sudder Court went further and thought that the provision would amount to 'a prohibition to preaching the Gospel'.[5]

Addressing these concerns, the commissioners opined that activities of Christian missionaries could not be considered to fall foul of the Indian Penal Code. '[I]n the very peculiar circumstances of this country', they wrote, 'discourse addressed to any person with the intention of converting him', if not insulting, 'should not be considered a crime'.[6] Significantly, they noted that in England, 'an attempt to convert any one from the religion of the country', even 'by the most gentle and dispassionate address', was 'by law an offence'.[7] To do so 'by contemptuous or vituperative language' was an offence that would be 'severely punished in practice' there, since conversion was not 'recognized as a legitimate object'. 'The law', they said resoundingly, 'assumes the truth of Christianity', but in British India 'it is manifest that the law and . . . legislature . . . cannot assume the truth of any religion'. They therefore opined that though this was not so in England, 'a bona fide attempt to convert' a person to another religion, 'ought not in this country to be treated as a crime', even though a missionary might '[wound] the religious feelings of the person addressed'.[8] In other words, a Christian missionary who wounded the religious feelings of a Hindu or Muslim in attempting to convert him did not, in the opinion of the law commission, commit an offence under the aforesaid provision.

Though the colonial government was nervous about the activities of Christian missionaries,[9] it enacted laws that sought to facilitate their attempts to convert others to Christianity. From 1813 onwards, Christian missionaries were able to enter British India quite easily.[10] In 1850, the Caste Disabilities Removal Act[11] said that any law in India would not be enforced if, under it, a person who converted to another religion lost his property or inheritance rights.[12] In other words, Hindus or Muslims who converted to Christianity would not thereby lose their property or inheritance. Further, entire groups of people were classified as 'criminal tribes', which encouraged them to convert to Christianity or Islam. For instance, in 1937, A.V. Thakkar, the general secretary of the Harijan Sevak Sangh, wrote to Rajendra Prasad and told him about the 'Maghahia Doms', who had been classified as a criminal tribe. 'When these Doms become Christians and take the shelter of missionaries,' he wrote, 'they are exempted from the roll-call and thus a regular encouragement is given, though indirectly, to their conversion to Christianity or Islam.'[13] Similarly, there were some areas in which only Christian missionaries could carry on their activities and not others.[14]

In England, a 'denial of the truth of Christianity in general, or of the existence of God' was considered to be 'blasphemy', a common law criminal offence which was a 'misdemeanour', punishable with imprisonment.[15] In 1885, an attempt to make the law in England similar to that in India failed.[16] Though blasphemy prosecutions in England were rare,[17] blasphemy only ceased to be a criminal offence in England in 2008.[18] The blasphemy law of England was far harsher than Section 298 of the Indian Penal Code. This was for three reasons.

Firstly, for much of the nineteenth century, blasphemy in England was considered by many jurists to occur when a person merely denied the truth of Christianity, even if he did so politely and without much fanfare.[19] It is probably for this reason that the Law Commission of India opined in 1846 that 'an attempt to convert any one from the religion of the country', even 'by the most gentle and dispassionate address', was 'by law an offence'. However, this was not the test for blasphemy under Section 298 of the Indian Penal Code, which required a deliberate intention to wound religious feelings. Though there were signs of the law having changed in England in the nineteenth century,[20] it was only in 1917 when the House of Lords conclusively held that an attack on Christianity amounted to blasphemy if it was accompanied by 'vilification, ridicule, or irreverence' of the Christian religion so as to be likely to give rise to 'a breach of the peace'.[21]

Secondly, the crime of blasphemy in England was one of strict liability.[22] In other words, it did not matter what the intent of the speaker was—if his words were blasphemous, then he would be said to have committed blasphemy. On the other hand, under Section 298 of the Indian Penal Code, a person was only guilty of blasphemy if he had the 'deliberate intention of wounding the religious feelings of any person'. This allowed a Christian missionary in India to argue that though his words might have insulted the religious beliefs of his listeners, his intent was not to hurt their feelings but to persuade them to convert to Christianity. No such defence might have been available to a Hindu preacher in England.

Thirdly, the blasphemy law in England applied only to attacks on the Church of England,[23] or to doctrines accepted by that church.[24] In a case decided in 1838, an English court took the view that 'a person may, without being liable to prosecution for it, attack Judaism, or Mahomedanism, or even any sect of the Christian religion (save the established religion of the country)'.[25] In India, Section 298 applied to all religious beliefs.

Sections 153A and 295A of the Indian Penal Code, enacted in 1898 and 1927 respectively, made it a crime to 'promote feelings of enmity or hatred between different classes of Her Majesty's subjects' or for any person to, with 'deliberate and malicious intention', 'outrage the religious feelings' or insult the 'religion or the religious beliefs' of any class of persons. These provisions were enacted to prohibit hate speech and not to prevent Christian missionaries from proselytizing.[26] In several princely states in India, however, laws were enacted to prevent or regulate conversion.[27] For instance, in Bhopal state, a statute made any Muslim who renounced Islam liable to being imprisoned for three years.[28] In Rewa, no Hindu could be converted to Islam without the sanction of the government.[29] Gandhi was opposed to this. 'Why should an adult of full understanding be obliged to obtain consent' and '[w]ho will determine the bona fides of such conversion?' he asked. He felt that a law which only required religious conversions to be registered would be 'sufficient insurance against bogus conversions'.[30]

'Like the Rose Its Scent'

However, forcible conversions often took place in colonial India, usually through threats of physical harm or by guile. During a communal riot, for instance, members of one religious group would attack another and force the victims to convert to the aggressors' religion. That apart, Christian missionaries were accused of preying on the vulnerable—the sick in hospitals, children in schools, and the poor.

Several forcible conversions took place due to violence. In 1921, there was an outbreak of violence in the south between members of the Moplah Muslim community and Hindus, as a result of which

Hindus were forced to convert to Islam.[31] During this time, Gandhi noted that there were around 1800 to 2000 instances of forcible conversions that were conducted in the following manner: Hindus were forced to repeat the *kalma*, Hindus' *chotis* were forcibly cut off, Hindu men were made to wear caps and Hindu women were forced to wear bodices or blouses.[32] Similarly, in September 1924, riots broke out between Muslims and Hindus in a town called Kohat in the North West Frontier Province, as a result of which many Hindus converted to Islam for fear of being attacked if they did not.[33] Gandhi referred to such conversions as 'forced conversions, or conversions so-called, i.e. conversions pretended for safety'.[34]

The Arya Samaj started a movement known as *shuddhi*,[35] of trying to convert lost Hindus back to Hinduism. A countermovement called *tabligh* was launched within Islam. Gandhi was opposed to both. He did not believe that there was any room for proselytization in Hinduism, and felt that the Arya Samaj was copying Christian missionaries.[36] He also felt that tabligh was not sanctioned by the Quran.[37] 'I am against conversion whether it is known as shuddhi by Hindus, tabligh by Mussalmans or proselytizing by Christians', he wrote. 'Conversion is a heart-process known only to and by God. It must be left to itself.'[38] There were also some instances of forcible conversions within these movements. 'I am told', Gandhi wrote in his newspaper in 1924, 'that both Arya Samajists and Mussalmans virtually kidnap women and try to convert them.'[39] 'Faith', he felt, 'spreads its aroma like the rose its scent' and is 'given through the language of the heart'.[40] However, Gandhi was not opposed to conversion, and he did not feel that conversions could be stopped as long as they were voluntary. In 1946, he assured the Bishop of Calcutta that even after Indian independence, conversions would continue, 'but there would be no State favouritism', i.e. in favour of Christian missionaries, 'as there has been during the British regime'.[41]

In 1927, a resolution was passed at the Madras session of the Indian National Congress, which said that when any person complained that he had been converted or reconverted to a religion 'in secrecy or by force, fraud or other unfair means', or if that person was under eighteen years of age, 'arbitrators' appointed by the Congress Working Committee would inquire into the matter and decide whether the conversion was genuine.[42]

Instances of forcible conversion through violence were reported with alarming frequency before and after India's partition while the Constitution itself was being drafted. In 1946, violence broke out in Noakhali in East Bengal, where Hindus were forcibly converted to Islam,[43] which greatly worried Nehru. In April 1947, Sardar Vallabhbhai Patel learned that about 100 Hindus had been killed in the Dera Ismail Khan district (now in Pakistan) and some had been converted.[44] In 1948, K.M. Munshi,[45] India's agent in Hyderabad, informed Patel that Hindus in Hyderabad were being forcibly converted to Islam.[46] But it was not merely Hindus who were being forced to convert to another religion during this time. That year, around 20,000 Muslims belonging to the Meo community complained that they had been forcibly converted to Hinduism. In fact, the governments of India and Pakistan reached an agreement that no conversions during the disturbances should be recognized.[47] In 1950, Muslims in East Punjab and PEPSU who had been forced to convert to Hinduism or Sikhism wished to revert to Islam. Nehru supported their cause and said that India was 'opposed to this business of forced conversions'.[48]

Several such forcible conversions were taking place in Pakistan. Indian intelligence had indicated to Patel that authorities and Muslim leaders in East Pakistan were forcing Hindus to either 'evacuate or embrace Islam'.[49] In March 1950, Prime Minister Nehru wrote a letter to Pakistan's Prime Minister, Liaquat Ali Khan, that if a person wanted to change his religion he should be 'perfectly free to do so', but 'compulsion in such matters is humiliation and destruction of the spirit of man'.[50] The Nehru–Liaquat Pact, signed in April 1950, called on both countries not to recognize forcible conversions and to punish those who were guilty of converting people forcibly.[51]

Against this backdrop, some provincial governments in India enacted laws that made converting from one religion to another difficult. In November 1947, the government of the Central Provinces and Berar enacted the Public Safety Act, which said that religious conversions could only take place in the presence of a magistrate. The Act, a temporary law, was enacted because of the 'large-scale forcible conversions' that were taking place in other parts of the country. As the Prime Minister of the province, R.S. Shukla, explained to Rajendra Prasad in a letter in April 1948, the 'circumstances at the time were such that any conversion of a Hindu to Islam, even if it was voluntary, was apt to be construed as forcible conversion and could easily have led to breaches of the peace'. He explained that the law was also meant to protect Muslims and aboriginals in the state.[52] In 1953, Prime Minister Nehru himself noted that '[n]othing excites people so much in India as religious conversion', adding that '[a] Hindu becoming a Muslim publicly would probably create a riot in Delhi'.[53] The anti-conversion clause in the CP and Berar statute was dropped a year later because it was no longer necessary.[54]

During the period of British colonialism in India, Indian leaders were concerned about how some Christian missionaries were getting converts by using methods that they considered unfair. In 1820, Raja Rammohun Roy wrote that among the 'few hundred' Indians belonging to the 'most ignorant class' who had been 'nominally converted to Christianity', he suspected that the majority had been 'allured to change their faith by other attractions than by a conviction of the truth and reasonableness of those dogmas'. This, he said, was because most of the Indian converts were either 'employed or fed by their spiritual teachers'. He wrote about how he had witnessed Indian converts to Christianity petition an ecclesiastical authority in Calcutta that they had been 'through false promises of advancement . . . induced . . . to give up their ancient religion'.[55]

Gandhi accused missionaries of 'buy[ing] children in days of famine and bring[ing] them up as Christians'.[56] He hinted that Christian doctors and teachers were asking their patients and students respectively to convert to Christianity. '[P]roselytizing under the cloak of humanitarian work is', he said, 'to say the least, unhealthy.'

'The methods of conversion must be like Caesar's wife above suspicion,' he added. He was unhappy with the fact that conversion had now 'become a matter of business', and remembered how 'a missionary report' set out 'how much it cost per head to convert' and presented a budget for 'the next harvest'.[57] Missionaries were accused of converting, en masse, groups of lower-caste Hindus by offering them money or assistance in litigation.[58]

However, these tactics did not significantly affect demographics in colonial India. In 1891, for instance, while 72 per cent of India's population was Hindu and 19.96 per cent Muslim, only 0.80 per cent consisted of Christians.[59] By 1941, Hindus were about 73.81 per cent of the population, Muslims were 24.28 per cent, and Christians 1.91 per cent.[60] According to 2011 census data, Hindus are 79.8 per cent of the population, Muslims 14.23 per cent and Christians 2.3 per cent.[61]

It was not only conversions to Christianity which occurred through guile. '[A]gents of the Aga-Khani movement', Gandhi wrote in 1924, 'lend money to poor illiterate Hindus and then tell them that the debt would be wiped out if the debtor would accept Islam.'[62] After India's partition, in March 1948, Rajendra Prasad learned that a Sikh official in Ludhiana (East Punjab) refused to allot houses to refugees from Pakistan unless they added 'Singh' at the end of their names and became Sikhs.[63]

'A Rather Obvious Doctrine'

In the Constituent Assembly, two issues arose over the question of conversion. The first was whether the freedom of religion included the right to propagate one's religion and proselytize. The framers decided that it did, and that this was covered by the right to free speech anyway. The second was whether there should be a specific provision in the Constitution barring forcible conversions. The assembly decided not to include this clause because it was obvious that such conversions would not be tolerated in independent India.

(a) 'Propagate'

On 17 April 1947, in a meeting of the Subcommittee on Minorities, M. Ruthnaswamy, a Cambridge-educated barrister and legislator from Madras,[64] asked that the right to 'propagate' one's religion be added to the right to the free exercise of religion.[65] '[C]ertain religions,' he said, 'such as Christianity and Islam, [are] essentially proselytizing religions, and provision should be made to permit them to propagate their faith in accordance with their tenets.'[66] Consequently, the draft approved by the subcommittee included the right to profess, practise and 'propagate' religion.[67] A few days later, the larger Advisory Committee met and discussed whether Christians and others should have the right to 'propagate' their religious beliefs. C. Rajagopalachari said that there was a 'sharp difference of opinion' over whether 'propagate' should be included in the Constitution, since it was already covered by the freedom of expression.[68] Some, like K.M. Munshi and Alladi Krishnaswami Ayyar,[69] opposed the inclusion of the word 'propagate' in the right to religion. Munshi said that the right to 'propagate' religion would include 'forced conversion', and the right to free speech included 'any kind of preaching' anyway.[70] Ruthnaswamy, on the other hand, supported the right to 'propagate' religion, and said that it included 'not only preaching but other forms of propaganda . . . like the use of films, radio, cinemas and other things'.[71] Govind Ballabh Pant, the prime minister of the United Provinces,[72] said that at the worst, the word 'propagate' was 'redundant' since it was covered by the right to free speech. He felt that it was better to include the word in the right to religion since 'so many members want it'.[73] Consequently, the word 'propagate' was accepted in the draft constitution.

Sometime between February and October 1948, when the draft constitution was offered for public comments, R.R. Diwakar[74] and S.V. Krishnamoorthy Rao,[75] who were both members of the Constituent Assembly, suggested that the right to 'propagate' religion be dropped from the Constitution.[76] Thereafter, on 3 December 1948,[77] Tajamul Husain, a congressman from Bihar,[78] moved an amendment to delete the word 'propagate', because religion, he said, was a 'private affair' and the right to free exercise of religion should not give a person the right to interfere with the religion of others.[79] K.T. Shah, an economics professor who had studied at the London School of Economics,[80] moved an amendment to prohibit missionaries and others from carrying out propaganda to convert people in publicly aided schools, colleges, hospitals and other places where 'persons of a tender age, or of unsound mind or body are liable to be exposed to undue influence from their teachers, nurses or physicians, keepers or guardians or any other person set in authority above them'. In moving this amendment, Shah said that the 'freedom of propaganda' which was being given to proselytizing religions 'should not be abused, as it has been in the past'. He said that he did not have any quarrel with those who changed their religions 'after full and mature consideration'. After all, he said, most religious beliefs 'are not . . . a matter of reasoned conviction; they are an acquired habit or an inherited prejudice which may not stand the strain of conviction on the opposite side'. However, he felt that fiduciaries like teachers, physicians, or guardians must not exercise 'undue influence' in converting their students, patients or wards. He said that he professed 'no particular religion' himself, which made him neutral.

Some members of the assembly supported these amendments.[81] Lokanath Misra,[82] whose brother later became the chief justice of the Supreme Court of India, recommended that the word 'propagate' be dropped. While opposing the amendments, K. Santhanam[83] said that mass conversions had been carried out by Christian missionaries to which 'great objection' had been taken in India, and that the government should have the right to regulate conversions to ensure that they were not brought about by 'money or by pressure or by other means'.

Others, however, opposed the amendments. T.T. Krishnamachari,[84] who later resigned as India's finance minister amidst a scandal, said that the right to 'propagate' religion was not being given only to

Christians, and that even members of the Arya Samaj would have the right to carry out shuddhi propaganda as part of their right to propagate Hinduism. He said that though he had studied for fourteen years in Christian institutions, no attempt had ever been made to convert him from his own faith and to adopt Christianity. He said that many Hindus from the lower castes had converted to Christianity because of the status it had given them. 'An untouchable who became a Christian became an equal in every matter along with the high-caste Hindu,' he said. Similarly, K.M. Munshi, who had originally opposed the insertion of the right to 'propagate' religion in the Advisory Committee, now opposed its deletion from the Constitution. He said that prior to 1938, under the old regime of British colonial rule, Christian missionaries had influence with Collectors of districts and utilized it to obtain converts. However, after 1938, when the Congress came to power in the provinces, much of that influence was lost. Since then, he said, conversions have taken place on the basis of 'persuasion' and not offers of 'material advantages'. He said that the right to propagate religion would be covered by the right to free speech anyway, and it should be retained since it was a compromise achieved by the Subcommittee on Minorities.[85] The amendments were consequently rejected by the assembly.

(b) Forcible conversion

In March 1947, K.M. Munshi's draft of the fundamental rights chapter of the Constitution contained two provisions that addressed forcible conversion. The first said that no person under the age of eighteen could change his religion 'without the permission of his parent or guardian'.[86] The second said that a religious conversion that was brought about by 'coercion, undue influence or the offering of material inducement' was prohibited and punishable by law.[87] By contrast, the draft prepared by Ambedkar guaranteed to every Indian citizen the right to 'profess, to preach and to convert within limits compatible with public order and morality'.[88] However, it was Munshi's draft which was accepted by the Subcommittee on Fundamental Rights.[89] Thereafter, the Subcommittee on Minorities suggested that a person under the age of eighteen should be entitled to convert when his parents have converted to another religion. It also recommended that no conversion should be recognized unless it had been attested by a magistrate after an inquiry.[90] In April 1947, Rajkumari Amrit Kaur, a Christian who later became the health minister in Nehru's cabinet,[91] prepared a note in which she said that since conversions by force or undue influence alone were barred, 'conversion of an adult to any religion by reason of conviction' would be permissible in independent India.[92]

When the Advisory Committee met to discuss Munshi's two clauses concerning conversion, they decided to drop the first clause (dealing with the religious conversion of minors).[93] Patel felt that such matters were better 'left to legislation'.[94] There was some debate about whether to drop the second clause (regarding fraudulent conversions) as well. Patel felt that this provision was 'unnecessary',[95] that there could not be a 'fundamental right for every conceivable thing'.[96] 'Forcible conversion is no conversion', said Patel, '[w]e won't recognise it.'[97] However, since other members of the committee[98] objected to this clause being dropped, it was included in the draft that went to the plenary assembly.[99]

Thereafter, on 1 May 1947, the fraudulent conversion clause of the draft Constitution was discussed in the Constituent Assembly.[100] During this debate, several members of the assembly expressed concern over forcible conversions in India. For instance, P.R. Thakur,[101] a barrister who belonged to the 'depressed classes' himself, said that victims of wrongful conversion were often members of the depressed classes. 'The preachers of other religions approach these classes of people,' he said, 'take advantage of their ignorance, extend all sorts of temptations and ultimately convert them.'[102] Algu Rai Shastri[103] said that a person should only be allowed to convert 'after he is convinced through cool deliberation that the new religion is more satisfactory to him than the old one' and not because of 'greed and temptation'. He said that he had 'a personal experience extending over a period of twenty-four years' of how 'the elders of the family are induced through prospects of financial gain to change their religion and also with them the children are taken over to the fold of the new religion'. He said that it was the practice of Christian missionaries to 'convert some influential persons by inducement and persuasion', by virtue of which others followed suit.[104] On the other hand, Purushottamdas Tandon said that he considered it altogether 'very improper to convert from one to another religion',[105] whether forcibly or otherwise.

Vallabhbhai Patel then said that it was well known in India that there had been 'mass conversions, conversions by force, conversions by coercion and undue influence'. On his recommendation, the fraudulent conversion clause was referred back to the Advisory Committee. Thereafter, in August 1947, after further deliberations, the Advisory Committee decided to drop it from the Constitution. '[T]his clause', they said, 'enunciates a rather obvious doctrine which it is unnecessary to include in the Constitution'.[106]

In short, the principle that the law would not recognize conversion from one religion to another if it was brought about by coercion or undue influence, thought the Advisory Committee, was an elementary principle, which did not need to be stated in the Constitution. On 30 August 1947, Patel informed the assembly that this was a subject better left to the legislature.[107]

Nehru and Conversion

Like Gandhi, Prime Minister Nehru did not want to stop interfaith conversions from taking place. In 1953, he reprimanded President Rajendra Prasad for attending an event where Christian missionaries were criticized for converting tribals by offering inducements. He told Prasad that the evangelical activities of Christian missionaries could not be stopped, unless they were 'conducted in the wrong way'.[108] More importantly, he told Prasad that whatever his 'personal views and convictions might be', as President he was 'above religion', the '[h]ead of a secular state, which treats all religions alike', and that Prasad's attendance at that event might affect how the state is viewed by Christians.[109] That year, he wrote to Home Minister K.N. Katju and asked him to ensure that applications for permits, made by Christian missionaries from the Swedish mission, were looked into. 'We must make a distinction', he wrote to Katju, 'between these very fine men and women who come here and give devoted service to India, without really caring for conversion, etc., and other missionaries who are politically or otherwise troublesome.'[110] Nehru instructed the home ministry of the Central government that visa applications by foreign missionaries could not be rejected on the grounds that they were planning on doing evangelical work in India.[111] In fact, a year later, the Supreme Court would hold that the freedom to profess, practise and propagate religion under Article 25 of the Constitution belonged not merely to citizens but to all persons,[112] including foreigners. Under Nehru's prime ministership, by 1953, the number of foreign missionaries in India nearly doubled since Independence.[113]

However, Nehru was also worried about the hidden political motives of some Christian missionaries in India. In October 1953, he told Amrit Kaur that some missionaries were engaging in politically subversive activities in India. For instance, a few Spanish Jesuits in Bombay, he told Kaur, were carrying on 'secret and intensive work against our policy in regard to Goa'.[114] A large number of missions had opened, he said, in border areas, where hardly any evangelical work was done.[115] He was also uncomfortable with American missionaries mixing with Indian students, because they represented the American viewpoint.[116] In a letter to a bishop that year, Nehru wrote that he was aware of the fact that there had been some 'wrong behaviour' on the part of a few missionaries, 'more especially in the tribal areas'—such things had happened even prior to Independence, he noted, and even the colonial government was compelled to take action.[117]

In the meantime, in April 1954, the government of Madhya Pradesh appointed a committee headed by M.B. Niyogi, a retired chief justice of the Nagpur High Court,[118] to enquire into Christian missionary activities.[119] The committee's report suggested that several dubious practices were being carried on by Christian missionaries in Madhya Pradesh.[120] It found that the Gospel was being inappropriately propagated through schools, hospitals and colleges.[121] For instance, an advocate who deposed before the committee complained that while his wife was at a mission hospital, a nurse tried to convince her to convert to Christianity. Another witness complained that he was asked either to pay Rs 35 or to allow his child (who was at a mission hospital) to be raised as a Christian.[122] Other patients at mission hospitals were asked to convert to Christianity if they wanted to be cured.[123] The committee found that some Roman Catholic missions were also carrying out moneylending activities. In the districts of Surguja and Raigarh, money was lent on the condition that the Hindu debtor agreed to chop off his *choti* (topknot). Only those who did not comply had to repay the money with interest. One witness said that people were offered loans and help in litigation in return for their conversion to Christianity.[124] Orphanages were run by missions in order to 'multiply the population of Christians'.[125] The committee opined that 'illiterate Adivasis, with families and children' were being nominally converted to Christianity by cutting their chotis off, though most of them did 'not know even the rudiments of the new religion'.[126] One such witness who was converted to Christianity did not know with what book the Bible began, with what book it ended, or even the Lord's Prayer.[127] Mass conversions were taking place because of inducements offered to vulnerable people, not because of any religious conviction.[128] Educational facilities like 'free gifts of books and education' were offered to secure the conversion of minors.[129] In other words, this did not amount to the exercise of the freedom of conscience by the converted. Instead, poor and vulnerable sections of Indian society were being taken advantage of.

The committee concluded that conversions were taking place due to 'undue influence'. In some questionable passages, however, the committee also said that conversion to Christianity was confusing the 'convert's sense of unity and solidarity with his society' and that there was 'a danger of his loyalty to his country and State being undermined'.[130] Christian missions were carrying out a 'vile propaganda' against Hinduism, which gave rise to 'an apprehension of breach of public peace',[131] said the committee, and Christian evangelization was aimed not at a spiritual transformation in India, but at 're-establishing Western supremacy'.[132] The Niyogi Committee report was criticized not merely by the National Christian Council of India but also by prominent non-Christian leaders like Dr Hare Krishna Mahatab, governor of Bombay.[133]

Despite the findings of the Niyogi Committee, in December 1955, Nehru spoke in the Lok Sabha against a private member[134] bill—the Indian Converts (Regulation and Registration) Bill—which was aimed at regulating conversions by providing for the licensing of persons who aided conversions, the reporting and registration of conversions, etc.[135] Nehru said that the bill would cause hardship to genuine missionaries. He felt that things like 'coercion, deception, etc.', if used by missionaries, could be dealt with under the existing law.[136] He also said, 'Christianity is as much a religion of the Indian soil as any other religion in India.'[137]

Keeping Hindus within the Fold

However, the Hindu Code, enacted by Parliament in 1955–56, set up disincentives against Hindus converting to Christianity.[138] For instance, children born to a Hindu after he or she converted to another religion were disqualified from inheriting the property of any of their Hindu relatives, unless the children were themselves Hindus.[139] A Hindu's conversion to another religion furnished a ground for divorce.[140] A Hindu who converted to another religion could no longer act as the natural guardian of his or her child.[141]

A Hindu did not require the consent of his or her spouse to adopt a child if the spouse had converted to another religion.[142] A Hindu wife was entitled to 'live separately' from her husband without forfeiting her right to claim maintenance if her husband had converted to another religion.[143] However, a Hindu wife lost that right if she was 'unchaste' or ceased to be a Hindu by conversion to another religion.[144]

Further, in 1950,[145] the President of India issued a list of recognized scheduled castes, whose members were entitled to benefits under the Constitution, like the ability to contest elections in reserved constituencies.[146] The presidential order initially specified that 'no person who professes a religion different from Hinduism' would be deemed to be a member of a scheduled caste.[147] This meant that members of the scheduled castes on the list who converted to another religion, like Sikhism, Christianity or Buddhism, in order to escape the inferior status they had been given in Hinduism,[148] were no longer entitled to contest reserved seats in elections. Though Sikhism and Buddhism were included in the list in 1956[149] and 1990 respectively, Christianity is still not on the list.[150] In other words, a member of a scheduled caste who converts to Christianity cannot contest an election in a reserved constituency unless he can show that he has reverted to Hinduism and to his original caste.[151] However, in some states, members of the scheduled castes who have converted to Christianity are considered to be members of the 'other backward classes' who are consequently entitled to other benefits, e.g., reservations in education and employment.[152]

In the 1960s, the states of Orissa and Madhya Pradesh enacted laws which sought to regulate conversions. They were euphemistically titled 'freedom of religion' statutes. The Madhya Pradesh law,[153] for instance, said that no person could 'convert or attempt to convert' anyone 'from one religious faith to another' by using force (which included a threat of divine displeasure[154]), 'allurement' (i.e. offering any gift or material benefit, whether in cash or otherwise[155]) or fraud.[156] The punishment for doing so was imprisonment for up to a year. However, the punishment extended up to two years if the victim was a minor, a member of a scheduled caste or scheduled tribe, or, for some inexplicable reason, even a woman.[157] The statute also required persons who engaged in conversion activities, like Christian missionaries, to intimate the district magistrate, within a prescribed period, when a conversion took place.[158] The Madhya Pradesh law was obviously designed to address the excesses of Christian missionaries which the Niyogi Committee had spoken of.

However, some of its provisions went a little too far. For example, it prescribed an enhanced punishment if the victim was woman. It is unclear why the law equated all women—not just *pardanashin* women or those belonging to lower castes—to those who were particularly vulnerable to conversion, like minors and scheduled castes. In other words, even if the most highly educated female CEO of a multinational company visiting Madhya Pradesh was told by a Christian missionary that she would not go to heaven unless she converted to Christianity, the law assumed that an offence had thereby been committed. The definition of 'allurement' was also overbroad as it included any gift or gratification, in cash or kind, or 'grant of any material benefit either monetary or otherwise'. It could therefore be argued that even if a person was given a free copy of the Bible in order to get him to convert to Christianity, this amounted to 'allurement' within the meaning of the law. Further, the definition of 'force' included the threat of divine displeasure—this meant that a Christian missionary could not tell his audience that God would be displeased if they did not convert to Christianity.

The Orissa[159] and Madhya Pradesh statutes were challenged in the respective high courts of those states and the issue eventually came up before the Supreme Court in *Stainislaus v. State of Madhya Pradesh*.[160] In the Orissa High Court, it was argued that the term 'inducement' (the Orissa statute used 'inducement' instead of 'allurement') was too broad, that it could include a person who merely sought to convert a person by invoking God's blessings or saying 'by His grace your soul shall be elevated'. The opponents of the law in that case argued that the inclusion of the threat of divine displeasure in the definition of force was unfair. Their argument was that 'Christians believe that satisfaction of the basic physical wants creates a wholesome basis for effectiveness of religion' and that an attempt was therefore made by missionaries to 'improve the economic condition of the "conversion-seekers" as an initial process of conversion'. They also argued that Christian missionaries make 'mild threats' to their audience, like 'You (non-Christians) shall go to hell', '[y]ou shall not obtain salvation', the '[w]rath of God shall come down upon you' or 'God will be displeased with you'.[161] In the Madhya Pradesh High Court, it was also argued that the definition of 'allurement' was too vague.[162] The Orissa High Court declared the law unconstitutional, holding that the right to propagate religion included the right of Christians to convert others to their own religion and that the term 'inducement' used in the law was too vague.[163] However, the Madhya Pradesh High Court took a contrary view and upheld the statute.

In the Supreme Court, it was argued that the provisions of the anti-conversion statutes violated Article 25(1) of the Constitution, i.e. the freedom of conscience and the right to 'propagate' religion. It was also pointed out that the right to 'propagate' religion included the right to convert someone from one religion to another.[164] The court almost cursorily rejected these arguments and held that Article 25 did not give 'the right to convert another person to one's own religion' but only 'to transmit or spread one's religion by an exposition of its tenets'.[165] It was held that there was 'no fundamental right to convert another person to one's own religion' as this would 'impinge on the "freedom of conscience" guaranteed to all the citizens of the country alike'.[166]

In upholding the Orissa and Madhya Pradesh statutes, the Supreme Court went too far. It could easily have held that the right to 'propagate' religion under Article 25 of the Constitution does not include the right to convert someone by force, fraud or undue influence. However, it went further and held that the right to propagate religion did not include the right to convert a person, even if the conversion proceeded voluntarily. In so holding, the court forgot that in any conversion, there are two people involved—the preacher and the listener. While the preacher's right to propagate religion may not include the right to convert the listener, the listener's right to conscience under Article 25 includes the right to convert to another religion after listening to the preacher. Therefore, while focusing only on the preacher's right to propagate, the court ignored the listener's right to conscience, which includes a right to listen to the preacher.

Anti-conversion laws are now in force in several states in India,[167] though arrests or prosecutions are rare.[168] In at least two such states, Gujarat and Jharkhand, the anti-conversion statute says that no conversion can take place without the prior permission of the district magistrate.[169] Unlike the Madhya Pradesh law, which merely requires the district magistrate to be intimated about a conversion, this is a drastic restraint which subjects a person's freedom of conscience to the discretion of a magistrate. Further, India's Intelligence Bureau, which collects information concerning national security, monitors the activities of foreign missionaries in India and the approximate number of conversions taking place in different parts of the country, since mass conversions can affect law and order.[170]

However, in 2018, the Supreme Court decided a case, *Shafin Jahan v. Asokan K.M.*,[171] involving the right of an adult female to convert to another religion and marry the man of her choice. A twenty-four-year-old Hindu woman, Akhila, converted to Islam, changed her name to Hadiya, and married a Muslim man, Shafin Jahan.[172] This was considered to be a case of 'love jihad'[173]—a phrase loosely used to describe the perceived fear that Hindu or Christian women will supposedly be lured into marrying Muslim men, through false expressions of love, for the purpose of converting them to Islam.[174] The phrase 'love jihad' also encapsulates an apprehension that foreign radical terror outfits provide funding to Muslim men in India to lure Hindu women so that they may be utilized for terrorism.[175]

Hadiya's father filed a habeas corpus petition in the Kerala High Court, alleging that she had been forcibly converted to Islam and that he thought she would be transported out of the country. The Kerala High Court inexplicably held that '[a] girl aged 24 years is weak and vulnerable, capable of being exploited in many ways'. It declared that her marriage was void and ordered a 'comprehensive investigation' by the police. Her husband filed an appeal in the Supreme Court. In the Supreme Court, Hadiya filed an affidavit 'expressly affirming her conversion to Islam and her marriage to Shafin Jahan'.[176] The court examined her and found that she was not being illegally confined. It held that the high court had committed an error in giving a father's wishes precedence over the marital choice of his adult daughter.[177] The objective of a habeas corpus petition, said one of the judges, was to trace an individual who was stated to be missing—once the individual appeared and asserted that she was not being illegally confined, the inquiry had to end there.[178] It was held that Hadiya had 'absolute autonomy over her person' and how she led her life was 'entirely a matter of her choice'.[179] The high court was held to have transgressed its jurisdiction in declaring her marriage void.[180] It was also held that '[c]hoices of faith and belief as indeed choices in matters of marriage lie within an area where individual autonomy is supreme', and that 'the Constitution protects personal liberty from disapproving audiences'.[181]

3

'I Cannot Vote for Mr Jinnah'

In this chapter, we will see that the colonial government quite possibly used secularism as part of its divide and rule policy to consolidate its hold over British India. From 1909 onwards, in order to ostensibly protect religious minorities, elections to legislative bodies were conducted on the basis of three principles: reservation, separate electorates, and weightage. Reservation meant that a fixed number of seats in legislatures were earmarked for different religious groups. For example, only a Muslim could get elected to a seat reserved for Muslims. 'Separate electorates' meant that voters were segregated on the basis of their religion. In other words, Hindu voters voted for the Hindu seats on legislative bodies, Muslim voters for the Muslim seats, and so on. This was considered by many leaders in the Congress to be responsible for the eventual partition of India, because it encouraged legislators to think only in terms of the narrow interests of their own religious communities, instead of national interests. Since the members of the Muslim League, for instance, only had to secure the votes of Muslim voters in order to get elected to power, they could demand the creation of Pakistan as they did not have to care about what Hindu voters felt.[1] As one legislator in colonial India astutely remarked in 1937, Hindu voters could not vote for Jinnah even if they wanted to because of separate electorates. 'Weightage' meant that religious minorities were given a higher proportion of seats in legislative bodies than their numbers in the general population.

We will see that in 1906, Viceroy Minto's administration bent over backwards to accommodate a demand for some of these measures in order to prevent Muslims from joining hands with the Congress. Thereafter, despite acknowledging that separate electorates were harmful to India's social fabric, the colonial government kept extending them to other minorities like Sikhs, Indian Christians, and the 'depressed classes'. This was done to protect religious minorities in India even though religious minorities in England, minorities like Catholics and Jews, were not given separate electorates there.

Why was the colonial government so eager to protect India's religious minorities even though separate electorates were not given to England's own religious minorities at home?[2] One possible answer, though perhaps not the only one, is that colonial secularism in British India was used as an instrument to divide and rule.

Though separate electorates were pernicious as they divided voters and leaders on the basis of religion, there was nothing inherently wrong in the mere reservation of seats for religious minorities on legislative bodies. In fact, in the colonial period, though the Congress wanted to abolish separate electorates, it promised to retain reservations for religious minorities in the legislative councils in order to ensure that their interests were sufficiently safeguarded. However, once India became independent, the Constitution not merely abolished separate electorates and weightage, but also abandoned the age-old Congress promise of reservation for religious minorities. Consequently, the proportion of Muslims elected to office in India is often lower than the proportion of Muslims in the general population.

In short, this chapter makes three arguments. Firstly, colonial secularism was possibly part of the policy of divide and rule in British India. Secondly, it was diluted in independent India because of its dubious origins as a colonial tool. Thirdly, the pushback against colonial secularism began much before the rise of India's Hindu right.

'A Possible Counterpoise to Congress Aims'

The governor general of British India and the governors of the provinces had legislative councils that made laws within their respective areas of authority. In the early years, the members of these councils were nominated by the governor general or governors themselves. Elections to these bodies were introduced for the first time under the Indian Councils Act, 1892.[3] For instance, the legislative council of Bombay had eight seats that were to be filled through elections among special interest groups. Only members of the corporation of Bombay, some other municipal corporations, district local boards, large landholders (called the Sardars of the Deccan), certain select associations of merchants, manufacturers and tradesmen, and the senate of the University of Bombay were permitted to vote in these elections.[4] These special interest groups alone had the right to vote in legislative council elections. Similarly, five seats on the governor general's legislative council were to be filled through elections conducted in the provincial legislative councils of Bengal, Bombay, Madras, the North-Western Provinces and Oudh, and in the Calcutta Chamber of Commerce.[5] The governor general and governors also had the power to nominate legislators to their respective councils by ensuring 'due representation of the different classes of the community'.[6] The principle behind this system was that 'each important class' was to 'have the opportunity of making its views known in council by the mouth of some member specially acquainted with them'.[7] However, there was no reservation, separate electorates or weightage under this system.

In 1906, Viceroy Minto[8] and Secretary of State John Morley[9] were getting worried that the Congress, which they saw as a predominantly Hindu body, was becoming too powerful. They believed that the British Empire in India would weaken if Muslims joined the Congress movement. Against this backdrop, they possibly devised a scheme to exploit the schism between Hindus and Muslims to consolidate the British hold over India, all in the name of secularism.

On 28 May 1906, Minto wrote to Morley and said that though 'we must recognize [the Congress] and be friends with the best of them, yet I am afraid there is much that is absolutely disloyal in the movement and that there is danger for the future'. 'I have been thinking a good deal lately', he continued, 'of a possible counterpoise to Congress aims.'[10] At this time, Minto thought that the Indian princes and landholders could be organized as an opposition to the Congress. On 6 June, Morley wrote back and said that his advisors were worried that Muslims would soon join the Congress movement, which would spell doom for the British Empire. 'Everybody warns us that a new spirit is growing and spreading over India', he wrote. 'Lawrence, Chirol, Sidney Low', who were his advisors, 'all sing the same song . . . Be sure that before long the Mahommedans will throw in their lot with the Congressmen against you', they had said to Morley.[11] On 27 June, Minto wrote to Morley about the 'disloyal tone of the Native Press' with which Congressmen were 'so largely connected'.[12]

On 26 July 1906, Morley made a speech in the House of Commons in which he hinted at reforms in the Indian legislative councils.[13] A few days later, on 4 August, the secretary of Aligarh College, Nawab Mehdi Ali Khan (better known as Mohsin-ul-Mulk[14]), wrote a letter to Mr W.A. Archbold, the British principal of the college, who was at the time spending his summer vacation in Simla.[15] In it, he asked whether it would be advisable for a delegation of Muslims to meet Viceroy Minto in order to speak to him about the rights of Muslims in India.[16] 'You are aware', he wrote, 'that the . . . young educated Mohammedans seem to have a sympathy for the "Congress", and [Morley's] speech [in the House of Commons] will produce a great tendency in them to join the "Congress".' He also wrote that if elections to the legislative councils were introduced under the new proposals, 'the Mohammedans will hardly get a seat while the Hindus will carry off the palm by dint of their majority'.[17] A few days later, this letter reached Viceroy's Minto's desk.[18] On 8 August, Minto forwarded the letter to Morley and told him that he was inclined to grant the 'proposed deputation' an audience.[19] This was unusual because very rarely, if ever, had a viceroy met a deputation consisting of only one religious community or group.[20] In 1901, for instance, Viceroy Curzon had refused to meet a deputation consisting only of Muslims, and no viceroy had met a deputation consisting only of members of the Congress.[21] Between 9–10 August, Archbold and J.R. Dunlop Smith, the private secretary to Viceroy Minto,[22] exchanged letters, in which Dunlop Smith informed Archbold that he had obtained permission for the Muslim delegation to visit Viceroy Minto.[23] On 10 August, a member of the Viceroy's Executive Council by the name of Denzil Ibbetson advised Minto to receive the deputation.[24] It could be a 'calamity', said Ibbetson, if the younger generation of Muslims were driven into the 'arms of the Congress party . . . for at present, the educated Mohammedan is the most conservative element in Indian society'.[25]

On 10 August, Archbold wrote back to Mohsin-ul-Mulk, and advised him to prepare a memorial to ask Viceroy Minto for special privileges for Muslims in elections to legislative councils. He wrote that the memorial must begin 'with a solemn expression of loyalty', perhaps to address Minto's unhappiness with the disloyal tone of the Congress.[26] The memorial was to say that elections 'would prove detrimental to the interest of the Muslim minority'. 'It should respectfully be suggested', he wrote, 'that nomination or representation by religion be introduced to meet Muslim opinion'. However, he warned Mohsin-ul-Mulk that Archbold's role in this process must not become publicly known. '[I]n all these views I must be in the background', he wrote, '[t]hey must come from you'. 'I can prepare for you the draft of the address or revise it', he wrote, since 'I know how to phrase these things in proper language'. A formal letter requesting an appointment with the viceroy should be prepared, he wrote, which 'should be sent with the signatures of some representative Mussalmans'. The deputation which goes to meet the viceroy, he added, must 'consist of the representatives of all the Provinces'.[27]

On 1 October 1906, thirty-five Muslim representatives from different provinces and princely states met Minto at his Viceregal Lodge in Simla.[28] The memorial, which had probably been edited[29] by Archbold, was read out to the viceroy by the Aga Khan. Among other things,[30] the memorial asked the viceroy for special privileges in elections. Muslim seats in the legislative councils, said the Aga Khan, 'should be commensurate, not merely with [the] political strength [of Muslims in India], but also, with their political importance and the value of the contribution which they make to the defence of the Empire'. '[D]ue consideration' must also be given, he said, 'to the position which [Muslims] occupied in India, a little more than a hundred years ago, and of which the traditions have naturally not faded from their minds'.[31] In other words, the Muslim delegation requested Viceroy Minto to give Muslims weightage in legislative councils because the Muslim community was politically important, because it contributed to the defence of the British Empire, and because Muslims were, before the British arrived, the ruling race in India.

Minto had been advised by Dunlop Smith and Archbold to give the deputation a 'reassuring reply'.[32] He responded by agreeing with the deputation's demands on the subject of elections and said that 'any electoral representation in India would be doomed to mischievous failure' if this were not so.[33] Later that day, Minto's wife received a letter from an official (probably Dunlop Smith[34]) which said that Minto's decision was a 'work of statesmanship' which prevented 'sixty-two millions of people from joining the ranks of the seditious opposition',[35] i.e. it prevented Muslims (there were 62 million Muslims in India at this time, according to the 1901 census[36]) from joining hands with the Congress. Dunlop Smith wrote a letter to another British official the following day in which he said that 'the [Muslims] declared to the [viceroy] that they would not join the Congress, [and] that they preferred appealing to their Ma Bap'.[37] The Muslim League itself was founded ninety days after this deputation met Minto[38] (though Muslim opposition to the Congress was decades old, spearheaded by Sir Syed Ahmed Khan).[39]

Tellingly, on 15 September 1909, Chief Justice Lawrence Jenkins wrote a letter to Morley, in which he said, '[F]rom all I hear . . . I incline to the view that the Muhammedan demand was prompted in the first instance from other sources, and has been skilfully engineered'.[40]

There is, therefore, some evidence that the Muslim demand for special protection in elections was devised by colonial officials as part of a divide and rule policy.[41] This was certainly the view taken by nationalist leaders and observers. On 4 October 1906, the *Amrita Bazar Patrika* wrote that this entire episode appeared 'to be a got-up affair and fully engineered by interested officials'.[42] In 1923, a Khilafat leader and president of the Congress, Maulana Muhammad Ali, called the Muslim deputation's visit to the viceroy a 'command performance', akin to a play being put up at the request of the royal family.[43] These words were repeated by Vallabhbhai Patel in the Constituent Assembly in May 1949.[44] Another member of the Constituent Assembly, K.M. Munshi, called this an 'unholy alliance' between 'British rulers' and 'the leaders of a section of the Muslims in North India', and a 'command performance' planned by Archbold and Dunlop Smith, 'among others'.[45] Of course, it cannot be said that the colonial British administration manufactured Mohsin-ul-Mulk's fears that Muslims would be left behind in the reformed legislative councils. However, colonial officials like the viceroy bent over backwards to accommodate the demands of the Simla deputation. In the words of historian B.R. Nanda, '[W]hat is surprising is not that the Muslim leaders should have wanted to lead a deputation and submit a memorial to the Viceroy, but that they should have been so warmly welcomed and given such wide-ranging assurances so hastily on constitutional issues of which the full implications were yet to be worked out by the Viceroy and his advisers'.[46]

Later, in May 1957, Prime Minister Nehru made a speech at a public meeting held in Delhi in which he said that separate electorates were introduced to colonial India because the British were worried about the 'havoc that the two united communities', the Hindus and

Muslims, 'could cause' to the empire. He said that Viceroy Minto had 'called a few of the top Muslim leaders and zamindars and asked them to come to him in a deputation seeking a separate electorate for the Muslims', and added that Minto 'indicated that he would agree to it'. 'You can appreciate the cunning of the Viceroy', said Nehru, '[h]aving instigated the demand, he made a pretence of considering it and eventually accepted it.' 'This is how the seeds of communal hatred and bitterness were sown', he added. '[E]ven today it is extremely dangerous to bring religion into politics and elections.'[47]

After the Simla deputation met the viceroy in 1906, the committee of the Viceroy's Executive Council suggested two changes to the electoral rules: firstly, it opined that a certain number of seats in the legislature should be reserved for Muslims, and, secondly, those seats should be filled by a separate Muslim electorate.[48] On 23 February 1909, Morley made a speech in the House of Lords in which he said that the Muslims essentially wanted two things, viz., 'an election of their own representatives', and 'a number of seats in excess of their numerical strength'. He informed the House that the government was 'quite ready' to meet these two demands 'in full'.[49]

Accordingly, under the Indian Councils Act, 1909,[50] the legislative council of the governor general was to consist of twenty-five elected members, of whom five (i.e. 20 per cent) were to be elected by Muslims from some of the provinces. The rest were to be elected by provincial legislative councils, landholders and chambers of commerce.[51] Similarly, separate electorates were set up for Muslims in the provincial legislative councils (except in Punjab and the Central Provinces[52]), where between two and five seats were reserved for Muslims, to be filled through votes cast by a separate Muslim electorate.[53] For example, in the Bombay legislative council, four out of the twenty-one elected members (i.e. 19 per cent) were to be elected by Muslims.[54] The rest were to be elected by special interest groups like the Bombay Chamber of Commerce, Bombay Millowners' Association, or landholders, or by bodies like the municipal corporation, university, etc.

Three features of the electoral system set up under the Indian Councils Act, 1909, stand out. Firstly, Muslims had a 'double vote'.[55] A Muslim could vote directly in an election for a Muslim seat in a legislative council. He could also vote for bodies like municipal corporations which, in turn, elected members on the legislative council. Of course, not all Muslims were entitled to vote—only those who owned sufficient property.[56] Secondly, Hindus could only vote once. Thirdly, Hindus could only vote directly (i.e. in the provincial or central legislative council elections) if they belonged to a special interest group, or indirectly by voting in elections for bodies like the municipal corporation which, in turn, voted in elections for members of the legislative council.[57]

'To Think as Partisans and Not as Citizens'

Separate electorates and weightage for Muslims, however, were not brought about entirely without Hindu cooperation. Gopal Krishna Gokhale, a Hindu Congress leader, conceded limited separate electorates for Muslims in order to ensure that the Indian Councils Act, 1909, would get enacted.[58] In September 1908, Gokhale had prepared a note on constitutional reforms for Morley, in which he had said that twenty-one of the twenty-five elective seats on the Viceroy's Legislative Council could be filled through a joint electorate, and the remaining four seats could be filled through separate electorates for Muslims.[59] However, Gokhale was shocked by the extent to which Muslims had been given representation in the councils under the 1909 statute. In a letter he wrote to a British official in December 1909, he said that the 'Mohammedan representation in the Viceroy's Council is so excessive as to be not only unjust but monstrously unjust'. He pointed out that out of the four members that the Bombay provincial legislative council would send to the central legislative council, three would be Muslims, though 'they are only one-fifth of the population of this presidency'![60] He was also irked by the fact that Muslims who had an annual income of £135 had the right to vote, while 'no Hindu or Parsee, however wealthy or whatever his position in other respects, has a vote unless he is a member of the three or four bodies which have been called upon to return a member'.[61]

However, separate electorates were further strengthened in 1916, as a result of a compromise between members of the Congress and the Muslim League, in a deal which is often referred to as the 'Lucknow Pact' or 'Congress-League Scheme'.[62] Under this arrangement, the Congress agreed that Muslims would get separate electorates with weightage, but in return, Muslims would have to give up their double vote and vote only once in separate electorates,[63] and Hindus would be entitled to direct voting as well.[64] Thereafter, in almost every province, except Bengal and Punjab where Muslims constituted more than 50 per cent of the population, Muslims got a greater proportion of seats in the legislative council than their proportion of the population. The following was the distribution of seats for Muslims relative to their strength in the population under the Lucknow Pact:[65]

Province	Percentage of Muslims in the general population	Percentage of Muslim seats proposed
Bengal	52.6	40
Bihar and Orissa	10.5	25
Bombay	20.4	33.3
Central Provinces	4.3	15
Madras	6.5	15
Punjab	54.8	50
United Provinces	14	30

In 1918, a report prepared under the joint authorship of Secretary of State Edwin Montagu and Viceroy Chelmsford[66] said that the issue of whether to continue with 'communal electorates' was 'the most difficult question' facing the government.[67] The report cited many reasons why separate electorates were harmful to India. 'We conclude unhesitatingly', the report said emphatically, 'that the history of self-government among the nations who developed it . . . is decisively against the admission by the State of any divided allegiance; against the State's arranging its members in any way which encourages them to think of themselves primarily as citizens of any smaller unit than itself.'[68] Dividing the electorate 'by creeds and classes' taught Indians 'to think as partisans and not as citizens', it said. It acknowledged that the 'British Government is often accused of dividing men in order to govern them', and that continuing with separate electorates would make the government look 'hypocritical or short sighted'.[69] Minorities who are given special representation in legislatures, it added, are lulled into a false sense of 'satisfied security', and they thereby lack the 'inducement to educate and qualify' themselves to improve their lot.[70]

However, after making these strong arguments against separate electorates, the Montagu–Chelmsford report concluded by saying that separate electorates could not be done away with 'until conditions alter' because any change to the system would 'rouse a storm of bitter protest' and 'put a severe strain on the loyalty' of Muslims to the British empire. It also noted that Muslims had been loyal to the British empire 'during a period of very great difficulty'.[71] Oddly, it then also recommended introducing separate electorates for Sikhs, though there had not been any separate electorates for Sikhs previously.[72]

Consequently, the electoral rules enacted under the Government of India Act, 1919,[73] continued the system of reservation, separate electorates and weightage. In Bombay, the Governor's Legislative Council was now to consist of eighty-six elected members, in addition to twenty-five nominated members and the ex-officio members of the Governor's Executive Council. While nominating members to his council, the governor had to ensure that the following communities and interests were represented, viz., the Anglo-Indian and Indian Christian communities, the 'laboring classes', 'depressed classes' and the cotton trade.[74] Elections in Bombay were conducted on the basis of three separate electorates, for Muslims, non-Muslims, and

Europeans. No person could vote in these unless he was a Muslim, non-Muslim or European respectively.[75] These constituencies were called 'general' constituencies.[76] For instance, the city of Bombay had two 'Non-Muhammadan Urban' constituencies, north and south, in which only non-Muslims and non-Europeans could vote. On the other hand, Bombay city had one Muslim constituency and one European constituency in which only Muslims and Europeans could vote respectively.[77] Not every adult Muslim, non-Muslim or European could vote in these constituencies. A voter had to have a place of residence within the constituency and had to either own land[78] or occupy land as a tenant where the annual rent or land revenue was more than a certain prescribed figure, pay income tax, or be a present or former officer in the armed forces.[79] As a result, only about 10 per cent of the adult male population in British India had the right to vote at this time.[80]

Interestingly, there was no literacy requirement for voting, and for this reason, pictorial symbols like a tiger or umbrella were used by candidates during the elections for the benefit of illiterate voters.[81] The idea was that illiterate voters could vote for candidates by recognizing their symbols. These pictorial symbols still have tremendous importance in Indian politics. The electoral rules under the 1919 Act did not expressly give women the right to vote, but allowed legislative councils to decide whether or not to allow them to vote.[82] By 1930, however, all the legislative councils had enacted rules allowing women to vote. Even so, less than 1 per cent of the adult female population had the actual right to vote.[83]

On the other hand, Bombay had several 'special' constituencies, which elected eleven members to the legislative council. These were landholders like the Deccan Sardars and Inamdars, Bombay University,[84] the Bombay and Karachi Chambers of Commerce, the Bombay Trades Association, Bombay Mill Owners' Association, Ahmedabad Mill Owners' Association, and Indian Merchants' Chamber and Bureau.[85] Unlike before, non-Muslims could also vote in the general constituency, and they too had a double vote.

On the whole, the Bombay legislative council had forty-six non-Muslim seats, twenty-five Muslim seats, two European seats, and eleven seats for special constituencies.[86] In other words, Muslims had 29.76 per cent of the seats in the legislative council, which was higher than their share of the general population in the province, which was around 20 per cent. Similarly, in the central legislative assembly, Muslims had a share of around 28 per cent of the elected seats,[87] which was much higher than their proportion in the population, which was around 18 per cent. There were separate electorates for elections to the central legislative councils as well. For instance, the province of Bombay had twelve seats in total in the central legislative assembly, of which two were Muslim seats, seven were non-Muslim seats, two were European seats, and one was a seat for the Indian Merchants' Chamber and Bureau.[88]

After 1919, with the exception of a few provinces, Hindus had fewer seats in the councils than their numbers in the population, while Muslims had a greater share of seats than their strength in the population. The following was the share of seats of non-Muslims in comparison with their proportion in the population:[89]

Province	Percentage of seats in the legislative council	Percentage of population
Madras	73.3	90
Bombay	53.5	78.9
Bengal	47.9	45.1
United Provinces	58.6	85.4
Punjab	25.5	32
Bihar and Orissa	61.2	88.2
Central Provinces and Berar	78	95.4
Assam	47.1	65.9

By contrast, the following was the share of the seats of Muslims in the legislative councils, in comparison with their share of the population:[90]

Province	Percentage of seats in the legislative council	Percentage of population
Madras	10.6	6.7
Bombay	25.4	19.8
Bengal	30.8	54.6
United Provinces	26	14.3
Punjab	40.4	55.2
Bihar and Orissa	18.5	10.9
Central Provinces and Berar	9.6	4.4
Assam	30.2	32.3

In 1930, the report of the Simon Commission[91] said, 'the gravest and most difficult of all the questions that arise in connection with the composition of Indian electoral assemblies' was that of whether to continue with separate electorates.[92] 'It is no exaggeration to say', said the report, 'that the answer . . . is regarded as of far more importance to large bodies of Indian opinion than any other matter involved in the structure of the councils.'[93] By this time, some reservations had been introduced in the legislative councils for members of the 'depressed classes', i.e. backward castes. So, for instance, seven out of forty-six non-Muslim seats in the legislative council of Bombay were reserved for 'Marathas and allied Castes', and in Madras, twenty-eight out of sixty-five non-Muslim seats were reserved for non-Brahmins.[94] However, while there was reservation for some 'depressed classes' in some of the provinces, no separate electorates had been introduced for them as yet, though separate electorates, by this time, had been introduced for Indian Christians and Anglo-Indians.[95]

The Simon Commission unanimously decided to continue with the system of separate electorates because it felt that the Muslim community was not prepared to give them up,[96] and it recommended that they could be done away with only when 'a substantial majority' of Muslims themselves agreed to do so.[97] It opined that 'mere reservation of seats' in a joint electorate was not sufficient to protect Muslim interests. This was because if a seat were reserved for a Muslim in a constituency in which the majority of the population consisted of Hindus, the Muslim candidate would then have to pander to Hindus in order to get elected.[98] However, the Simon Commission did not recommend separate electorates for the 'depressed classes'. Instead, it suggested that they be given reserved seats in a non-Muslim constituency.[99]

The political battle lines were drawn, and while the Muslim League propounded separate electorates, the Congress sought their abolition. In 1928, at a special session of the Muslim League, Jinnah formulated fourteen points that he wanted the Indian National Congress to agree to, one of which was that separate electorates should be continued in India.[100] By contrast, a statement published in July 1931 by the Working Committee of the Congress in Bombay said that the aim of the Congress was to have 'joint electorates' (i.e. a single electoral roll, with no distinction between voters based on their religion), but with '[r]eservation of seats' for religious minorities.[101]

However, despite acknowledging that the system of separate electorates was divisive and harmful, in 1932, Prime Minister Ramsay MacDonald declared his 'Communal Award', by virtue of which even the 'depressed classes' were given reservations and separate electorates.[102] To protest the Communal Award, Gandhi undertook a fast unto death in September 1932.[103] It was because of Gandhi's fast that, only a few days later, the 'Poona Pact' was signed, as a result of which the depressed classes, led by Dr B.R. Ambedkar, agreed to give up separate electorates in return for a greater share of reserved seats in the provincial legislatures.[104] So where the Communal Award had reserved seventy-one seats in the provincial legislatures for members of the depressed classes on the basis of separate electorates, the Poona Pact gave them

148 seats.[105] The Poona Pact also set up a system of primaries for members of the depressed classes. Under this system, a panel of four depressed class candidates would be elected in the primaries consisting only of members of the depressed classes. These candidates would then contest elections in reserved constituencies but in a joint electorate, i.e. the electorate would consist of voters who were Hindus regardless of their caste, and not merely of members of the depressed classes.[106]

The Government of India Act, 1935,[107] which was the last substantial constitutional document before Indian independence, continued the system of reservations, separate electorates and weightage. Under it, Muslims were given a share of 32.6 per cent of the seats in the Council of State and 32.8 per cent in the Federal Assembly, both of which constituted the central legislature.[108] However, the 1935 statute accepted the Poona Pact and did away with separate electorates for scheduled castes, while adopting the system of primaries for electing scheduled caste candidates.[109] Muslims still had separate electorates, and were given the following proportion of seats in the provincial legislative assemblies:[110]

Province	Percentage of Seats in the Legislative Assembly
Bombay	17.14
Madras	13.48
Bengal	47.6
United Provinces	28.94
Punjab	49.14
Bihar	26.31
Central Provinces and Berar	12.5
Assam	31.48
North West Frontier Province	72
Orissa	6.66
Sind	56.6

Yet again, not every adult could vote in these elections. In the province of Bombay, for instance, a person could vote only if he or she resided within the constituency and was either assessed to income tax during the previous financial year, held property (or occupied it as a tenant) of a certain value, passed the matriculation or school leaving examination of Bombay university,[111] or was a present or former member of the armed forces. Additionally, women in Bombay province were also eligible to vote if their husbands satisfied those criteria, or if the woman in question was a pensioned widow or the mother of a member of the armed forces.[112]

'I Must Vote for My Friend, Mr Bhulabhai Desai'

The Minto–Morley reforms were seen by Indian nationalist leaders as being an integral part of the British divide-and-rule policy. Minto's term as viceroy came to an end in 1910. Several decades later, at the Round Table Conference held in London in the early 1930s, Viceroy Minto's wife asked Gandhi if he still remembered her name. 'Remember your name!' Gandhi is said to have exclaimed, 'The Minto–Morley Reforms have been our undoing. Had it not been for the separate Electorates then established we should have settled our differences by now.'[113] While inaugurating the Berar Provincial Congress Conference in January 1940, Vallabhbhai Patel said that the 'Morley–Minto Reforms were first devised to divide India on religious basis'.[114] In December 1946, in a letter to a Christian lawyer, Patel wrote that the system of separate electorates 'given to the Muslims has done irreparable damage to the cause of India: this was done deliberately as a policy of divide-and-rule, and we are paying dearly the price for this act of mischief'.[115]

After the Government of India Act, 1935, was enacted, several Congress leaders made speeches protesting against its retention of separate electorates. In June 1936, Patel delivered a speech in Ahmedabad in which he said that the colonial government had brought about separate electorates in order to 'create dissensions' among different religious communities.[116] In March 1937, a report prepared by Rajendra Prasad and Govind Ballabh Pant noted that separate electorates which divided 'the two major communities into watertight compartments undoubtedly presented great difficulties' to the Congress party, which typically did not do well in elections in Muslim constituencies.[117] In September that year, S. Satyamurti, a Congress leader, made a speech in the central legislative assembly in which he said, 'what is the madness—I cannot vote for Mr Jinnah; even if I wanted to vote for him, I must vote for my friend, Mr Bhulabhai Desai, because Mr Desai and I are Hindus and Mr Jinnah is a Muslim.'[118]

Satyamurti later explained to Gandhi in a letter that separate electorates made 'communal leaders . . . exist and flourish at the expense of national-minded leaders'. This is because, he said, 'an average Hindu' would vote 'for a Hindu who promised to protect Hindu as against Indian rights', while 'an average Muslim' would vote 'for the Muslim who goes to the legislature to protect Muslim rights as against Indian rights'.[119] However, Satyamurti did not want the Congress to abolish all electoral protection for religious minorities. He hoped to replace separate electorates with 'joint electorates with reservation of seats for minorities for the time being'.[120]

In the years leading up to Indian Independence, Patel was convinced that separate electorates would have to be abolished. In 1945, Patel made a speech at Shivaji Park, Dadar, in which he said that the colonial government had 'granted separate electorates to the Muslims with the intention of making us fight each other'.[121] In April 1946, Patel wrote a letter to a fellow congressman in which he said that 'joint electorates would reverse the process of the spread of communal hatred and distrust'.[122]

On the other hand, Nehru was of the opinion that separate electorates could not be abolished in India without the consent of Muslim leaders. In a letter he wrote to Jinnah in April 1938, he said that though communal electorates were 'anti-national' and against 'national unity', joint electorates could 'not be imposed on unwilling groups'.[123] In November 1939, the Congress passed a resolution calling for a constituent assembly to be set up, in which it said that the assembly 'should be elected on the basis of adult suffrage, existing separate electorates being retained for such minorities as desire them'.[124] In fact, members of the Constituent Assembly itself were later appointed on the basis of separate electorates.

However, even members of religious minority groups were beginning to ask for the abolition of separate electorates. For instance, in December 1946, the Young Men's Muslim Association at Baliapatnam passed a resolution in which it condemned the proposal of the Madras government to conduct elections to local boards and municipal councils on the basis of separate electorates, saying that this was 'a very painful affair to the nationalist Muslims' and that 'such a proposal would be detrimental to the best interests of the country as a whole and of Hindu–Muslim unity'.[125] In December 1946, a Christian lawyer, V.K. John, wrote a letter to Patel in which he said that in his view 'the Indian Christian community should not ask for separate electorates or even joint electorates with reservation but ought to sink its identity with the general electorate'. He wrote that this view was 'shared by a very large section of the community, particularly by the younger members of the community'.[126] 'Let us hope', wrote Patel in reply, 'that all communities will realise in course of time that it is more in the interest of the country and of the community as a whole to fall in line with the general national regeneration of the country'.[127]

Separate Electorates Abolished

In March 1947, Ambedkar prepared a draft Constitution which mounted a defence of separate electorates. Ambedkar wanted the Poona Pact to be replaced by separate electorates for scheduled castes in independent India.[128] In an explanatory memorandum, he wrote that there were essentially two problems with the Poona Pact. The first was that the scheduled caste man who won the primary election (i.e. the person who was at the top of the table) usually did not win the general election. This was because the broader Hindu electorate used to elect a more moderate candidate as opposed to the one who ended up on top in the primaries. The second was that the primary election, in many cases, was not really being conducted. It was 'for the most part a fiction and not a fact', wrote Ambedkar. In the previous election, only forty-three primaries out of 151 reserved seats were actually held. 'This is because it [was] impossible', said Ambedkar, 'for the Scheduled Castes to bear the expenses of two elections—primary and final.' Ambedkar believed that the system of 'joint electorates and reserved seats' which was being proposed by the Congress was 'much worse', because the broader Hindu electorate was only likely to elect moderate candidates.[129]

'To insist that separate electorates create anti-national spirit', wrote Ambedkar, 'is contrary to experience.' He gave the example of the Sikhs, who had been given separate electorates, and argued that 'no one can say that the Sikhs are anti-national'. He pointed out that despite being elected under a system of separate electorates, Jinnah 'was the apostle of Indian nationalism up to 1935'. Indian Christians too had separate electorates, he said. 'Nonetheless a good lot of them have shown their partiality to the Congress if they have not been actually returned on the Congress ticket.' 'Obviously,' he concluded, 'nationalism and anti-nationalism have nothing to do with the electoral system. They are the result of extra-electoral forces.'[130]

In fact, in a book published in 1945, Ambedkar had denounced Gandhi's 'fast unto death' which had resulted in the Poona Pact which abandoned separate electorates for the depressed classes. In it, he wrote:

There was nothing noble in the fast. It was a foul and filthy act. The fast was not for the benefit of the Untouchables. It was against them and was the worst form of coercion against a helpless people to give up the constitutional safeguards of which they had become possessed under the Prime Minister's

Award and agree to live on the mercy of the Hindus. It was a
vile and wicked act. How can the Untouchables regard such
a man as honest and sincere?[131]

However, in the months that followed, it became clear that Ambedkar
was in the minority in the Constituent Assembly on this question. In May
1947, some members of the Provincial Constitution Committee opined
that separate electorates should be replaced with '[j]oint electorates with
reservation of seats'.[132] On 7 July 1947, a little more than a month
before Independence, Nehru wrote a letter to Mountbatten in which he
said, 'All our troubles, or nearly all, have been due to separate electorates
and the system of weightage, originally introduced for the Muslims. It
became clear that this did little good to the minority concerned and
only created separatist tendencies.' However, Nehru conceded that
'without weightage and separate electorates some kind of reservation'
could still be retained for religious minorities.[133]

On 22 July 1947, the Minorities Sub-Committee of the Advisory
Committee decided by a majority of 28-3 to abolish separate
electorates for elections to the legislatures.[134] However, that following
day, the subcommittee decided, by a majority of 23-3, that there
should be some reservation of seats for religious minorities.[135] On
28 July 1947, the larger Advisory Committee, chaired by Patel, decided
by a huge majority (with only three members dissenting) to accept
the recommendations of the subcommittee.[136] The report prepared
by the Advisory Committee said that separate electorates had 'in the
past sharpened communal differences to a dangerous extent' and had
'proved one of the main stumbling blocks to the development of a
healthy national life'.[137] It recommended that 'seats for the different
recognized minorities shall be reserved in the various legislatures on the
basis of their population'.[138] In other words, though separate electorates
and weightage were done away with, reservation was to be maintained,
though it would be reconsidered after a period of ten years.[139]

On 27 August 1947, Patel placed the report of the Advisory
Committee before the Constituent Assembly. The move to abolish

separate electorates and weightage was opposed by two members of the Muslim League in the assembly, B. Pocker Sahib Bahadur and Chaudhuri Khaliquzzaman, both of whom had been elected to the assembly on the basis of separate electorates. Bahadur, whom Patel later referred to as 'the no-changer and confirmed Muslim Leaguer',[140] said that the 'institution of separate electorates' ought to be retained since it had been 'enjoyed by the Muslim community' for the past forty years. Khaliquzzaman, who later moved to Karachi before the Constitution was adopted,[141] said that the argument that separate electorates helped consolidate the British hold over India no longer applied once the British left India. Later, Patel would refer to Khaliquzzaman as 'the great Muslim leader, who swore loyalty to the Constitution in this House and immediately after packed off to Karachi'.[142]

However, apart from these two lone voices in the assembly, there was a chorus of support for the abolition of separate electorates. 'Did not the Italians, the Frenchmen, the Spaniards and others come together in the continent of America?' asked M. Ananthasayanam Ayyangar.[143] 'Therefore it is up to us to create a secular State.' Govind Ballabh Pant said that separate electorates isolated minorities from the majority, and there could not be any 'divided loyalty' in a democracy. Patel responded to the critique of the Muslim Leaguers and asked, 'Can you show me one free country where there are separate electorates? If so, I shall be prepared to accept [them].' The assembly voted in favour of the abolition of separate electorates and for their substitution with joint electorates and reservation.[144] The Drafting Committee of the Constitution decided to insert a clause into the Constitution itself which made this clear.[145]

'A Few Anxious Moments of Silence'

We have seen that for long, the Congress had advocated the abolition of separate electorates and weightage but the retention of reservations for religious minorities on legislative bodies. However, in a sudden and mysterious meeting held in May 1949, the Advisory Committee decided to drop reservations for minorities as well.

It all began on 30 December 1948, when some members of the Advisory Committee suggested that conditions in India had 'vastly changed' since 1947. They opined that 'it was no longer appropriate in the context of free India and of present conditions that there should be reservation of seats for Muslims, Christians, Sikhs or any other religious minority'. Reserving seats for religious minorities, they felt, would 'lead to a certain degree of separatism' and was 'contrary to the conception of a secular democratic State'.[146] Thereafter, some members of the Advisory Committee, including Dr H.C. Mookherjee (a Christian), Tajamul Husain (a Muslim), and Lakshmi Kanta Maitra, gave notices of resolutions seeking to recommend to the Constituent Assembly that there should no longer be any reservation of seats on legislative bodies for religious minorities in India.[147]

Ambedkar opposed these notices in the Advisory Committee and said that the matter would have to be placed before the plenary body of the Constituent Assembly.[148] However, sometime in early 1949, Patel, who chaired the Advisory Committee, overruled Ambedkar and allowed the discussion to proceed at a meeting of the Advisory Committee itself.[149] The spokesperson for the nationalist Muslims in the committee, Maulana Hafizur Rahman, was in favour of retaining reservations for Muslims. On the other hand, another Muslim member of the committee, Tajamul Husain, made a caustic speech in which he criticized the nationalist Muslims, attacked their leader, Maulana Azad, and urged them to drop reservations.[150] Begum Aizaz Rasul, a member of the Muslim League who had not relocated to Pakistan, said that after Partition, it would now be better for the Muslims who had stayed behind not to isolate themselves through reservations. Patel 'sat in stolid silence' during this meeting and then adjourned the proceedings in order to give time to the Muslim members of the committee to reach a unanimous conclusion on the issue.[151]

The Advisory Committee met again on 11 May 1949.[152] Strangely, no minutes were kept of this meeting, or if they were, no record of them is now readily available. 'It was a critical situation', wrote K.M. Munshi, a member of the committee. Tajamul Husain, the vociferous Muslim proponent of abolition, was absent. Begum Aizaz Rasul 'could not summon up courage to speak' as she was 'afraid of being severely attacked by the Nationalist Muslims', wrote Munshi later. 'The representatives of the Nationalist Muslims sat silent.' The committee members expected the nationalist Muslims to stick to their earlier position of seeking reservations. However, apparently, Maulana Azad had instructed them not to argue in favour of reservations for religious minorities.[153] 'There was no one to propose that the Muslims did not want reservation', wrote Munshi, 'and the fate of the most important issue—joint electorates without reservations—hung in the balance'. The matter was called out, and 'there were a few anxious moments of silence'. Patel then looked at Munshi, who whispered to Begum Rasul, sitting next to him, that Patel 'expected her to speak'. She then 'summoned up courage', 'walked up to the lecturn' and 'pleaded in a very hesitant manner for abolition of reservations for Muslims left in India'. 'No sooner had she resumed her seat than [Patel]', wrote Munshi, 'who perhaps was aware of Azad's instructions, said: I am very glad that the Muslims are unanimously in favour of joint electorates without reservations. We will now adjourn.'[154]

In this mysterious manner, the Advisory Committee decided to drop reservations for religious minorities in elections, by a vote of 58-3,[155] reversing what had been a part of the Congress plan for decades.[156] The Advisory Committee in its report to the Constituent Assembly opined that it had made this recommendation since conditions in India had 'vastly changed since August 1947', though it is not clear what those conditions were, and since 'the minorities themselves feel that in their own interests, no less than in the interests of the country as a whole, the statutory reservation of seats for religious minorities should be abolished'.[157]

The Advisory Committee's new recommendation to abolish reservation for religious minorities was discussed in the Constituent Assembly on 25–26 May 1949. The move was opposed by a few of its members. Mohamed Ismail Sahib, for example, said that he was in favour of retaining separate electorates and reservations. Z.H. Lari asked why reservations were being maintained for scheduled castes if they were 'against the national interests'. He said that the Muslim members of the Advisory Committee did not have 'any hold' over the opinion of the Muslim minority in the country, and suggested that Patel convene a meeting of all the Muslim members of the assembly in order to discuss this issue.

Syed Muhammad Saadulla raised concerns over the mysterious meeting held on 11 May. He said that he was a member of the Advisory Committee and he was unable to attend that meeting due to 'domestic trouble'. He then said that only four members of the Muslim minority were present at that meeting, of whom only one had made a speech supporting the resolution to abolish reservations. Another Muslim member of the committee voted against the measure. The third Muslim member of the committee, Maulana Abul Kalam Azad, remained neutral during the proceedings and by his example, the fourth Muslim member, Maulana Hafizur Rahman, was also neutral. He therefore argued that the resolution only had 'the solitary support of Begum Aizaz Rasul'. He reminded the house that he and all the other members of the assembly had been elected on the basis of separate electorates.

However, there was once again a strong chorus of support for the move to abolish reservations for religious minorities, even among the Muslim members in the assembly. For instance, Naziruddin Ahmad, a Muslim, said that adopting reservations for religious minorities 'would only serve to perpetuate the unpleasant memory of . . . separate electorates and all the embitterments . . . that accompanied them'. He felt that no Hindu candidate standing for elections in India would be able to 'ignore the Muslims'. 'In fact,' he said, 'for one seat there will be at least two Hindu candidates, and in case of a contest, the Muslims will have an important role to play, and they may well be able to tip the scale, by playing the part of an intelligent minority, suitably aligning themselves with one side or the other.' He felt that Muslims would 'have a decisive voice in the elections'. Dr H.C. Mookherjee, a Christian, said that it was the 'path of wisdom for the minorities to trust the majority'. Rev. Jerome D'Souza agreed. Begum Aizaz Rasul said that reservation would '[keep] up the spirit of separatism and communalism'. She too said that she could 'not visualise any political party in the future putting up candidates for election ignoring the Muslims'. 'The Muslims comprise a large part of the population in this country', she said, adding, 'I do not think any political party can ever ignore them'. Sardar Hukam Singh, a Sikh, also supported the move. Several others added to this list of supporters.

Muhammad Ismail Khan, a Muslim from the United Provinces, contradicted Saadulla and said that Begum Aizaz Rasul was not the only Muslim member of the assembly who opposed reservations, and that there were 10–12 Muslim members who had, a few months previously, expressed an opinion that reservations for religious minorities must be done away with. He made the point that Muslims no longer needed protections like separate electorates and reservations since they could go to the Supreme Court of independent India if their fundamental rights were violated. 'We can vindicate our rights in future not in the legislature,' he said, 'but in the Supreme Court . . . '

Tajamul Husain concurred. He said that if Muslim members of the Advisory Committee like Maulana Azad wished to oppose the resolution in the meeting held on 11 May, then they would have done so. Their silence meant, in his opinion, that they had agreed with the resolution. He said that of the seven Muslim members of the committee, only two were opposed to the resolution, viz., Saadulla and Jafar Imam. He asked members of the assembly to '[r]emove the term "minority" from your dictionary', as it was the British who had 'created minorities'. He said that minorities should rise 'as part and parcel of the whole Indian community' and not on the strength of 'communal or racial labels'. He added that Muslim minorities were not poor, weak and uneducated like the scheduled castes.[158]

Nehru spoke as well, saying that he wished to associate himself 'with this historic turn in our destiny'. He said that earlier, the assembly had 'reluctantly' decided to continue with 'some measure of reservation' for two reasons: firstly, reservations could not be done away with without the consent of religious minorities; secondly, the government was unsure of how people would operate in the absence of reservations. Neither of these two conditions, he said, remained valid now. Such protections, he added, were only necessary 'where there is autocratic rule or foreign rule'. By continuing with a system of reservations, Nehru said, India would be isolating its religious minorities. He was in favour of abolishing reservations even for the scheduled castes, though he said that 'in the present state of affairs in India that would not be a desirable thing to do'.

Patel concluded the proceedings by making a speech in which he hinted that one possible reason why reservations were being done away with was because the Muslim League was thinking of reviving itself in India. He said that Muslim Leaguers in India were claiming that 'they might get some big chunk' of the funds of the Muslim League in India, funds which had yet to be settled and apportioned between the Muslim League in Pakistan and India. 'There is no place here', he said, 'for those who claim separate representation.'

Eventually, the Constituent Assembly decided to delete reservations for religious minorities in legislatures. On 26 November 1949, Rajendra Prasad made a speech in the Constituent Assembly, in which he expressed his satisfaction with the fact that the Constitution was able to 'get rid of separate electorates which had poisoned our political life for so many years', and that reservation for religious minorities was given up as well.[159] In 1952, Nehru even wrote a letter to the chief ministers of the states in which he alerted them of a law that was being enacted in East Africa by the 'European planter element' to introduce 'separate communal electorates' there, and said that this was clearly 'meant to weaken various popular elements in East Africa and to make it easier for the European planters to hold on to their special interests and position'.[160]

Conclusion

Writing her autobiography many years later, Begum Aizaz Rasul explained why she had voted against reservations for Muslims on legislative bodies. The atmosphere in post-Partition India was tense and Muslims felt especially vulnerable. Mahatma Gandhi, who had advocated Hindu–Muslim unity, was assassinated in January 1948 'on this account'.[161] A few months later, after Jinnah's death in September 1948,[162] Pakistan started mistreating its religious minorities. Hundreds of thousands of refugees consequently arrived in India, which made Indian Muslims feel worried that retaliatory action might be taken against them. Had Pakistan kept its promise of protecting its religious minorities, she wrote, 'it would have made our position stronger and enabled us to speak from strength'.[163] Instead, the environment at that time was such that '[e]ven a broken knife found in a Muslim house could send the family to jail'.

Under these circumstances, '[w]hat difference would a few seats more or less in the legislatures have made for the Muslims if reservation had been retained?' Rasul wrote. Instead, '[i]t was the goodwill of the majority that was essential'.[164] 'It is most unfair and unjust of Muslims of the post-Independence generation to pass judgement on our actions of those times', she wrote. 'It is not possible for the Muslims of today to visualize the conditions of those days'.[165] In other words, in the immediate aftermath of Partition, Indian Muslims were worried about their own safety and wellbeing in India and they gave up reservations in order to earn the goodwill of the majority Hindu populace, to ensure that they continued to be secure in post-Partition India.

However, after the system of reservation, separate electorates and weightage was abolished under the Constitution, the share of

Muslim representation in legislative bodies in India has drastically reduced. After the 1951–52 elections, Muslims held only 4 per cent of the seats in the Lok Sabha (i.e. obtaining twenty-two out of 500 seats).[166] They received an even smaller percentage of seats in the 1962 elections.[167] According to the last census conducted in 2011,[168] approximately 14.22 per cent of the population of India consists of Muslims. However, among roughly 524 sitting members of the Lok Sabha elected in the 2014 general elections, only fourteen (i.e. 2.67 per cent) could be identified as Muslims.[169] Among 542 members elected to the Lok Sabha in the 2019 general elections, only around eighteen (i.e. 3.3 per cent) could be identified as Muslims.[170] Similarly, out of 244 sitting members of the Rajya Sabha as on 28 December 2018, only seventeen (i.e. 6.96 per cent) were Muslims.[171]

True, the Indian Constitution succeeded in abolishing the pernicious system of separate electorates and weightage, which had possibly been adopted by the British with the aim of dividing the populace under the guise of secularism. However, in doing so, while abandoning reservations for religious minorities on legislative bodies as well, the Constitution has failed to ensure adequate representation for religious minorities like Muslims on legislatures in India commensurate with their share of the population. Seen today, with the benefit of hindsight, some of the speeches made by the Muslim members of the Constituent Assembly conceding the abolition of reservations seem naive. Naziruddin Ahmad and Begum Aizaz Rasul argued in the assembly that no Hindu candidate or political party would be able to ignore Muslims. Perhaps this is no longer entirely true. In December 2014, a leading national political party in India had only four Muslim members of state legislative assemblies among a total of 1016 legislators in its party ranks across the country.[172]

Of course, communal reservations might have harmful effects, but they are not the only methodology which may be employed to ensure that Muslims are given adequate representation on legislative bodies.[173] Even in the Constituent Assembly, some members suggested alternatives to reservations. M.R. Masani[174] and Z.H. Lari[175] had suggested instituting a system of proportional representation with cumulative voting in multi-member constituencies.[176] However, these suggestions were dismissed as 'intellectual abstractions'.[177] Consequently, the systemic failure to provide adequate representation for religious minorities in public office was accomplished much prior to the rise of India's Hindu right.

4

Temple and State

In this chapter, we will see that the seeds of secularism were sown in colonial India in 1833, when the East India Company felt that it must distance itself from 'heathen' and 'false' Indian religions. England itself had an established church at the time (which is so even now)— the Church of England. Senior clergy members like the Archbishop of Canterbury were appointed by the monarch. Salaries of members of the clergy were paid at least in part through tithes collected from the people. By contrast, in the middle of the nineteenth century, the colonial government in British India decided to let Hindu and Muslim religious endowments be managed (and often mismanaged) by local 'trustees'.[1] When Indian legislators eventually came to power in the provinces after 1919, they rejected this colonial secularism which had grown out of a Christian evangelical sense of revulsion towards Indian religions. They enacted laws that enabled the government to heavily regulate and administer religious institutions, especially Hindu temples. While debating the draft Constitution, the Constituent Assembly mysteriously dropped the 'establishment clause', which was akin to the one contained in the first amendment to the US Constitution. State governments thereafter enacted laws by which Hindu temples virtually became departments of the government,[2] and the Supreme Court usually upheld those laws, even though they inextricably entangled the government with the affairs of religious institutions.

Secularism as Colonial Revulsion

When the East India Company started conquering and taking control of territories in India, England was not a secular country with a wall of separation between church and state. Instead, the Church of England was the established church in the realm. King Henry VIII established the Church of England, and broke away from the Pope.[3] Since 1520, every ruler of Great Britain bore the official title 'Defender of the Faith'.[4] The 'Act of Supremacy' enacted in 1534 declared that the British monarch was the 'Supreme Head of the Church of England'.[5] The 'Act against the Pope's Authority' in 1536 dissolved the Pope's authority.[6] The Archbishop of Canterbury, or the most senior bishop in the Church of England,[7] and other high-level church officials were all appointed by the government.[8] The incomes of members of the clergy were supported by compulsory tithes or taxes imposed on some agricultural products.[9] New monarchs were crowned by a high-ranking member of the clergy, and senior bishops were represented in the House of Lords.[10] Even today, the House of Lords consists of the 'Lords Spiritual and Temporal'—the 'Lords Spiritual' are senior members of the clergy like the Archbishops of Canterbury and York.[11]

Similarly, pre-colonial rulers in India were intricately involved in the administration of religious institutions like temples and mosques. In 1790, for instance, Tipu Sultan, the Muslim ruler of Mysore, issued an order to his officials that Hindu temples were under their management, and that they were to ensure that 'the offerings to the gods and the temple illumination are duly regulated . . . out of the government grants'.[12] According to one scholar, Tipu Sultan was following 'a pattern imposed by centuries of history' in India.[13]

When the East India Company took over, it continued administering religious institutions that had been managed by prior, pre-colonial governments, partly because it was a good source of revenue and partly because it lent legitimacy to the ruling dispensation.[14] For instance, in 1796, the British collector of Madras took over the administration of Hindu temples at Conjeevaram (Kanchipuram).[15] In 1801, it was declared that all temples and servants at Tirupati were under the control and administration of the District Collector of North Arcot, who could punish any temple servant for misappropriating funds.[16]

The colonial government soon started enacting laws for administering temples and other religious institutions. In 1806, the government issued regulations for the 'superintendence and management' of the Jagannath Temple in modern-day Odisha.[17] Interestingly, the British referred to this temple as the 'Juggernaut' Temple. The English word 'juggernaut' is derived from this nomenclature,[18] which can probably be attributed to an Anglican chaplain, Reverend Claudius Buchanan. In June 1806, Buchanan was horrified to see a Hindu pilgrim sacrificing himself to the idol at Jagannath. The pilgrim, said Buchanan, lay on the ground with his 'arms stretched forwards' and was 'was crushed to death by the wheels of the tower' carrying the idol.[19] He wrote a book about his experiences at the 'Juggernaut' Temple, which became quite popular.

The 1806 regulations reintroduced a pre-colonial tax on pilgrims who visited the temple.[20] The tax was to be used, among other things, for paying the salaries[21] of temple officials though this did not bar them from 'receiving presents or gifts' voluntarily offered by devotees.[22] The 'superintendence of the temple . . . and its interior economy', and 'the entire control over [its] priests, officers and servants' was vested in an 'assembly of pundits or learned Brahmins',[23] consisting of three members, who were appointed by the government.[24] The pundits held their office during good behaviour,[25] but could be removed by the government 'on proof of misconduct'.[26] Like the monarch appointing the Archbishop of Canterbury for the established Church of England, the colonial government thus exercised the power to appoint senior priests at the Jagannath Temple.

However, this arrangement did not last very long. In 1809,[27] only around three years later, the management of the Jagannath Temple was transferred to the rajah of Khoordah, who was appointed the trustee of the temple. The government still retained some control over the temple. The rajah of Khoordah held his office as trustee of the temple only so long as he conducted himself with 'integrity, diligence and propriety' and could be removed by the government for failing to do so.[28] Some temple officials called *dewul purchas* were to be appointed by the British collector of Cuttack,[29] who also exercised control over the pilgrim tax.[30]

Soon thereafter, the colonial government enacted rules in Bengal, Madras and Bombay, for regulating the administration of temples and mosques. In 1810,[31] a law was enacted for Bengal that opened by saying that 'considerable endowments' or sizeable donations and contributions which had been made by past governments and individuals in favour of mosques and temples were being misappropriated and embezzled by the managers of those institutions.[32] The 'general superintendence of all lands granted for the support of mosques, Hindoo temples . . . and for other pious and beneficial purposes' was therefore vested in the colonial government.[33] It became the duty of the government to ensure that religious endowments were not mismanaged by local managers of mosques and temples.[34] Wherever a pre-colonial government had exercised the power of appointing trustees at religious institutions, the colonial government would now be able to exercise that power.[35]

A similar law was enacted in Madras in 1817.[36] In Bombay, in 1827,[37] a law was enacted which said that lands that were exempt from paying taxes because they were being used for religious establishments would be liable to be taxed 'if the conditions of the grant are not fulfilled', i.e. if the manager of the institution was misappropriating funds.[38]

Over the years, the colonial government got itself intricately entangled with the administration of religious institutions. Officers and attendants at temples were appointed by government officials.

For instance, on one occasion, the tahsildar of Palachy wrote a note to the acting principal collector at Coimbatore informing him that the dancing girl employed at the Pagoda of Kolandai had died, and that he had appointed her daughter in that position.[39] Members of the government presented offerings to Hindu idols and were present at Hindu and Muslim festivals, where British troops were made to attend as guards of honour.[40] Royal salutes were fired from the batteries of Fort St George in Madras at the celebration of Pongal and at Ramzan.[41] Under the orders of the public officer of the district, a religious offering was made at temples for ensuring a good monsoon.[42] At government offices, prayers were offered to the Hindu goddess Saraswati by worshipping account books and other records on some festival days.[43] By 1833, the Madras government reported that it was in charge of the administration of 7600 Hindu temples.[44]

All this annoyed Christian missionaries and members of the Christian clergy in Britain and India who put pressure on the government to end these practices.[45] Consequently, in 1833, the 'Court of Directors' (like the modern-day board of directors) of the East India Company wrote a long letter of instructions[46] to the government in India outlining its policy towards India's religions.[47] The directors wrote that all 'religious rites and offices' that were 'harmless' in the sense that they were 'not flagrantly opposed to rules of common humanity or decency . . . ought to be tolerated, however false the creed by which they are sanctioned'.[48] However, they continued that while it was necessary to provide some police protection at large festivals, '[i]t is not necessary that we should take part in the celebration of an idolatrous ceremony, or that we should assist in the preparations for it, or that we should afford to it such systematic support as shall accredit it in the eyes of the people'.[49] The exhibition of 'British Power in such intimate connexion with the unhappy and debasing superstitions' at Hindu and Muslim religious institutions, they wrote, gave the people of India the impression either that 'we admit the divine origin of those superstitions; or, at least, that we ascribe to them some peculiar and venerable authority'.[50]

The fact that the pilgrim tax was being used in making repairs at temples and paying the salaries of priests annoyed the directors.

'From being simply conservators of the public peace . . . we are become the chief agents in sustaining an idol establishment', they wrote.[51] They therefore ordered that 'the interference of British Functionaries in the interior management of native temples, in the customs, habits and religious proceedings of their priests and attendants, in the arrangement of their ceremonies, rites and festivals, and generally in the conduct of their interior economy, shall cease.'[52]

The directors expressed their dissatisfaction with the 1809 regulations, which, they noted, still left the colonial government a large degree of control over the 'interior concerns' of the Jagannath Temple.[53] They opposed the pilgrim tax at Jagannath, not because they thought that it was an unfair imposition on the religious rights of Hindus, but because they were revolted 'at the idea of deliberately making a profit of practices, the existence of which we must deplore, and of tenets which we cannot but entirely disapprove'.[54] They wrote that the pilgrim tax gave the government an incentive to promote and encourage 'the superstition, out of which the tax is derived'.[55] '[A]t Juggernauth', they wrote, 'the most gorgeous part of the decorations with which the cars at the festival are embellished, consists in cloths directly supplied by our own warehouses.'[56] They concluded by directing the government that the pilgrim tax should be abolished and that 'in all matters relating to their temples, their worship, their festivals, their religious practices, their ceremonial observances, our native subjects be left entirely to themselves'.[57]

It was in this manner that the seed of secularism was sown in India. Unlike Britain, which had an established church, the colonial government was directed to disentangle itself from 'superstitious' Indian religious institutions, because Indian religions were considered heathen and false. Importantly, it was not the 'Mutiny' in 1857 which set British India on a course towards secularism, but the 1833 letter of instructions from the Court of Directors which did so.[58] However, the government did not seek to distance itself from all religions. The Church of England in India was still established. Most of the senior members of its clergy were appointed by the Crown and paid their salaries by the government in India.[59] In 1927, though the formal relationship between the Church of England and its Indian counterpart came to an end,[60] chaplains and bishops continued to receive payments from the government, and churches which had been built by the government were maintained and repaired by it.[61] It was only after India attained independence that these arrangements came to an end.[62]

The 1833 instructions were not meant to be immediately implemented. However, they were virtually ignored for five years.[63] In 1838, the court of directors sent a reminder to the colonial government in India, after which the process of disentanglement began.[64] The pilgrim tax at the temple of Jagannath was revoked in around 1840.[65] In 1841, military bands and the firing of salutes were barred at religious festivals.[66] The government started actively looking for Indian trustees whom they could transfer their powers of administering temples and religious institutions to—trustees like the rajah of Khoordah at Jagannath.[67]

In February 1862, a bill was introduced in the legislative council of the Viceroy, the stated objective of which was 'to enable the Government to divest itself of the management of Religious Endowments'.[68] The mover of the bill in the council, Cecil Beadon, said that it was 'the last of a series of measures taken by the Government during several years for divesting itself of the management of religious trusts'. The bill sought to repeal the 1810 and 1817 regulations in Bengal and Madras.[69] The government was washing its hands off Hindu and Muslim religious endowments. Later that month, while the bill was being referred to a select committee of legislators, an Indian member of the Viceroy's Legislative Council, Rajah Deo Narain Singh, praised the Bengal and Madras regulations. He said that Hindu and Muslim endowments 'had been misapplied and misappropriated to other uses' and that after these regulations were enacted, the government had 'most honestly and efficiently administered them' in 'strong contrast' to even Hindus and Muslims, 'who before the dominion of the British destroyed each other's temples whenever they were sufficiently powerful'. He said that there was no real need for enacting Beadon's bill, but since it was being introduced, he hoped that the courts would continue to exercise powers of management over religious endowments.[70] In other words, the government's involvement in the administration of religious endowments was not necessarily seen as interference— Singh thought that the government's efficient management of those institutions evidenced its neutrality towards religion.

The bill was passed in February 1863.[71] The 1810 and 1817 regulations in Bengal and Madras were repealed as far as they related to 'endowments for the support of Mosques, Hindoo Temples, or other religious purposes'.[72] After the enactment of the 1863 law, where the government had hitherto exercised the power to appoint trustees of religious endowments, those powers were transferred to a newly constituted set of committees, whose members were elected and had to profess the same religion as the one of the endowment they were put in charge of.[73] On the other hand, for those religious endowments in which the government had not exercised any right of appointing trustees, all powers of administration were handed over to the trustees themselves.[74] However, it was the duty of the trustees to maintain accounts,[75] and any person interested in the endowment could sue the trustees in court for breach of trust.[76] Section 22 was the lynchpin of the 1863 Act. It said that it would no longer be 'lawful' for 'any Government in India, or for any Officer of any Government' in his official capacity, to take over the 'superintendence of any land or other property' belonging to a 'Mosque, Temple, or other religious establishment', to take part in the 'management or appropriation of any [religious] endowment', to nominate or appoint any trustee in a religious institution, 'or to be in any way concerned therewith'. Referring to this provision in the legislative council, the lieutenant governor of Bengal said that '[n]othing less than this would seem to mark the determination of the Government to rid itself of a burden which had been bequeathed to it by the former Rulers of India, and to abstain from all further concern with Religious establishments'.[77] Colonial officials thus spoke of secularism in terms of getting 'rid' of the nuisance of having to manage indigenous religious institutions in whose tenets the Christian colonial government did not believe.

The 1863 law was ineffective and the general feeling was that trustees of temples had a free hand in appropriating or misappropriating the funds of religious endowments.[78] This was primarily because the elected committees set up under it had limited powers. Committee members were not paid a salary, and if trustees did not obey their directions, the only option was filing a lawsuit which was expensive.[79] In fact, the withdrawal of the government from the management and administration of religious endowments was 'bitterly criticized by many Indians'.[80]

Thereafter, courts began to exercise limited powers of superintendence over religious endowments. They did so under section 539 of the Code of Civil Procedure, 1877, which was modelled on the English Charities Procedure Act, 1812.[81] The English law said that whenever there was a breach of any trust 'created for charitable purposes',[82] 'two or more persons' could file a petition and the court could then 'make such order therein . . . as to [it] . . . shall seem just'. The petition had to be certified by the attorney general or solicitor general.[83] However, the 1812 English law did not work because Lord Chancellor Eldon interpreted it in a very narrow manner.[84] Though the Charity Commission was eventually appointed in Britain in 1853 to oversee charities,[85] no comparable law was enacted in colonial India.

Section 539 of the Indian code said that whenever there was a breach of a trust 'created for public charitable purposes', either the advocate general or 'two or more persons having a direct interest in the trust' (after obtaining the consent of the advocate general in writing) could institute a suit. The court had vast powers and could pass orders such as 'appointing new trustees of the charity', 'settling a scheme for its management', 'or granting such further or other relief as the nature of the case may require'. This provision, slightly modified, still stands in the present-day Code of Civil Procedure, 1908.[86]

Thus, for instance, one such case was decided by the Bombay High Court in 1887.[87] Manohar Ganesh Tambekar was the hereditary manager of the temple of Shri Ranchhod Raiji at Dakor, built in 1772 by his ancestor. He sued a group of 150 hereditary *shevaks*, or priests, who performed daily services, and kept custody of all the cash, ornaments, clothes and daily offerings made by pilgrims to the deity. They were paid Rs 150 each year out of the revenues of the foundation, but the pilgrims donated a sum of about Rs 1 lakh each year to the idol. Tambekar asked the court to pass various orders, like directing the shevaks to give accounts of all the money they had received, appointing new shevaks, etc. The defendants (i.e. the shevaks) objected to the court's jurisdiction. The court rejected their contention and said that even under the previous 'native system of government', 'the State in its secular executive and judicial capacity habitually intervened to prevent fraud and waste in dealing with religious endowments'.[88] 'The cases in which Hindu foundations and charitable (including religious) trusts have been enforced,' said the court, 'and the persons connected with them made accountable by the Civil Courts are too numerous to mention.'[89] Since the 'religion of the Hindu population' was 'jurally allowed', the 'duties and services connected with it' were 'deemed objects of public concern', and those duties were enforceable in a court of law 'at least as to their physical and secular elements'.[90] Relying on Roman law, the court held that the idol was a legal person, a 'juridical person symbolized or personified in the idol at Dakor', and that the donations made by pilgrims were not the property of the shevaks, but of the idol itself.[91] The court held that the shevaks were accountable for the money they had received from pilgrims on the theory of an implied trust.[92] The shevaks, said the court, were 'answerable as trustees even though they have not consciously accepted a trust'.[93] The court directed the district judge of Ahmedabad to take steps to guard the property of the temple (by appointing a court receiver or otherwise), to take an account of the temple property, to recover amounts misappropriated by the shevaks, and to 'draw up a scheme for the future management of the temple and its funds, giving due consideration to the established practice of the institution and to the position of the shevaks and of other persons connected with it'.[94] On appeal, the Bombay High Court's decision was affirmed by the Privy Council.[95]

However, the colonial vision of secularism expressed as government disentanglement from the management and administration of religious endowments was rejected by Indian political leaders once they came to power at the provinces in British India. The constitution enacted in 1915[96] said that a local legislature in a province could not, without the previous sanction of the governor general, make any law 'affecting the religion or religious rites and usages of any class of British subjects in India'.[97] The Madras government repeatedly tried to introduce laws for improving the administration of religious endowments, but the governor general prohibited it from doing so.[98] In a letter written to the government of India in 1918,[99] the Madras government complained that this clause 'unnecessarily restricts the power of the local Governments'. However, under the Government of India Act, 1919, the power to legislate on matters relating to 'religious and charitable endowments' in the provincial list (or the list of governmental duties which were within the domain of the provincial governments) was 'transferred' to elected ministers, and not 'reserved' for the British colonial governor alone.[100]

Consequently, the Madras legislature in colonial India, manned by Indian political leaders, enacted a far-reaching law which virtually took over the management and administration of Hindu temples in the province of Madras.[101] Though there were various previous versions of it, the Madras Hindu Religious Endowments Act, 1926,[102] was the one that stuck until a little after Independence. It established 'boards' of Hindus appointed by the government.[103] The trustees of temples were now bound to obey instructions issued by these boards.[104] They had to furnish accounts to the boards.[105] The surplus funds of temples could now be spent by the boards themselves, on any 'religious, educational or charitable purposes not inconsistent with the objects' of the temples.[106] Boards had the power to settle a scheme for the administration of a temple, which included fixing the number of trustees, removing any hereditary or non-hereditary trustees and appointing new trustees. These powers were far broader than those previously exercisable by courts under the Code of Civil Procedure. While courts could only act where there had been a 'breach of trust', the boards under the Madras law could settle a scheme merely where they were 'satisfied' that it was necessary to do so 'in the interests of the proper administration of the endowments of a temple'.[107] In other words, like the monarch in England appointing the Archbishop of Canterbury, the Madras law, enacted by Indian leaders in the provincial legislature, gave the government the power to appoint, through its boards, trustees and managers of Hindu temples.

The Constituent Assembly Drops the Establishment Clause

In March 1947, Ambedkar prepared a draft on fundamental rights that was to be used as a template for drafting the Constitution. Importantly, that draft contained an 'establishment clause', akin to the one in the first amendment to the US Constitution. It said that '[t]he State shall not recognize any religion as State religion'.[108] A draft prepared by K.T. Shah also said that the state would be 'entirely a secular institution', which would 'maintain no official religion [or] established church' and would 'observe absolute neutrality in matters of religious belief, worship, or observance'.[109] If these clauses found their way into the Constitution, the Madras Hindu Religious Endowments Act, 1926, might quite possibly have been found unconstitutional.

That month, when the subcommittee on fundamental rights within the Constituent Assembly met, it decided to adopt a draft drawn up by the constitutional adviser to the assembly, Sir B.N. Rau. Rau's draft gave '[e]very religious denomination' the right to 'manage its own affairs in matters of religion', to 'acquire and administer property immovable and movable', and to 'establish and maintain institutions for religious or charitable purposes'. These rights were to be exercised 'consistently with the rights guaranteed' under the Constitution.[110] The subcommittee also agreed to adopt the following establishment clause, which was only a stylistic modification of Ambedkar's draft: 'Neither the Union nor any unit thereof shall recognize any religion as the State religion.'[111] Rau's notes on the draft said that the former clause was based on Section 44(2)5 of the Irish Constitution, while the latter one was based on the first amendment to the U.S. Constitution, and on Article 137(1) of the Weimar Constitution.[112]

Then, something odd happened. On 14 April 1947, the subcommittee discussed the establishment clause, and both K.M. Munshi and K.M. Panikkar[113] promised that they would redraft it, 'so as to provide for those cases where religion is already accepted as a State religion.'[114] Two days later, when the subcommittee presented its report on fundamental rights to the Advisory Committee,[115] the establishment clause had unceremoniously vanished, never to return again. The silent deletion of Ambedkar's establishment clause from the draft constitution was quite mysterious. However, Ambedkar did not submit any minute of dissent in protest.

About a week later, the Advisory Committee of the Constituent Assembly met to discuss the draft clauses of the fundamental rights. Alladi Krishnaswami Ayyar, a prominent advocate from Madras, suggested that the right of religious denominations to manage their own affairs be made '[s]ubject to any law as to maladministration of funds.'[116] Perhaps Ayyar had the Madras Hindu Religious Endowments Act, 1926, in mind when he suggested this change.[117]

After the draft Constitution was prepared in February 1948,[118] comments were received from B. Pattabhi Sitaramayya[119] and others[120] who wanted to reintroduce an establishment clause along the following lines: 'No religion shall be recognized as a State religion nor shall any tax be levied for the promotion or the maintenance of any religion.'[121]

Commenting on this suggestion, constitutional advisor Rau said that '[t]he proposed amendment involves a question of policy'.[122] Nothing further happened on this suggestion. The entire debate in the Constituent Assembly on the provision in the draft constitution dealing with the rights of religious denominations to manage their own affairs occupies no more than a few pages. Ambedkar merely concluded the discussion with the words: 'I have nothing to say'.[123]

In the Constituent Assembly, H.V. Kamath[124] tried to move an amendment to introduce an establishment clause into the draft constitution to the following effect: 'The State shall not establish, endow, or patronize any particular religion.'[125] In support of this amendment, Kamath said that he did not want to be 'misunderstood' as saying that 'a State should be anti-religious or irreligious'. '[T]o my mind', he said, 'a secular state is neither a Godless State nor an irreligious nor an anti-religious State.'[126] Another member said that non-establishment was 'the essence of a secular state'.[127] During the debate, Ambedkar rose and simply said: 'Mr. Vice-President, Sir, I have nothing to add to the various speakers who have spoken in support of this article.' Ambedkar rejected most of the amendments which were proposed, including Kamath's. Kamath objected to this and said that Ambedkar had to offer reasons why he was not accepting each amendment. However, the vice-president, who was presiding over the debate, said that Ambedkar could not be compelled to speak.[128] Kamath's amendment was put to vote and rejected.

Consequently, Article 26 of the Constitution gives to every religious denomination or a section of it, subject to 'public order, morality and health', the right to 'establish and maintain institutions for religious and charitable purposes', to 'manage its own affairs in matters of religion', to 'own and acquire movable and immovable property', and to 'administer such property in accordance with law'. Importantly, the Constitution itself said that the state could interfere in the management of religious institutions in the interests of 'public order, morality and health'. Further, for some unknown reason, the Constitution contained no establishment clause.

Religious and Secular Practice

It was Munshi's draft which was used as the template for what eventually became Article 25 of the Constitution. In his March 1947 draft, he gave all citizens the 'freedom of conscience' and the 'right freely to profess and practise religion' though 'in a manner compatible with public order, morality or health'.[129] This language was derived from the Irish Constitution.[130] Munshi later explained why his draft included a right to 'practice' religion, instead of a mere right to worship, by saying that many things ought to be covered by the freedom of religion which do not amount to worship but are nonetheless religious practice. For instance, he invoked the example of the 'immersion procession of Ganapathi'. 'It is not worship,' he said, 'but practice of religion.'[131] However, Munshi's draft also contained an exception that 'economic, financial or political activities associated with religious worship' would not be included in the freedom to religion.[132] It was this draft which was adopted by the subcommittee on fundamental rights on 26 March 1947.[133] Thus, Munshi's draft drew a line between protected religious 'practice' on the one hand, and secular 'economic, financial or political activities' which, though 'associated with religious worship', were not to be protected.

Rajkumari Amrit Kaur objected to Munshi's draft and said that it might invalidate legislation which sought to terminate anti-social customs.[134] The following month, Sir Alladi Krishnaswami Ayyar too suggested that provision be made for ensuring that the government could enact laws for 'the social betterment of the people'.[135] He believed that it would be impossible to 'separate social life from religious life', that Hinduism involved an 'inter-mixture between religion and the social fabric of society'.[136] Consequently, an explanation was added to the draft that the freedom of religion would not 'debar the State from enacting laws for the purpose of social welfare and reform'.[137] At Munshi's suggestion, an explanation was also added that the government could enact laws to '[throw] open Hindu religious institutions of a public character to any class or section of Hindus'[138] (which was later broadened to Sikhs, Jains and Buddhists).[139] Soft secularism in independent India therefore contemplated state interference in and reform of religion.[140]

The thin line drawn in Munshi's draft between protected religious practice and unprotected secular activity would be one which the Supreme Court would explore in the years to come. The question that lay at the forefront of all these cases was: does the right of trustees to manage and administer Hindu temples amount to a practice integral to the religion, or to a secular activity incidental to it?

The Supreme Court Permits Entanglement

The 'essential-to-the-religion' test

Both central and state legislative bodies in India are permitted, under the Constitution, to enact laws relating to 'religious endowments and religious institutions'.[141] After the constitution came into force, several states enacted laws which allowed the government to heavily regulate religious institutions (usually Hindu temples). Some such statutes covered all the temples in the state, while others were concerned only with a specific temple.[142] By 1960, there were only four states in India where a law governing Hindu temples did not exist.[143] Through these statutes, the state government often interfered and got inextricably entangled with the administration of Hindu temples, and provisions which allowed them to do so were mostly upheld by the Supreme Court on the theory that the management of a religious institution is a secular function which is not essential to religion. In short, the colonial secularism of the Court of Directors of the East India Company, born out of a sense of revulsion towards 'false' Indian religions, has been repeatedly rejected by law-makers and courts in independent India.

Both Articles 25 and 26 of the Constitution use the term 'religion'.

Under Article 25, everyone (and not merely Indian citizens) has 'the right freely to profess, practise and propagate religion'. Under Article 26(b), every religious denomination has the right 'to manage its own affairs in matters of religion'. Each of these provisions is subject to public order, morality and health.[144] The Supreme Court has held that the word 'religion' essentially means two things. Firstly, it means liberty of religious opinion and belief.[145] In other words, everyone has the freedom to decide which God to worship, or not to worship any God at all. So if the government tells a temple devoted to Vishnu to start praying to Brahma, this would clearly fall foul of the right to freedom of religion understood as liberty of opinion and belief. The fact that Article 25 speaks not merely of a right to 'religion', but also to 'freedom of conscience' suggests that even atheists and agnostics have the right to believe what they do. 'Religion', the Supreme Court has said, is not necessarily theistic, since there are religions in India like Buddhism and Jainism which do not believe in the existence of God.[146]

Secondly, religion includes acts done in pursuance of religious belief. However, these are protected so long as they are integral or essential to the religion.[147] In the early years, the court would ask itself whether the practice in question was religious in nature, i.e. whether it was 'essentially religious' as opposed to secular.[148] Now, the court asks itself whether the practice, even if religious in nature, is 'essential to the religion'. In deciding whether something is essential to a religion, the court takes into account the views of the denomination in question, but those views are not determinative.[149] Only the 'core beliefs' of a religion are essential to it.[150] A practice is considered to be essential if the religion itself would fundamentally be altered in its absence. A practice is essential if it has not been changed in any way.[151] Similarly, a practice is essential if it is obligatory.[152] For instance, the Supreme Court has held that a 'mosque is not an essential part of the practice of the religion of Islam and *namaz* (prayer) by Muslims can be offered anywhere, even in [the] open'.[153]

A 'code of ethical rules', 'rituals and observances, ceremonies and modes of worship', or even 'matters of food and dress' could be essential to a religion.[154] So if the government orders all Jains of the Swetambara sect that they can no longer wear white clothing, this would be unconstitutional, even though the order relates to a mere matter of dress, since clothing to this sect is integral to religious belief. Likewise, if the government orders the Sai Baba Temple in Shirdi to no longer conduct the early morning Kakad Aarti, or prayer, this too would be unconstitutional, because the prayer is an act done in pursuance of religious belief, and is integral to religion. The mere fact that a prayer involves the 'expenditure of money', the 'employment of priests and servants', or the 'use of marketable commodities' does not mean that it ceases to be a religious act and becomes secular.[155] Equally, merely because an activity takes place inside a temple or is connected to a temple does not make it religious and integral to religion.[156]

However, courts get to decide if a system of belief is religious or if a practice is essential to religion. In one case, for instance, the Supreme Court held that the followers of Sri Aurobindo were not a religious denomination, since his teachings, said the court, were a philosophy, not a religion.[157] In another case, the Supreme Court said that the power of the Syedna, or the head of the Dawoodi Bohra community of Shia Muslims, to excommunicate members was an integral part of the religion.[158] The test it laid down in that case for coming to this conclusion was that the court must examine the doctrine[159] of the religion and consider whether the religious community itself considers the practice to be essential.[160] Since the power of excommunication was based on religious grounds, like 'lapse from the orthodox religious creed or doctrine' or the 'breach of some practice considered as an essential part of the religion by the Dawoodi Bohras in general', it was considered to be a part of the management of the community, through its religious head, 'of its own affairs in matters of religion'.[161]

However, the right of religious denominations to manage their own affairs in matters of religion under Article 26(b) of the constitution gives way to social welfare laws enacted by the government under Article 25(2). So if the government enacts a social welfare measure to prohibit excommunication on grounds other than religious ones, e.g. the power to excommunicate a member for breaching 'some obnoxious social rule or practice', then this would be permissible under the Constitution.[162] For instance, if the government enacts a law that prohibits a religious leader from excommunicating his followers if they refuse to allow *khatna* or female genital mutilation (circumcision) to be performed on their daughters, the law might not be unconstitutional.[163] Similarly, a law which threw open Hindu temples to members of 'excluded classes' was held to be valid, though it was held that temples could exclude outsiders during certain religious services.[164]

In its recent Ayodhya judgment, the Supreme Court has set the ball rolling for eradicating the essential-to-the-religion test. The question in this case was whether the Babri Masjid was indeed a mosque under Islamic jurisprudence. It was argued that several theologically prescribed principles of Islamic law, e.g. that no graves should be situated close to a mosque, were not observed there, which denuded it of the character of a mosque. Rejecting this argument, the Supreme Court held that it would be inappropriate for the court to 'enter upon an area of theology and to assume the role of an interpreter of the Hadees'. The 'true test', wrote the court, was 'whether those who believe and worship have faith in the religious efficacy of the place where they pray.' 'This Court', the five-judge bench unanimously wrote, 'as a secular institution, set up under a constitutional regime must steer clear from choosing one among many possible interpretations of theological doctrine and must defer to the safer course of accepting the faith and belief of the worshipper.'[165]

Though the Ayodhya case was a title dispute that did not directly involve the fundamental right to religious freedom, the court's judgment in the case might eventually undo the essential-to-the-religion test. Under that test, when a person claims that her freedom of religion has been violated by government action, the court first examines her religion's doctrines in order to determine whether the right claimed by her is essential to her religion. After the Ayodhya judgment, the court may have to accept the devotee's claim that a certain course of conduct is essential to the religion and instead investigate only whether the government infringement of that right falls within the permissible restrictions.

The power of courts to investigate whether a practice is essential to religion has recently been referred to a larger bench of seven judges of the Supreme Court.[166]

Secular interference

The line between integral religious practice and non-essential secular activity is often hard to draw. The Supreme Court has said that courts must take 'a common sense view' and be practical while deciding such questions.[167] '[S]ome amount of control or supervision over the due administration of religious endowments, the court has held, is permissible.[168] However, over the years, the Supreme Court has permitted not merely 'some amount' of government interference in religious (especially Hindu) institutions, but quite a lot of it. Though the government cannot interfere with rituals and prayers at temples, it can regulate the amount that temples spend on such things,[169] especially if the expenditure is 'likely to deplete the endowed properties or affect the stability of the institution'.[170] So provisions in a Madras law which said that trustees of Hindu temples had to get their scale of expenditure approved by a government official, and that additions or alterations to a Hindu temple's budget could be made by a government official, were found to be constitutionally valid.[171] The government can require trustees of religious endowments to maintain accounts and ensure that those accounts are audited.[172] It can prohibit religious endowments from investing money in anything except a list of approved securities.[173] A law which says that the trustee of a religious endowment cannot transfer immovable property without the consent of a government official is valid,[174] as is one which requires religious trusts to be registered.[175] The 'right to manage the properties of [a] temple', it has been held, 'is a purely secular matter'.[176] A rule which excluded women between the ages of ten and fifty from entry into the Sabarimala Temple in Kerala was found to be an unconstitutional non-essential religious practice.[177]

In *Raja Bira Kishore Deb v. State of Orissa*,[178] the Supreme Court was concerned with whether the provisions of the Shri Jagannath Temple Act, 1954, were valid. The law vested the administration of the famed Jagannath Temple and its endowments in a committee called the Shri Jagannath Temple Managing Committee.[179] The committee was to be composed not merely of the raja of Puri (i.e. the original trustee, formerly known as the rajah of Khoordah), as its chairman, but also government officials like the collector of the district of Puri and some other members nominated by the state government.[180] This committee, composed almost entirely of nominees of the state government, then had the power to organize the materials necessary for performing prayers at the temple, and to even ensure that the priests performed their religious functions properly. The court found the law to be constitutionally valid.[181]

The government has the power to enter temple premises, but only so long as it respects the rules of the temple. The legislature of the state of Madras enacted a law in 1951 called the Madras Hindu Religious and Charitable Endowments Act, which replaced the colonial-era Madras Hindu Religious Endowments Act, 1926. The new law allowed the government-appointed commissioner to enter the temple to inspect it. The Supreme Court struck the provision down, in the classic case of *Commissioner, Hindu Religious Endowments, Madras v. Sri Lakshmindra Thirtha Swamiar of Sri Shirur Mutt* (the '*Shirur Mutt case*'),[182] on the grounds that it gave an 'an unregulated and unrestricted right of entry in a public temple' to 'persons who are not connected with the spiritual functions'.[183] The court noted that it was 'a traditional custom universally observed not to allow access to any outsider to the particularly sacred parts of a temple as for example, the place where the deity is located'. Temples also had 'fixed hours of worship and rest for the idol when no disturbance by any member of the public is allowed'. The Madras law, on the other hand, did not take into account these traditions. It did not confine the commissioner's right of entry to only 'the outer portion of the premises', leaving it open for him to enter even the temple's 'inner sanctuary'.

In other cases, however, laws which gave powers to the government to enter temple premises were upheld if the government had to respect the temple's traditions. For instance, in one case, a law which said that a government official had to give a 'reasonable notice' to a religious institution before entering it, and had to respect the 'religious practice and usages' of the institution, was upheld.[184] On the other hand, in another case, a law allowed the state government to depute any person, including a non-Hindu, to inspect the 'movable or immovable property, records, correspondence, plans, accounts and other documents relating to the temple and its endowments'. It did not say that the officer had to respect the traditions and usages of the temple, or even that a reasonable notice had to be given prior to the inspection. Even so, the Supreme Court upheld the law on the grounds that the 'power of inspection is necessarily incidental to the power to administer the properties'.[185] The court considered it 'far-fetched and imaginary' that the government would appoint a non-Hindu to inspect the premises.

The appointment of priests in Hindu temples has been held to be a secular activity, which the government can regulate. In many Hindu temples, priests acquire their positions on a hereditary basis. A state law that abolished hereditary priesthood was held to be constitutionally valid since a priest is a servant of the temple who is subject to the disciplinary control of the trustee.[186] In one case, it was held that a statutory board was within its power to appoint a non-Malayala Brahmin to the post of priest in a Hindu temple, even though traditionally, Brahmins alone held priesthoods at the temple. What was required, said the court, was that priests must be well-versed in the prayers.[187] The collection of offerings made by devotees to the idol at Hindu temples has been held to be a purely secular act. So a law that required the temple administration to install *hundi*s, or collection boxes, in the temple and said that *sevak*s or temple attendants could have no share in those collections was held to be constitutionally valid.[188]

The government exercises broad powers not merely over low-level temple officials like priests and sevaks, but also over the trustees themselves. A law enacted in Andhra Pradesh[189] said that when the position of the head of a 'math' or Hindu monastery became vacant, due to the death, resignation, or removal of the old one, the customary successor could not assume his office unless he had the 'permission' of the government-appointed commissioner. The commissioner could refuse his permission on grounds like if he felt the successor lacked 'basic knowledge of the Hindu religion and philosophy', 'unquestionable moral character', or even a 'religious temperament with implicit faith in discipline and practice'. In other words, the commissioner could decide to reject the successor on the grounds that he did not have sufficient knowledge of Hinduism. That would be like a government official rejecting the appointment of the Pope on the grounds that he was not pious enough. The provision was upheld by the Supreme Court.[190] The commissioner's decision, however, was held to be subject to judicial review by a court.[191] Another provision in the Andhra Pradesh law which allowed the commissioner to reject a person nominated by the *mathadhipati*, or the head of the monastery, to be his successor was upheld.[192] It was held that the commissioner had to test whether the nominee was 'a fit person to hold the office of mahant and to manage and administer the math according to the tenets, Sampradayams, usage, customs and philosophy of the math and the properties attached to it'.[193] A provision which allowed the commissioner to remove the mathadhipati if certain conditions specified in the law were met, e.g. if the mathadhipati lost his mind, violated the custom of celibacy or committed breach of trust, was also held to be constitutionally valid.[194]

Such powers have not merely been wielded by the government over Hindu temples. In a case involving the tomb of Khwaja Moin-ud-din Chishti of Ajmer, the Supreme Court was considering the constitutional validity of a law[195] that allowed a statutory committee (whose members were appointed entirely by the central government[196]) to decide the privileges of the 'Khadims' and to regulate their presence in the Durgah.[197] The law also allowed the committee to determine the functions and powers of the 'Sajjadanashins'.[198] The Khadims[199] were the custodians and protectors of the Durgah, while the post of Sajjadanashin was a spiritual office.[200] The provision was upheld, especially since the committee had to follow the rules of Muslim law applicable to Hanafi Muslims in India, and the tenets of the Chishti saint.[201]

Though there is no central law for Hindu temples,[202] the Waqf Act, 1995, a central law, regulates Muslim religious endowments. Each state has a statutory board that exercises powers of 'general superintendence' over all waqfs or Muslim religious endowments in a state. The board has to ensure that waqfs are 'properly maintained, controlled and administered', and that their income is applied to the objects for which the waqf was created. In doing so, the board has to act in conformity with the purposes of the waqf and take into account any usage or custom of the waqf sanctioned by the school of Muslim law to which it belongs. The board can give directions, settle schemes, sanction the lease of immovable property belonging to waqfs, scrutinize and approve budgets submitted by *mutawallis* and arrange for them to be audited, and even 'to appoint and remove mutawallis'.[203] However, the statute ensures that the board is not entirely state-controlled. The board has to have a majority of elected members over members nominated by the state government. The elected members of the board are picked by an electoral college consisting of the following persons: Muslim members of parliament in the state, Muslim members of state legislatures, Muslim members of the bar council, and mutawallis of waqfs with an annual income of Rs 1 lakh and above.[204]

Usurping religious property

Religious denominations have the right, under Article 26(d) of the Constitution, to administer their movable and immovable property 'in accordance with law'. However, like the other rights under Article 26, this right belongs not to individuals[205] or to just about any group of people, but to 'religious denominations'. So a Hindu temple which does not belong to a denomination does not have any fundamental right under Article 26. Relying on the *Oxford Dictionary*, the Supreme Court has held that a 'denomination' is a sect or body which is defined by three features, viz. that it: (i) has a common faith (ii) has a common organization, and (iii) is recognized by a distinctive name.[206] The commonality in the group must be based on religion, not purely on caste, community or social status.[207] Gowd Saraswat Brahmins were held, in one case, to be a denomination,[208] but the Vellala community was held not to be a denomination in another.[209] Adherents of the Shaiva form of worship were held not to be denominational worshippers in yet another.[210] Likewise, worshippers of Lord Ayyappa were held not to constitute a denomination.[211] However, if a temple does belong to a religious denomination so defined, the fact that other Hindus are allowed to worship there does not take away from its denominational character.[212]

While the government can regulate a religious denomination's right to administer its own property, it cannot altogether take over the administration of its property. In *Ratilal Panachand Gandhi v. State of Bombay*,[213] the Supreme Court was considering the constitutional validity of the Bombay Public Trusts Act, 1950. The case was brought by a *vahivatdar* (or manager) of a Jain public temple or *derasar*, and by the trustees of the Parsi panchayat. The statute set up the office of the charity commissioner in the state of Bombay, with whom all public religious and charitable trusts had to be registered. One of its provisions allowed the court to appoint a new trustee for a trust, and the court could even decide to make the charity commissioner the sole trustee.[214] The Supreme Court held that a law which 'takes away the right of administration altogether from the religious denomination and vests it in any other or secular authority' violates Article 26(d) of the Constitution. The impugned provision was therefore struck down. The Supreme Court also said that if courts could decide to appoint the charity commissioner as the 'mathadhipati' or 'spiritual superior' of a math, this would be 'disastrous' and 'amount to a flagrant violation of the constitutional guarantee'.[215] This is because a mathadhipati did not merely exercise secular functions for administering math property. He was the spiritual head of the monastery. The very object of a math, said the court, was 'to maintain a competent line of religious teachers for propagating and strengthening the religious doctrines of a particular order or sect'. '[T]he substitution of the Charity Commissioner for the [mathadhipati]', said the court, 'would mean a destruction of the institution altogether.' The fact that the charity commissioner could be appointed as the sole trustee was also problematic. Allowing the charity commissioner to function like a *shebait* in a temple or a mathadhipati in a math would be an 'interference with the religious affairs' of these institutions, said the court.

Similarly, in the *Shirur Mutt case*,[216] the government-appointed commissioner was authorized by a provision in the Madras law to call upon the trustee of a Hindu religious institution to appoint a manager to administer its secular affairs, failing which the commissioner could appoint a manager himself. The commissioner had the power to do so even where there was no breach of trust or misappropriation of funds by the trustee. While striking it down, the Supreme Court found that this was a 'provision of an extremely drastic character'.[217] The manager so appointed had to 'practically . . . do everything according to the directions of the Commissioner and his subordinates'. The court found that the commissioner was 'at liberty at any moment he chooses to deprive the *mahant* of his right to administer the trust property even if there is no negligence or maladministration on his part'.[218] This, said the court, would 'cripple' the mahant's authority, and 'reduce his position to that of an ordinary priest or paid servant'.[219]

In another case, it was held that the government could only take over the management of a religious endowment for a limited period of time, in order 'to rectify and stump [sic] out the consequences of maladministration', after which the administration had to be handed back to the trustees.[220] In many cases, the Supreme Court has held that the government has the power to appoint a transitory board until the permanent board is constituted or an interim trustee during a temporary vacancy.[221]

In *Ratilal's case*, the Supreme Court struck down provisions[222] in the Bombay Public Trusts Act, 1950, which stretched the doctrine of 'cy pres' beyond its usual limits. Ordinarily, the author of a trust donates money to the trust with the intent that it be utilized towards a certain purpose. Where that purpose fails or where the purpose has been exhausted and there are surplus funds left over, the funds may be utilized for some other purpose, as nearly as possible to the intent of the donor. This is known as the doctrine of 'cy pres'. However, the Bombay law allowed the charity commissioner and court to altogether ignore the intent of the author of the trust even where the purpose for which the money was donated could be carried out. It was, said the court, 'a violation of the freedom of religion' and of the right of religious denominations to manage their own affairs, 'to allow any secular authority to divert the trust money for purposes other than those for which the trust was created'. 'The State can step in', it was held, 'only when the trust fails or is incapable of being carried out either in whole or in part', or where there are surplus funds left over after exhausting the intent of the author of the trust.[223]

In the *Shirur Mutt case*, the Madras law said that if a Hindu religious endowment had a surplus of funds, those could only be utilized by the trustee according to the directions of the commissioner.[224] The Supreme Court struck this provision down and said that the trustee could be 'guided but not fettered by such directions' issued by the commissioner on how to spend surplus funds, particularly since the statute itself specified how the trustee could spend those funds, and a trustee could not spend temple funds on himself.[225] Another provision in the Madras law said that the trustee could spend surplus funds on any of the purposes specified in the statute only after obtaining the previous sanction of the government.[226] The Supreme Court struck this provision down as well, holding that it constituted 'a burdensome restriction' upon the property rights of the mahant, which were 'sanctioned by usage'. The provision, said the court, had 'the effect of impairing [the mahant's] dignity and efficiency as the head of the institution'.[227]

The government cannot interfere with the personal property of the head of a temple or math, like a mahant or *shebait*. In the *Shirur Mutt case*, the Madras law required 'pathakanikas' or personal gifts made to the mahant to be spent only for the purposes of the math, and required the mahant to maintain accounts for those gifts. The Supreme Court struck the provision down and said that it was an unwarranted restriction on his right to property.[228] However, in another case it was later held that if a personal gift is given to a mahant in his capacity as the head of the math, then it is in reality a gift to the math. So a law which required mahants to maintain accounts for such gifts, and to spend those gifts only according to the customs and usages of the institution, was held to be constitutionally valid.[229] However, a trustee, custodian or manager of a temple does not stand in the same position as a mahant of a math or a shebait of a temple, and does not have a comparable right to property.[230] Similarly, priests have no proprietary rights over offerings made by devotees to the temple, since they cannot be compared to a mahant or shebait either.[231]

The right of religious denominations to administer property in accordance with law, under Article 26(d) of the Constitution, does not prevent the government from acquiring land belonging to them,[232] unless the acquisition destroys their right to survive.[233]

Drastic takeovers

However, the Supreme Court has upheld drastic takeovers of Hindu temples despite the principles set out above. In *Raja Bira's case*, for instance, concerning the Jagannath Temple, the impugned law[234] allowed the government of Orissa to appoint an administrator for the temple. The administrator then had vast powers to exercise functions like appointing all officers and employees of the temple, leasing out the lands and buildings of the temple, and ordering emergency repairs.[235] The administrator exercised his powers under the 'control' of the statutory committee which, we have seen, was composed almost entirely of state government nominees. Even so, the statute was upheld.[236]

In *Tilkayat Shri Govindlalji Maharaj v. State of Rajasthan*,[237] the Supreme Court was considering the constitutional validity of the Nathdwara Temple Act, 1959, relating to the temple of Shri Shrinathji at Nathdwara in Rajasthan. The statute gave possession of the temple and all its endowments (including all offerings made to the deity) to a statutory board.[238] The existing trustee of the temple, the 'Goswami',[239] was an ex-officio member of the board. The Collector of Udaipur district was an ex-officio member of the board, even if he was a non-Hindu. However, the remaining members of the board were all appointed by the state government from amongst persons belonging to the Pushti-Margiya Vaishnava community.[240] The state government had the power to remove any member for some prescribed reasons, e.g. if the member was absent from more than four consecutive meetings of the board without obtaining leave, or guilty of corruption or misconduct in the administration of the endowment.[241] The state government could even dissolve the board entirely and constitute a new board.[242] The board was responsible not merely for managing the properties and affairs of the temple but also for arranging the conduct of the daily worship, ceremonies and festivals in the temple, though according to the customs and usages of the Pushti-Margiya Vallabhi Sampradaya. However, a provision in the statute said that the law did not affect any tradition, custom or 'established usage' of the temple.[243] The state government had the power to remove difficulties in the operation of the statute by issuing such directions as appeared to it to be necessary.[244] Even though all this amounted virtually to a complete government takeover of the temple, the provisions of this statute were fully upheld by the Supreme Court.[245]

The fact that the board was to consist of members, though appointed by the government, but of the same religious denomination as that of the temple, weighed in favour of the constitutionality of the law in *Tilkayat's case*.[246] The fact that even a non-Hindu Collector could be a member of the board, who would have a voice in administering the temple, did not render the statute unconstitutional,[247] perhaps because all the other members belonged to the temple's religious denomination. In another case, the Supreme Court also took the view that members of a statutory committee meant to administer a temple must belong to the same religious denomination as that of the temple itself.[248] So Digambar Jains could not be appointed to the positions of chairman and members of a statutory committee of management in a Swetambar temple.[249]

However, in the case[250] involving the tomb of Khwaja Moin-ud-din Chishti of Ajmer, the court took a seemingly contrary view. The law in that case required all the members of the statutory committee to be Hanafi Muslims.[251] The petitioners in that case contended that all Hanafi Muslims were not necessarily members of the Chishtia order of Sufis, to which the shrine belonged. The Supreme Court rejected this argument on the grounds that the tomb had historically been managed by the government, and the Chishtia order never had the right to administer the tomb's properties.[252]

Provisions in statutes which enable a government-official to frame a scheme for a religious institution have been upheld, so long as there are procedural safeguards in place. In the *Shirur Mutt case*, for example, the court was evaluating a provision in the Madras statute which allowed the government-appointed deputy commissioner to frame a scheme for a Hindu religious endowment if he felt that it was necessary to do so. The deputy commissioner also had the power to appoint a Hindu executive officer for a math, whose salary was to be paid out of the funds of the math. The court upheld the provision because it had 'ample safeguards' to 'rectify any error or unjust decision', including an appeal before the commissioner, the right to file a suit against the decision of the commissioner, and a further appeal to the high court. [253]

Wall of Separation

The entanglement of state governments with religious institutions in India would be impermissible in the US. The first amendment to the Constitution there prohibits Congress from making any law 'respecting an establishment of religion' or 'prohibiting the free exercise thereof'.[254] So the freedom of religion in the US has two essential limbs: non-establishment and free-exercise. In a letter written in 1802, President Thomas Jefferson had advanced the idea of a 'wall of eternal separation between Church [and] State'[255] in the US,[256] which has become a widely used metaphor.

In fact, it is tempting to surmise that the deletion of Ambedkar's establishment clause had something to do with an important case which was decided by the US Supreme Court only a few months before the deletion, in February 1947. A town in New Jersey was reimbursing parents for money spent by them in sending their children to schools by the public transportation system, even if they were being sent to Catholic parochial schools. In the first significant case concerning the establishment clause of the First Amendment to the American Constitution,[257] *Everson v. Board of Education*,[258] the Supreme Court found that there was nothing wrong with this practice. The court held that though a government must be 'neutral' towards religion, it is not required to be hostile against it.

Speaking for the court, Justice Black also explained the scope of the establishment clause. He wrote that it meant that the government could not 'set up a church', 'pass laws which aid one religion, aid all religions, or prefer one religion over another', and that '[n]o tax in any amount, large or small, can be levied to support any religious activities or institutions'. He added that a government could not, whether 'openly or secretly, participate in the affairs of any religious organizations or groups and *vice versa*'. The clause required that a government could neither 'handicap' nor 'favor' a religion. Evoking Jefferson, he concluded by holding as follows: 'The First Amendment has erected a wall between church and state. That wall must be kept high and impregnable. We could not approve the slightest breach.'

The establishment clause was dropped from Ambedkar's draft only a few months after this decision was delivered by the US Supreme Court. It is unclear if the framers of the Constitution were aware of this case when the establishment clause was deleted, but if they were, one can understand why they did so. The US Supreme Court had held that the establishment clause prevented governments from participating in the affairs of religious organizations and this might have rendered the Madras temple statute invalid in India.

Thereafter, in *Lemon v. Kurtzman*,[259] the US Supreme Court adopted a three-pronged test to determine whether a law was consistent with the first amendment, viz., 'First, the statute must have a secular legislative purpose; second, its principal or primary effect must be one that neither advances nor inhibits religion . . . finally, the statute must not foster "an excessive government entanglement with religion".' However, the court noted that the 'line of separation', between church and state, 'far from being a "wall," is a blurred, indistinct, and variable barrier'.

The rigidity of the Lemon test itself has been diluted by the court in subsequent years.[260] However, excessive entanglement of the government with religion remains barred in the US. In *Lynch v. Donnelly*,[261] Justice O'Connor in her concurring opinion wrote that the establishment clause prohibits two things: firstly, 'excessive entanglement with religious institutions, which may interfere with the independence of the institutions, give the institutions access to government or governmental powers not fully shared by nonadherents of the religion, and foster the creation of political constituencies defined along religious lines'; and secondly, 'government endorsement or disapproval of religion'. Endorsement 'sends a message to nonadherents that they are outsiders, not full members of the political community, and an accompanying message to adherents that they are insiders, favored members of the political community'.

According to Donald Eugene Smith, in the US, governments exercise 'practically nil' financial supervision of church property.[262] 'In a secular state in the West', he says, 'a church has the right to manage its own affairs in all respects—in doctrine, discipline, and administration of property.'[263] That having been said, Smith wrote that Western secularism 'presupposes the existence of well-organized churches with a tradition of self-government', whereas the Indian model 'presupposes largely unorganized religious institutions over which the state has traditionally exercised considerable regulation and control'.[264]

The state laws we have seen in this chapter all involved excessive government entanglement in religious institutions. However, entanglement with Indian religions was what the Court of Directors of the East India Company tried to avoid in 1833, because of their discomfort with 'heathen' and 'false' Indian religions. This vision of colonial secularism was rejected by Indian political leaders before Independence, and has been rejected by the Supreme Court of India thereafter.

5

To Divorce Religion from Personal Law

This chapter explores how the notion of 'personal law'[1] emerged in British India and why colonial legislators did not enact a uniform civil code in family matters. We will see that the British government adopted a policy of non-interference in religious laws, inspired by the Roman Empire where the customs of conquered people were left intact as far as they were compatible with the conqueror's norms. However, the colonial government then repeatedly violated its own policy and legislated on religious issues. It faced almost no opposition when it enacted statutes that supplanted Hindu and Muslim laws in the public sphere—laws dealing with subjects like contracts, evidence and crime. However, orthodox Indians repeatedly complained whenever the government tried to interfere with personal laws concerning the family, even if those laws were benevolent and well-conceived, like those abolishing sati or raising the age of consent for sexual intercourse from ten to twelve years. We will therefore see that the absence of a uniform civil code in India has its origins not in the principle of non-interference by the government in religious matters (since religious laws in the public sphere on subjects like contracts and evidence were freely altered during the colonial period), but in the principle of freedom from interference in the home and family.

After 1935, Indian leaders became members of the legislature in large numbers, and the colonial government abandoned its policy of non-interference in personal religious matters which had held sway since the time of Warren Hastings in 1772. Thereafter, the Constitution of independent India also formally renounced colonial secularism by making the enactment of a uniform civil code a directive principle of state policy. The existence of separate personal laws was seen by the framers of the Constitution (and subsequently by the courts of independent India) as one of the factors inhibiting national unity. However, in the decades thereafter, while the courts have attempted to reform Muslim personal law, the Government of India has relapsed into an informal policy of retaining the personal law of Muslims on questions like marriage and inheritance. In other words, the informal policy of the government of independent India towards Muslim personal law has been much the same as the formal policy of Governor General Warren Hastings towards Hindu and Muslim personal law.

In this chapter, we will also see that while enacting statutes dealing with personal law (e.g. those abolishing sati or permitting Hindu widows to remarry), colonial legislators expressly investigated whether the religious practice that was sought to be reformed was essential to the religion in question or not. This set the tone for what the Supreme Court would hold in *Shirur Mutt's case*, which we have seen in the previous chapter, and in cases like *Shayara Bano*, which will be examined herein, as to whether a practice constitutes an integral part of religion.

Personal Law in British India

A Uniform Civil Code in England

During the period of British rule in India, England did not (and continues not to)[2] have a separate set of personal laws, i.e. laws dealing with family matters like marriage, divorce, inheritance and adoption for its different religious communities like Protestants, Catholics and Jews.[3] In 1836, while some accommodation was given to Catholics and others to carry out marriages according to their own rites, the fundamental rules of marriage in England (e.g. that marriages had to be monogamous and heterosexual) applied to everyone regardless of their religion.[4] The Divorce and Matrimonial Causes Act, 1857, the first comprehensive law of divorce in England, did not contain exemptions for Catholics, Jews or Muslims.[5]

The term 'personal law' was used in England in a private international law context.[6] When a foreigner came to England, his capacity to marry was governed by his 'personal law', i.e. the law of his domicile.[7] In other words, the different religious groups of England did not have a separate personal law, only foreigners had a personal law (which was the law of their domicile) in some matters. However, even the personal law of foreigners was not absolute. In *Ogden v. Ogden*,[8] the Court of Appeal in England was considering the question of whether a marriage between an Englishwoman and a Frenchman was valid. The marriage took place in England, but the Frenchman, who was less than twenty-five years old, had not taken the consent of his parents as required under French law which was his 'personal law'. The marriage was nonetheless held to be valid. 'Why should it be recognized', asked the Court of Appeal, 'that a person who comes over to this country and validly enters into a marriage with one of its inhabitants according to English law should be held unable to do so here because of the regulations of a foreign system of jurisprudence which places upon him a personal incapacity to contract unless he complies with formalities required by the foreign law?'[9] Similarly, in the nineteenth and early twentieth centuries, foreign polygamous marriages were not recognized in England, as they were considered contrary to public policy, even though they might have been valid according to the personal law of the foreigner concerned.[10]

It is, even today, a part of the public policy of England that there should be a 'unified and single set of legal principles' of family law, applicable 'to all regardless of race or creed'.[11] Though some accommodation is given to different religious groups (e.g. various religious marriage ceremonies are recognized),[12] there is a uniform law of marriage, divorce, inheritance and adoption, in England. When a person dies without leaving a will, for instance, it does not matter whether he was a Protestant, Catholic, Jew, Muslim, or Hindu—the uniform law of intestate succession in England applies to him.[13] Though some religious communities in England have their own tribunals (e.g. Sharia Councils for Muslims and the Beth Din for Jews), these are not binding ecclesiastical courts but centres for alternative dispute resolution.[14]

The Hastings Plan

Though this was not the practice in England, in 1772, the first governor general of British India,[15] Warren Hastings, declared a plan in which he said that in all civil suits concerning 'Inheritance, Marriage, Caste, and all other religious Usages or Institutions', the laws of the Quran with respect to Muslims, and 'those of the Shaster' (or shastras) with respect to Hindus, would be 'invariably adhered to'.[16] Initially, Hindu and Muslim priests were hired by British courts to interpret the personal laws of those communities, but soon, religious texts were translated into English and applied by British courts without the aid of those intermediaries.[17] This rule of non-interference in the civil personal laws of Indians was the avowed formal policy of the Raj for much of the colonial period.[18]

In 1833, while debating the new charter of the East India Company, which sought to give the legislature in British India the power to enact codes of law, Thomas Babington Macaulay said in Parliament that the new charter did 'not mean that all the people of India should live under the same law: far from it'. 'We know how desirable that object is', he said, 'but we also know that it is unattainable.' He said that though 'respect must be paid to feelings generated by differences of religion, of nation, and of caste', much could 'be done to assimilate the different systems of law without wounding those feelings'. In enacting law codes in India, said Macaulay, the government was not proposing any 'rash innovation', and it was not their idea to 'shock' the populace in India. 'Our principle is simply this', Macaulay said famously, 'uniformity where you can have it—diversity where you must have it—but in all cases certainty.'[19] The Charter Act enacted by Britain's parliament that year gave the legislature in India the power to enact law codes, but the 'rights, feelings, and peculiar usages of the people' and the 'distinction of castes, difference of religion, and the manners and opinions prevailing among different races' had to be respected,[20] or at least that was the formal policy of the government.

After the Mutiny (which has also been referred to as the First War of Indian Independence) in 1857, Queen Victoria's proclamation in November 1858 added to what Warren Hastings and Macaulay had said earlier.[21] The proclamation declared that though the colonial government believed in the 'truth of Christianity', no person in India would be 'favoured . . . molested or disquieted by reason of their Religious Faith or Observances', that Christianity would not be imposed on the Indian populace, and that colonial government officials would incur the Queen's 'highest Displeasure' if they did not 'abstain from all interference with the Religious Belief or Worship' of her Indian subjects.[22] Thereafter, no law affecting religion or the religious rites of Indians could be introduced in any legislative body in British India without the previous sanction of the governor general.[23] The proclamation was even broader than the Hastings plan of 1772. It included not merely civil personal laws, but all laws, civil as well as criminal.

This policy contained in Queen Victoria's proclamation was formally adopted until the Government of India Act was enacted in 1935. In 1930, for instance, the Indian law member of the Viceroy's Executive Council, B.L. Mitter, explained to the central legislative assembly that it was a 'fixed principle of the Government of India not to interfere in any way whatsoever with the personal laws and customs of the different peoples of India' unless the government had 'very strong and conclusive evidence that the change is desired by the people who are affected'.[24]

When in Rome

The professed policy of the British in India was that of non-interference in personal religious matters. This meant that Indians would be governed by their own religious laws in their family environment—laws dealing with subjects like marriage, divorce, inheritance and adoption. But where did this idea come from? If England always had a uniform civil code, then why is it that colonial officials applied a different set of 'personal laws' to the different religious groups in India, treating Indians like foreigners in their own country, and members of India's different religious groups like citizens of separate countries, according to the principles of private international law in England?

In 1776, only a few years after Warren Hastings declared his plan, a code of Hindu law was prepared by one of his officials in India by the name of Nathaniel Brassey Halhed.[25] Halhed's preface to this code sheds some light on why Hastings might have adopted his policy of non-interference in personal religious matters. Halhed wrote that the Romans had pursued a policy of 'Toleration in Matters of Religion' and of adopting the laws of the conquered country which did not 'immediately clash' with their own. He said that much of the success of the Roman Empire could be attributed to the fact that the Romans had 'allowed . . . their foreign Subjects' to freely 'Exercise . . . their own Religion' so long as it was 'compatible with their own System'. It was with a view to obtaining the 'same political Advantages', said Halhed, that Hastings had asked him to prepare his translated code of Hindu law.[26] In other words, the British in India were formally pursuing the Roman policy of accommodating the religious beliefs of the conquered territories, so long as those beliefs were compatible with their own system. This was a strategy adopted by a conqueror to govern a conquered territory.[27] However, Halhed's preface does not explain why the colonial government decided only to retain religious personal laws while legislating in the public sphere.

On this principle, over the years, several personal laws which were incompatible with the British legal system were gradually legislated out of existence.[28] The most famous of these was the practice of 'suttee' or sati, according to which a Hindu widow would immolate herself on the funeral pyre of her dead husband, often after being drugged or forced by the husband's family members to do so. Though this practice was clearly incompatible with the British legal system, it took more than fifty years after the Hastings plan for sati to be abolished by law in India. This was largely because British colonial officials feared that there would be unrest in the Indian army if the government interfered in personal religious practices like sati.[29]

In 1789, the British collector of Shahabad, M.H. Brooke, wrote a letter to Governor General Cornwallis and said that though the 'rites and superstitions of the Hindu religion should be allowed with the most unqualified tolerance', a practice like sati was one 'at which human nature shudders'. He therefore asked for instructions on what to do when Hindu families asked him for permission to commit sati.[30] Brooke was told that though he could dissuade Hindus from committing Sati, he could not resort to coercive measures or exert any 'official powers' to prevent it from taking place.[31]

Around 1799,[32] a Christian missionary by the name of William Carey witnessed the practice of sati being committed in Bengal. As he wrote in his diary later on, he tried to beg the perpetrators to stop the practice. 'I talked till reasoning was of no use,' he wrote, 'and then began to exclaim with all my might against what they were doing, telling them that it was a shocking murder.' Instead, the onlookers at the event told Carey that sati 'was a great act of holiness'.[33] Carey and others collected data on sati and placed it before the governor general, Lord Wellesley,[34] who served as such between 1797 and 1805.[35] Wellesley asked the judges of the appellate company court in Calcutta, the Nizamut Adalat, whether sati could be abolished. The judges replied that while it could not be abolished altogether, it could be regulated.[36]

During Lord Minto's tenure as governor general of India, sometime between 1807 and 1813,[37] colonial officials started regulating the practice of sati. Whenever someone wanted to commit sati, they had to inform the nearest magistrate or police officer. It was then the duty of this official to ascertain whether the Hindu widow was going to commit sati of her own free will. No widow could commit sati if she was under sixteen years of age or pregnant. Widows could not be drugged before committing sati. Police officers had to be present while sati was being committed in order to ensure that the widow was committing the act voluntarily.[38]

In 1823, Lord Hastings (not Warren Hastings), who was governor general during 1813–23,[39] wrote to a friend in England and said that more than 800 Hindu widows had committed sati during his tenure. He called the practice of sati an 'outrage against humanity', but said that it was dangerous to 'suppress forcibly a practice so rooted in the religious belief of the natives'. To abolish the 'horrid superstition' of sati without the 'real concurrence' of Indians in the army, he said, 'would be distinctly perilous', as the custom was linked to 'family honour' and 'points of faith'. Though Hastings felt that he could have obtained the 'assent of the army' for abolishing sati, on account of his 'peculiar influence over the Native Troops', he did not abolish the practice during his tenure either.[40]

Sati was eventually abolished in 1829 because of the force of public opinion generated by Christian missionaries in England.[41] In his popular book which we have seen in the previous chapter, which introduced Britons to the 'Juggernaut' Temple, Reverend Claudius Buchanan wrote a chapter on sati, in which he said that between 15 April and 15 October 1804—in six months—around 115 Hindu widows had committed sati in an area within thirty miles around Calcutta alone.[42] English legislators started taking notice. In 1813, William Wilberforce[43] made a speech in the House of Commons against sati. The efforts of the missionaries gained momentum. In December 1828, the Society for Promoting the Abolition of Human Sacrifices in India was formed in Coventry,

England.[44] It published literature shedding light on the practice of sati in India.[45]

In the meantime, Indian intellectuals like Dwarkanath Tagore and Ram Mohan Roy argued that sati was not sanctioned by Hindu law.[46] For instance, Roy wrote an essay in around 1826, in which he said that Hindu women, by force of circumstances, seemed to have only three options once their husbands died: first, to 'live a miserable life, as entire slaves, without indulging any hope of support from another husband', second, to 'walk in the paths of unrighteousness for their maintenance and independence' (i.e. perhaps by resorting to prostitution or entering into a relationship not recognized by society), and, third, to 'die on the funeral pile of their husbands, loaded with the applause and honour of their neighbours'.[47] He urged Indians to place even 'greater confidence in the honest judgment of . . . European gentlemen' than 'in that of their own countrymen' on issues such as these.[48] Interestingly, in such debates which concerned women, the voices of women were rarely heard.[49]

It was against this backdrop that in November 1829, Lord William Bentinck, governor general,[50] wrote a minute[51] in which he made a case for abolishing sati.[52] He wrote that he was torn between sending 'year after year . . . hundreds of innocent victims to a cruel and untimely end', and hazarding 'the very safety of the British Empire in India' by abolishing sati.[53] On balance, he felt that by retaining sati, he would be guilty of 'the crime of multiplied murder'.[54] He believed that by regulating sati in the past, the colonial government had lent legitimacy and its tacit consent to the practice, which was reprehensible.[55] He set out several reasons why abolishing sati would not disturb the foundations of British rule in India. Firstly, powerful Indian rulers had now been defeated by the East India Company, and the position of the British in India was secure.[56] Secondly, he believed that the people of India would not rise up in 'insurrection or hostile opposition' if sati were done away with, because they lacked 'courage and . . . vigour of character' and were used to 'the habitual submission of centuries'.[57] In any event, the British had 'created a vast body of rich landed proprietors', zamindars, who were 'deeply interested in the continuance of' British rule in India, who had 'complete command over the mass of the people', and who would not revolt if sati were abolished.[58] Bentinck had also consulted forty-nine officers in the Indian army, and noted that 'few entertain any fear of immediate danger' if the practice were ended.[59] However, he made it clear that he was not in favour of converting Hindus to Christianity, and he believed that the views he had expressed in his minute were in accordance with what 'many enlightened Hindus think and feel'.[60]

Accordingly, on 4 December 1829, the legislative council of Bengal passed a law[61] which made practising sati a crime. The law opened by saying that the practice of sati was 'revolting to the feelings of human nature', that it was not observed 'by a vast majority' of the people of India, and that it was not a necessary ingredient of Hinduism, which only required that widows lead 'a life of purity and retirement'.[62] However, the law also made it clear that the colonial government was not 'intending to depart from one of the first and most important principles of the system of British government in India', that all people be allowed to observe their 'religious usages', as long as their beliefs did not violate 'the paramount dictates of justice and humanity'. Compelling a widow to commit sati was in some cases made punishable with the death penalty.[63] Similar laws were enacted in Bombay and Madras in 1830.[64]

Surprisingly, the abolition of sati had several opponents in India. Petitions were submitted to the Privy Council by several Hindus asking for Bentinck's law of 1829 to be repealed. To counter those petitions, Dwarkanath Tagore and Ram Mohan Roy[65] wrote petitions arguing that the abolition of sati had been received well in India.[66] Eventually, in around 1832, the Privy Council ratified the law.[67]

In short, the British formally pursued a policy in India of not interfering with the personal religious practices of the local populace that affected Indian families at home unless those practices were repugnant to British principles of morality and justice. However, even if Indian religious practices were morally offensive, the stability of the British Empire came first, and the objectionable practices would be retained until such time as colonial officials were secure that their abolition would not cause an insurrection or unrest, especially in the army.

Over the years, other measures were brought about which interfered with religious practices that were repugnant to British notions of morality and justice. In 1802, a law[68] was enacted that criminalized the practice of sacrificing children by drowning them or causing them to be devoured by sharks along the Ganges. The law said that this practice was 'not sanctioned' by Hindu law or by any of the previous Hindu or Muslim governments in India. In 1795, 1804, and 1870, laws were enacted against female infanticide to prevent Indians from killing their daughters.[69] In 1817, an exemption given to Brahmins in Banares from receiving the death sentence for murder was lifted as it was 'obviously repugnant to the principles of equal justice'.[70] This was despite the fact that the code of Manu prohibited Brahmins from receiving the death sentence.[71]

Opposition to Reform

Despite the fact that these regulations were a step in the right direction, many conservative Hindus objected to their enactment.[72] We have already seen that the anti-sati law generated opposition, which was eventually resolved by the Privy Council in 1832. Even laws that sought to allow Hindu widows to remarry or that raised the age of consent for sexual intercourse from ten years to twelve years garnered conservative opposition.

In 1856, while the legislative council of the governor general was debating a bill to allow Hindu widows to remarry, it received over forty petitions against the proposed bill, signed by 50,000 to 60,000 persons, and only around twenty-five petitions, signed by some 5000 people, in favour of the bill.[73] The opposition to the bill was on the grounds that it would interfere with the Hindu religion. Those who supported the bill, on the other hand, said that the prohibition against Hindu widows remarrying was 'not in consonance with the true interpretation of their religious books' and that it was 'absurd, unjust, cruel, and, in its consequences, immoral'. Members of the legislative council who spoke in favour of the bill said that it did not interfere with religion because Hindu widows who did not wish to remarry were free not to do so even after its enactment. Eventually, those in support of the bill won the day. The law which was enacted in 1856 took note of the fact that 'many Hindoos believe' that the bar against widow remarriage was 'not in accordance with a true interpretation of the precepts of their religion'.[74]

The age of consent controversy offers an even starker example of the opposition that presented itself whenever the colonial government attempted, even benevolently, to interfere with personal religious law. Section 375 of the Indian Penal Code dealt with the offence of rape. It said that sexual intercourse between a man and his wife who was ten years of age or above did not amount to rape. An eleven-year-old Hindu girl called Phulmani Bai died from lacerations she suffered as a result of intercourse with her husband.[75] In January 1891, a bill was introduced to raise the age of consent for sexual intercourse from ten years to twelve years for both married and unmarried girls. The mover of the bill in the legislative council, Sir Andrew Scoble,[76] said that Hindu law itself said that it was unlawful to have sexual relations with 'an immature girl'.[77] He said that raising the age of consent to fourteen years would involve 'too abrupt a fundamental revolution in the social life of India'.[78] In support of the bill, the governor general said that its object was 'simply to afford protection to those who cannot protect themselves'.[79]

Sir Romesh Chunder Mitter, a retired Indian judge of the Calcutta High Court,[80] opposed the bill and said that it was 'likely to cause widespread discontent in the country' and that it would be 'a departure from the wise and just policy of the Government . . . because it would interfere with the religious rites and duties of the orthodox Hindus.'[81] He believed that the law would violate the guarantee contained in Queen Victoria's proclamation,[82] and said that it would be akin to a law being enacted in England mandatorily requiring the dead to be cremated instead of buried, on grounds of hygiene.[83]

In response, Scoble said that Queen Victoria's proclamation did not bar the legislature from interfering with religious practices 'on grounds of humanity and morality'.[84] Similarly, Governor General Lansdowne said that the proclamation did not prohibit legislation on matters of 'public health, public morality and the general comfort and convenience of the Queen's subjects'.[85] He said that the Queen's proclamation had to be read with two limitations. Firstly, where religious practices were 'inconsistent with individual safety and the public peace, and condemned by every system of law and morality in the world, it is religion, and not morality, which must give way'.[86] Secondly, in the event a religious practice conflicted with morality, the legislature could distinguish, if possible, 'between essentials and non-essentials', i.e. whether the religious practice in question was essential or non-essential to the religion, whether it was one of the 'fundamental principles' of the religion or one of its 'subsidiary beliefs and accretionary dogmas', and whether it was of 'first-rate importance and absolutely obligatory' or only 'of minor importance and binding only in a slight degree'.[87]

In this speech, Governor General Lansdowne anticipated a test that would be adopted by the Supreme Court of independent India decades later in *Shrirur Mutt's case*. Lansdowne then said that in Hinduism, every act was considered religious, and this would prevent the legislature from instituting measures of reform, since every law touching on social matters would be considered an interference with religion.[88] However, he also said that the government was not willing to invalidate child marriages with girls under the age of twelve. That change, he said, had to come from within the Hindu community.[89]

The bill was eventually passed in March 1891.[90] Eventually, in 1929, a law was enacted which criminalized marriages between a male below the age of eighteen and a female below the age of fourteen.[91]

In short, when the government sought to interfere with
Hindu religious family law, no matter how benevolent or well-
conceived the proposed law was, it was often bitterly opposed by
conservative elements within the community who saw the measure
as government interference with religion and a violation of Queen
Victoria's proclamation. Further, it is interesting that when the
legislature enacted a law abolishing a regressive Hindu religious
family practice, it often said that the practice was not really
sanctioned by the religion in question. The statute criminalizing
sati said that sati was not essential to Hinduism. The widow
remarriage law said that the prohibition on widow remarriage was
considered by many Hindus to be contrary to Hinduism. While
debating the age of consent for sexual intercourse, Governor
General Lansdowne expressly called upon legislators to investigate
whether a religious practice was essential or non-essential to the
religion. Such an investigation set the tone for what the Supreme
Court would do in *Shirur Mutt's case*, which we have seen in the
previous chapter.

The colonial government violates its own policy

It was not merely family law, however, which was religious in nature.
There were several rules in Hinduism and Islam which dealt, for
example, with the law of contracts, evidence and crimes.[92] Despite
overtly adopting a policy of non-interference in religious laws, the
colonial government repeatedly violated this policy and enacted
secular statutes on subjects in the impersonal sphere.

Under some treatises in Hindu law, for instance, a contract could
be considered invalid if a contracting party was full of 'anger, lust, [or]
grief' at the time that the contract was signed.[93] This principle was
done away with under the Indian Contract Act, which was enacted
in 1872. Similarly, under Hindu law, if one family member incurred
a debt and another family member later promised to pay that debt,
the subsequent promise would be considered contractually binding

despite the fact that it lacked consideration. This rule too was done away with under the Contract Act.[94]

Hindu law allowed hearsay evidence to be admitted. If a witness to a transaction explained the circumstances of that transaction to another, that other person could be admitted as a witness.[95] It also said that a woman,[96] a 'Juggler', or a person 'constantly employed in Games of Dice and Chances'[97] could not be witnesses. It required both the cross-examiner and witness to bathe before the cross-examination and for questions to be asked in cross-examination with differing levels of respect, depending on the caste of the witness concerned.[98] Similarly, under Muslim law, in criminal cases, the evidence of two men was required to secure a conviction, and the testimony of women was not admissible, 'on account of their defect of understanding, their want of memory, and incapacity of governing'.[99] All these religious rules were done away with by the Indian Evidence Act, 1872. In fact, while debating the Evidence Act, the law member of the Viceroy's Executive Council, James Fitzjames Stephen, said that the Muslim Hedaya was full of 'arbitrary rules of evidence', like '[s]uch a fact must be proved by two eye-witnesses; such another by four; such another by seven'.[100]

Likewise, under Hindu law, when a person killed a goat, horse or camel, a magistrate could punish him by cutting off one hand and one foot.[101] The punishment for kidnapping a person of 'superior' caste was that the perpetrator would be tied up and burned alive.[102] All these religious sanctions were done away with under the Indian Penal Code, 1860. After preparing his draft of the Indian Penal Code, Macaulay wrote that Hindu criminal law had mostly been replaced by Muslim criminal law, and was 'the last system of criminal law which an enlightened and humane Government would be disposed to revive'.[103] In turn, Muslim criminal law had incrementally been replaced by English law, even before the Indian Penal Code had been drafted. In Bengal and Madras, he wrote, Muslim criminal law had 'gradually been distorted to such an extent' that it could no longer earn 'the religious veneration of Mahomedans'.[104] 'In substance', he wrote, the criminal law of Bengal and Madras differed 'at least as widely from the Mahomedan penal law, as the penal law of England differs from the penal law of France.'[105] In Bombay, the entire criminal law had been replaced by a British code.[106] This had not caused much unrest in the Indian community. 'Throughout a large territory, inhabited to a great extent by a newly-conquered population,' Macaulay wrote, 'all the ancient systems of penal law were at once superseded by a code, and this without the smallest sign of discontent among the people'.[107]

Why is it that the British colonial government interfered with religious Hindu and Muslim laws in the public sphere—laws governing subjects like contracts, evidence and crime, without worrying about its own formal policy of religious non-interference?

One possible explanation is that the Hindu and Muslim religious injunctions dealing with subjects like contracts and evidence were not exhaustive. As a professor at the University of Oxford and a former law member of the Viceroy's Legislative Council in India, Sir Henry Maine, wrote, 'there were many branches of law in which the political officers of the British Government could find few positive rules of any sort'. 'Thus there was no law of Evidence, in the proper sense of the words,' he said, 'hardly any law of Contract; scarcely any of Civil Wrong.' 'The civil procedure,' he added, 'consisted in little more than vague directions to do justice.'[108] In the absence of comprehensive Hindu and Muslim rules on these subjects, courts in British India started applying principles of the English common law of evidence and contracts. In Maine's words, '[i]nto all the departments of law which were thus scantily filled the English law steadily made its way'.[109]

Another explanation is that it was harder for the colonial government to enact legislation affecting Hindu or Muslim personal laws than impersonal ones. For some reason, British colonial interference with religious laws in the public sphere did not generate much opposition from the orthodox community. We have seen that even benevolent laws which sought to interfere with religious practices affecting the family were bitterly opposed by many Hindus, for instance, who saw those laws as an interference with their religion. On the other hand, when secular laws were enacted to supplant religious laws in the public sphere, they met with little or no opposition.[110] What this tells us is that the lack of a uniform civil code in India can be attributed not to religion but to privacy. Hindus and Muslims were not bothered much when their religious laws of contract, evidence and crime were replaced by the British. They did object, however, when the government attempted to legislate on matters governing their personal, family lives. What they were asserting, therefore, was not a right to the free exercise of religion, but a right to freedom from interference in family matters.

One more explanation is that while the British enacted secular laws to deal with subjects in the public sphere like contracts, evidence and crime, they retained religious laws in the personal sphere in order to deliberately create fissures among the different religious communities in India. There is some historical evidence to suggest that the British actually created the cohesive conceptual category of 'Hindu', which did not exist prior to colonialism.[111] After the Mutiny in 1857, Governor Elphinstone of Bombay suggested that the Indian army should not have regiments consisting of Indians from different regions. In his view, each regiment ought to have been recruited from one geographic location and not others. '[O]ur safety consists in forming our regiments of the most discordant materials', he wrote.[112] If this were done, Elphinstone believed that a mutiny in one regiment could be contained. '*Divide et impera* was the old Roman motto,' he wrote, 'and it should be ours.' He continued:

> The safety of the great iron steamers . . . is greatly increased by building them in compartments. I would ensure the security of our Indian empire by constructing our native army upon the same principle; for this purpose I would avail myself of those diversities of race and language which we find ready to our hands.[113]

To be sure, the colonial government did not leave personal laws, even those that did not conflict with British notions of morality and justice, entirely intact. Instead, the colonial encounter substantially altered the personal laws of the populace.[114] For instance, ancient Hindu law did not recognize wills.[115] The Supreme Courts of British India first sanctioned them and by 1857, they were such a regular feature of Hindu inheritance that the Privy Council held that they were valid under Hindu law.[116] Further, colonial officials sometimes modified personal law by misconstruing it altogether. For instance, they placed an undue emphasis on scriptural, written law over custom and practice.[117] The translations of religious texts were sometimes riddled with errors. English law was incorporated into personal law. For example, courts in British India applied English trust law doctrine to Hindu religious endowments,[118] and judges in colonial India used the notion of 'justice, equity and good conscience' to apply English law to religious personal law.[119] For this reason, scholars sometimes speak of 'Anglo-Muhammadan law' and 'Anglo-Hindu law' instead of Muslim or Hindu personal law respectively.[120] Colonial secularism did not stop the government from enacting statutes for Parsis (who lobbied for the legislation themselves) and Christians in India.[121] Therefore, wittingly and sometimes unwittingly, the colonial government certainly violated its own stated policy of not interfering with the personal laws of the people.

Non-Official Bills

The Government of India Act, 1935 loosened the formal policy of non-interference in religious matters, which had been adopted since the time of Warren Hastings. After its enactment, the prior approval of the governor general was no longer required for passing statutes affecting personal law. We have already seen in the previous chapter that after 1919, Indians started filling up the central and provincial legislative assemblies, and they rejected colonial secularism by enacting laws for administering Hindu temples. This was true even in the personal law sphere, where private member bills or 'non-official bills' started being introduced into the legislative assembly by Hindu and Muslim legislators to reform their own religious personal laws, and those bills were often passed as law.

So, for instance, in 1937, the central legislature of British India enacted the Muslim Personal Law (Shariat) Application Act,[122] which made the Shariat applicable to all Muslims (except those in the North-West Frontier Province) on personal law subjects like intestate succession, marriage, divorce, maintenance, dower, and so on,[123] instead of customary and Anglo-Muslim law.[124] The Shariat would only apply to questions of adoption, wills and legacies, if a Muslim declared his intention to be bound by it on those points.[125] This law was enacted despite the fact that there were several Muslims in India who considered themselves governed not by the Shariat in personal law matters, but by their own customs which were analogous to Hindu personal law.

The bill was introduced by a private, non-official member of the central legislative assembly, Hafiz Mohammad Abdullah, a member of the All India Muslim League.[126] Many Muslim members of the assembly supported the bill in principle. For instance, Abdul Qaiyum, a Muslim member of the assembly from the North-West Frontier Province, said that he wanted 'the Muslims in India in matters affecting them to follow the personal law of the Muslims as far as they can'.[127] Muhammad Anwar-ul-Azim, a Muslim member from Chittagong, said that it was 'a singular pity that the Government of India . . . should have sat still for such a long time' and that 'it should have been left to my esteemed friend from the Punjab, the Hafiz Sahib, to introduce this Bill'.[128] Khan Bahadur Shaikh Fazl-i-Haq Piracha, from North-West Punjab, said: 'I feel it my pleasant duty to give my wholehearted support to the Shariat Bill, the necessity of which is so much being felt by the Muslim community of the country, especially the Punjab.' M.A. Jinnah made a speech which highlighted the fact that this was a non-official bill. 'I thought I would wait until I heard the Government view on this Bill', he said, 'but evidently Government have no views at all.'[129] The colonial government's attitude in such cases ranged from 'benign neglect'[130] to 'grumbling' support.[131]

Similarly, in 1939, the central legislature passed the Dissolution of Muslim Marriages Act, 1939, which recognized the right of Muslim women to obtain a divorce on certain enumerated grounds,[132] and said that the conversion of a Muslim woman to another religion did not automatically dissolve her marriage.[133] Earlier, since Muslim women were not able to obtain a divorce, and their conversion to another religion was considered as automatically dissolving their marriages, Muslim women who wanted to obtain a divorce had no option but to convert to another religion.

This statute was also moved as a private member bill by Qazi Muhammad Ahmad Kazmi, a Muslim member of the central legislative assembly from Meerut.[134] The bill, he said, 'only removes a very grave defect and is calculated to meet a very great necessity and a very great demand of the Muslim community'.[135] The bill did not meet with much opposition, in principle, from Muslim legislators. Abdul Qaiyum[136] said that it was 'a very important measure, and if there is any measure the need of which has been so very strongly felt by the Muslim community in India, it is this measure'. '[I]t is a very good thing that my Honourable friend, Mr Kazmi, has brought out all those points', he said, and added, 'when this Bill becomes law, a long-felt need of the Muslim community will have been met'.[137] Sir Muhammad Zafrullah Khan, leader of the house, later a judge of the Federal Court of India and judge (subsequently president) of the International Court of Justice,[138] said that there was 'not the slightest doubt' that the Bill was 'an extremely important measure'.[139]

Official members of the legislative assembly lent their tacit support to the Bill in principle. One such member who had been nominated by the government, J.A. Thorne, said that it was 'entirely in accord with Government practice that any Bill which proposes to alter social or religious usages or custom of a community should be ventilated as widely as possible', i.e. widely disseminated for soliciting public opinion, 'before this House proceeds to consider it'.[140] In other words, the colonial government seemed to have abandoned its formal policy of non-interference in personal religious matters, since the interference was at the hands of Hindus and Muslims themselves, who were now members of the legislative assembly. The words of praise lavished on the bill by Sardar Sant Singh, a Sikh from Punjab, are revealing. 'Here is a provision', he said, 'by which the author of this Bill wants to interfere in the Muslim law of his own community.'[141] Such laws were not seen as interference by the British government in personal religious matters, but as interventions made in personal law by members of the religious community itself.[142] Gone was the opposition of orthodox sections of the community when the government attempted to reform personal law. Sir Nripendra Sircar, who was the law member of the Viceroy's Executive Council, did not move the Bill, but he did not oppose it in principle either.[143]

Constitutional Unity or Diversity?

Likewise, the framers of India's Constitution did not adopt the earlier formal British policy of non-interference in religious matters which was articulated by Hastings, Macaulay and in Queen Victoria's proclamation. We have already seen in the previous chapter that the Constitution did not have an establishment clause. That apart, the Constitution contained a provision, Article 44, in the non-binding directive principles of state policy, which required the state to 'endeavour to secure' for its citizens 'a uniform civil code throughout the territory of India'. Standing in direct contrast to the policy of non-interference in personal law that had hitherto been followed,[144] this clause was prepared because the framers of the Constitution saw the existence of religious personal laws as something which divided the country. A uniform civil code, they thought, was necessary to consolidate and unify India. At the same time, Ambedkar's interventions in the debate on the uniform civil code in the Constituent Assembly reveal that he advocated a cautious approach—he did not want a uniform civil code to be enacted overnight.

On 30 March 1947, the subcommittee on fundamental rights met and, in the absence of any Muslim member, decided that India should endeavour to have a uniform civil code for its citizens.[145] Three members of the sub-committee, M.R. Masani,[146] Hansa Mehta[147] and Amrit Kaur, felt that this clause did not go far enough. They wanted the state to mandatorily enact (rather than merely 'endeavour' to do so) a uniform civil code within five to ten years. They believed that the different religious personal laws in India had been responsible for '[keeping] the nation divided into watertight compartments in many aspects of life'.[148]

However, when the subcommittee on minorities met on 19 April 1947, it recommended that the uniform civil code, though 'eminently desirable', ought to be restricted and made applicable 'on an entirely voluntary basis'.[149] In other words, if a person wanted to be bound by his own personal laws rather than the uniform civil code, he should be free to do so, thought the subcommittee on minorities.

The clause in the draft constitution dealing with the uniform civil code was debated in the Constituent Assembly on 23 November 1948.[150] Several Muslim members of the assembly opposed the clause. They advanced many arguments to contend that it ought to be dropped, viz. that interfering with personal law would amount to an interference with a way of life;[151] rather than producing 'harmony through uniformity', the uniform civil code would create discontent;[152] the British colonial government had not interfered with personal laws, and the Indian government should not immediately do so either;[153] personal laws were 'dear and near to certain religious communities' and Muslims would not abide by the uniform civil code because it was not in accordance with the religion that they had practised for centuries;[154] personal laws must be respected in a secular state;[155] there was no clarity on which system would be made the basis of the uniform civil code;[156] and a uniform civil code would be contrary to other fundamental rights.[157] Echoing the Roman principle articulated by Halhed in the time of Warren Hastings, B. Pocker Sahib Bahadur argued that 'one of the secrets of success' of the British Empire was that the colonial government had not interfered with the personal laws of the various communities.

However, two Muslim members of the assembly, Naziruddin Ahmad and Hussain Imam, supported the provision but suggested that the enactment of a uniform civil code should be gradual and not immediate. Imam said that it could only be enacted 'when the whole of India has got educated, when mass illiteracy has been removed, when people have advanced, when their economic conditions are better'.

Three of the leading voices in the Constituent Assembly, K.M. Munshi, Sir Alladi Krishnaswami Ayyar and B.R. Ambedkar, supported the clause dealing with the uniform civil code.

Munshi said that even in 'advanced Muslim countries' like Turkey or Egypt, the personal laws of minorities were not 'recognised as so sacrosanct as to prevent the enactment of a Civil Code', and minorities in those countries were not permitted to follow their own laws. In European countries too, he argued, even minorities had to submit to a civil code. The Shariat Act imposed Muslim law on Khojas and Cutchi Memons, he said, who used to follow Hindu customs. Much in the same manner, the uniform civil code would impose a uniform system of law on the populace. He could not understand what matters like inheritance or succession had to do with religion, and felt that he wanted to 'divorce religion from personal law'. He believed that the British were responsible for making Indians feel that 'personal law is part of religion'. The uniform civil code, he said, would affect not merely minorities, but also Hindus, who had different systems of law throughout the country. He said that even the Muslim ruler Allauddin Khilji had adopted laws which 'offended against the Shariat', in the 'best interests' of his kingdom. He believed that a uniform civil code was necessary to 'unify and consolidate the nation'. He elaborated this by saying:

Religion must be restricted to spheres which legitimately appertain to religion, and the rest of life must be regulated, unified and modified in such a manner that we may evolve, as early as possible, a strong and consolidated nation. Our first problem and the most important problem is to produce national unity in this country.

Alladi too agreed that the personal law system had contributed to 'differences among the different peoples of India'. '[W]e want', he said, 'the whole of India to be welded and united together as a single nation.' He astutely pointed out that the British had enacted laws that contradicted the religious laws of Hindus and Muslims. 'Muslim law covers the field of contracts, the field of criminal law,' he said, and that had not stopped the colonial government from introducing 'one criminal law in this country which [was] applicable to all citizens, be they Englishmen, be they Hindus, be they Muslims.' Despite this, Muslims did not 'take exception' or 'revolt against the British for introducing a single system of criminal law'. Likewise, no exception was taken to the Muslim law of contracts being superseded by 'Anglo-Indian jurisprudence'. There could therefore be no objection to a uniform civil code. He too said that in continental European countries like France, Germany and Italy, there was no system of 'different personal laws'.

Ambedkar made the same point as Alladi about India having 'a uniform code of laws covering almost every aspect of human relationship', such as a uniform criminal code and statutes governing the law of property and negotiable instruments. The 'only province' which had not been legislated upon in colonial India, he said, was 'Marriage and Succession', and it was with 'this little corner' that the clause of the Constitution dealing with the uniform civil code was concerned. He made the same point as Munshi and said that until 1937, in various parts of India, like the United Provinces, Central Provinces and Bombay, Muslims were governed by Hindu law in matters of succession. The 1937 Shariat Act enacted by the central legislature constituted an imposition on this personal law system. In North Malabar, he said, the matriarchal Marumakkathayam law applied to both Hindus and Muslims. Analogously, he said, there could be no objection if 'certain portions' of Hindu law were applied to all communities in India, not because they were Hindu in origin but 'because they were found to be the most suitable'.

However, Ambedkar also advocated caution. He said that the clause in the Constitution on the uniform civil code did not make the enactment of the code mandatory. Further, it was 'perfectly possible', he said, that a 'future parliament' would enact such a code on a voluntary basis, making it applicable only to those who agreed to be bound by it, at least in the initial stages, as was done by certain portions of the Shariat Act of 1937. 'We must all remember', he said later,[158] 'that sovereignty is always limited'. In a speech reminiscent of Halhed's invocation of the Roman principle, Ambedkar said that 'sovereignty in the exercise of that power must reconcile itself to the sentiments of different communities.' 'No Government', he said, 'can exercise its power in such a manner as to provoke the Muslim community to rise in rebellion.' '[I]t would be', he continued, 'a mad Government if it did so.' 'In Europe there is Christianity', he said, 'but Christianity does not mean that the Christians all over the world or in any part of Europe where they live, shall have a uniform system of law of inheritance.' 'No such thing exists', he said. In a speech reminiscent of Governor General Lansdowne's intervention in the age of consent debate, Ambedkar said that in India, '[t]here is nothing which is not religion', and adopting a policy of non-interference would prohibit social reform legislation.

A Code for Hindus

In December 1949, when Ambedkar was the law minister, the Constituent Assembly of India debated a comprehensive Hindu

Code Bill which would have codified Hindu personal law on matters like marriage and divorce, succession, minority and guardianship, and adoptions and maintenance.[159] The Bill was opposed by many members of the Assembly, including a person by the name of Hari Vinayak Pataskar.[160] Pataskar objected to the Bill on the grounds that it violated the constitutional principle of a uniform civil code.[161] He felt that by seeking to push through the Hindu Code Bill, India was going 'backward rather than forward'.[162] Instead, he said, '[a]ll the inhabitants of India should be welded into one' and that nothing 'should be done for Hindus alone in such matters'.[163] He said that the British had pursued a policy of 'noninterference in religious or semi-religious matters' for 'their own purposes', so that they could keep the different communities in India apart. Now, he said, 'our ideal is to unite all our people in the nation'.[164] 'By the present Bill,' he told the government, 'you are giving the exclusive right to a Muslim to have as many wives as he likes or at any rate up to four.'[165]

The Hindu Code Bill was very close to Ambedkar's heart, and he eventually resigned as Law Minister in 1951 when it was not passed.[166] Ironically, when the Bill was broken up into different statutes and passed by Parliament in 1955–56, Pataskar, formerly a vocal opponent of the Hindu Code, was the law minister, who, in the absence of a uniform civil code, now had to defend the enactment of a law for Hindus only. A Hindu Mahasabha[167] leader in the Lok Sabha, N.C. Chatterjee, then strongly objected to these measures on the very grounds that Pataskar had raised in 1949, viz. that the Constitution bound India to a uniform civil code, and these statutes constituted a violation of that principle.[168] Chatterjee called the statutes a '[c]ommunal measure', and said that the government did not have the 'courage to implement' the uniform civil code. 'Your secularism', he said to the government, 'is skin-deep and your democracy is slogan-mongering.'[169]

On the other hand, Pataskar said that the Hindu law statutes that were being enacted were applicable not merely to Hindus but also to other minorities like Sikhs and Jains. The statutes, he said, were therefore 'applicable to a large mass of our [population], about 85 per cent'. He believed that if the Hindu law statutes were 'suitable and beneficial', they could eventually be extended to the remaining minority communities in India, viz. Muslims, Christians, Parsis, etc., but he recognized that this was a 'slow process'. He said that he, for one, was 'satisfied with this small measure of uniformity which our government has succeeded in bringing now' and he was confident that 'the rest of the 15 per cent population without any compulsion on our part, without any force, may in time which will shortly come fall in line'.[170]

The statutes that constitute the Hindu Code did not merely give statutory shape to existing Hindu laws, but they attempted to reform the law and make it uniform.[171] Thus, for instance, inter-caste marriage was recognized and monogamy was made mandatory.[172] Perhaps for this reason, Hindu law is often perceived to be secular law.[173] Pataskar was right in saying that the several statutes that constitute the Hindu Code apply not merely to Hindus but also to Jains, Buddhists and Sikhs.[174] In fact, the code applies by default to anyone who is not a Muslim, Christian, Parsi or Jew by religion.[175] In other words, though there is a uniform civil code for Hindus, Jains, Buddhists, Sikhs and others in India, there is none for Muslims, Christians, Parsis and Jews.[176]

However, Hindu personal law has not been entirely codified. For instance, much of the law relating to partition of joint family properties by 'metes and bounds' and the right of the *karta* of a Hindu undivided family to sell joint family property are subjects that are still within the realm of uncodified personal law. Further, personal law still governs marriage and succession among Muslims.[177]

The Ghost of Narasu[178]

In independent India, it is often the courts that have interfered with and attempted to reform the personal law of Muslims and other groups,[179] somewhat similarly to what courts in British India would do.[180] However, the extent of judicial interference in personal law is limited because personal law cannot be challenged on the grounds that it violates the Constitution. This is because of a judgment delivered by the Bombay High Court in the case of *State of Bombay v. Narasu Appa Mali*,[181] a case which dealt with a law that made polygamy among Hindus illegal. One of the lawyers in that case argued that polygamy in Muslim personal law was altogether unconstitutional because it allowed men to have more than one wife though women could not have more than one husband, thereby discriminating between men and women.[182] This argument was rejected by the court, which held that personal laws were not amenable to being challenged under the Constitution.[183] The law laid down by the Bombay High Court in this case has been accepted by the Supreme Court in a few cases.[184] In this manner, for some odd reason, personal laws in India enjoy a higher status than even laws enacted by India's Parliament or ordinances promulgated by the President of India. While statutes and ordinances can be tested on the touchstone of the Constitution, religious practices, no matter how regressive they may be, which exist under a prevalent system of personal law, are immune from Constitutional scrutiny. In other words, personal laws enjoy, in our country, a higher sanctity than even the Constitution. However, if personal law is codified, the constitutional validity of the statute can then be tested.[185]

In *Mohd. Ahmed Khan v. Shah Bano Begum*,[186] the Supreme Court was faced with the question of whether Section 125 of the Code of Criminal Procedure, 1973, applied to divorced Muslim wives. Section 125 permitted a magistrate to direct a husband of sufficient means to make a monthly payment of maintenance to his divorced wife who was unable to maintain herself. The earlier colonial-era Code of Criminal Procedure, 1898, did not contain a similar provision permitting a court to grant maintenance to a divorced wife.[187] However, Section 127(3)(b) of the 1973 code said that if a woman had received a sum payable on divorce to her under any 'customary or personal law', then Section 125 did not apply.[188]

The judgment in Narasu Appa Mali's case did not come in the way since the court was not really concerned with whether a practice under Muslim personal law violated the Constitution.

Shah Bano and her husband, a lawyer, were married in 1932. They had five children. The husband then divorced Shah Bano and said that he owed her nothing—he had already paid her maintenance during their marriage, and deposited an amount of Rs 3000 in court by way of dower during the period of *iddat* (explained below). The magistrate directed him to pay Shah Bano an amount of Rs 25 per month as maintenance, which the High Court enhanced to Rs 179.20. The husband appealed to the Supreme Court.

Upholding the decision of the High Court, the Supreme Court found that Section 125 of the code applied regardless of the religion of the wife and husband.[189] After reviewing textbooks on Muslim law, the court came to the conclusion that there was no Muslim personal law that barred a husband from giving an alimony to his divorced wife if the wife were unable to maintain herself, and that there was no conflict between Muslim personal law and Section 125 of the code.[190] The court then went a step further, read verses of the Holy Quran, and came to the conclusion that the Quran itself required Muslim men to provide for their divorced wives.[191] It found that Section 127(3)(b) did not apply to Muslims, since *mahr* was not an amount payable on divorce.[192] The court considered it unreasonable for a divorced Muslim wife unable to maintain herself to be forced to rely on her own relatives for maintenance.[193]

While concluding its judgment, the court expressed a 'regret' that Article 44 of the Constitution, dealing with the uniform civil code, 'has remained a dead letter'.[194] It held that a uniform civil code would 'help the cause of national integration by removing disparate loyalties to laws which have conflicting ideologies'.[195]

However, thereafter, the Rajiv Gandhi government enacted the Muslim Women (Protection of Rights on Divorce) Act, 1986,[196] which sought to undo the Shah Bano judgment. Under this statute, a divorced Muslim woman is only entitled to the following from her husband: (i) a 'reasonable and fair' amount of maintenance to be paid by the husband only during the *iddat* period, i.e., three menstrual cycles or three lunar months after the divorce;[197] (ii) if the wife maintains her own children, a 'reasonable and fair' amount of maintenance for the children until they reach the age of two; (iii) the sum of *mahr* or dower agreed to be paid at the time of marriage; and (iv) all the properties given to the wife before, during or after the marriage by her relatives or friends, by her husband, or by the relatives or friends of her husband.[198]

In other words, under the 1986 Act, a divorced Muslim woman was not entitled to receive a monthly amount of maintenance from her husband under Section 125 of the Criminal Procedure Code, 1973.[199] She could, however, under certain circumstances, petition a court to ask her own relatives (or the State Waqf Board) to provide her a 'reasonable and fair maintenance'.[200] However, several years later, in *Danial Latifi v. Union of India*,[201] the Supreme Court diluted the 1986 Act and held that a Muslim husband is bound to provide for his divorced wife even beyond the iddat period until she remarries, though the amount had to be paid during the iddat period.[202]

After Shah Bano's case, in several decisions, the Supreme Court has expressed the hope that Parliament will enact a uniform civil code, which will aid in fostering national integration, while also holding that it has no powers to direct Parliament to do so. For instance, in *Jorden Diengdeh v. S.S. Chopra*,[203] a case involving divorce under Christian law, the Supreme Court noted that the law relating to divorce was 'far from uniform', and the time had come for a uniform law.[204] Similarly, in *Sarla Mudgal v. Union of India*,[205] Justice Kuldip Singh expressed his disappointment over the fact that Article 44 of the Constitution had been kept in 'cold storage' as he felt that a uniform civil code would constitute 'a decisive step towards national consolidation'.[206] '[N]o community', he wrote, can 'claim to remain a separate entity on the basis of religion'.[207] He held that Article 44 of the Constitution was 'based on the concept that there is no necessary connection between religion and personal law in a civilised society'.[208]

While Article 25 guaranteed religious freedom, he wrote, 'Article 44 seeks to divest religion from social relations and personal law.'[209] He considered '[m]arriage, succession and like matters' to be of a 'secular character' that were not guaranteed by the constitutional freedom of religion.[210] He asked the government to take a 'fresh look' at Article 44 and to even file an affidavit in court explaining the steps it had taken towards enacting a uniform civil code.[211]

However, Justice Sahai in his 'concurring' judgment in Sarla Mudgal's case disagreed with Justice Kuldip Singh over the question of a uniform civil code and the secular character of personal law. He felt that personal laws are 'religious in nature and content' and though a uniform civil code was desirable, it could 'concretize only when [the] social climate is properly built'.[212] He held that the government could consider enacting a law which barred a married man from taking on a second wife after converting to another religion unless he divorced his first wife.[213]

Thereafter, Chief Justice V.N. Khare, in *John Vallamattom v. Union of India*,[214] while echoing Justice Kuldip Singh's views in Sarla Mudgal's case, said that a uniform civil code would 'help the cause of national integration by removing the contradictions based on ideologies'. In *Lily Thomas v. Union of India*,[215] it was later clarified that the Supreme Court does not have any power to direct the government to enact a uniform civil code.[216]

However, in *Pannalal Bansilal Pitti v. State of Andhra Pradesh*,[217] the Supreme Court sounded a note of caution, though in a slightly different context. The question in that case was whether the government should enact a uniform law dealing with all religious and charitable endowments, and not a uniform civil code. Though the court said that uniformity in those matters was 'highly desirable', it found that a uniform endowment law would possibly be 'counter-productive' to the 'unity and integrity of the nation', where 'gradual progressive change' was necessary. The court held that instead of enacting a uniform law 'in one go', it was preferable to remedy 'acute' defects in the law, through a 'slow process' of legislation.[218]

Doubts have been expressed over the correctness of the Bombay High Court's judgment in Narasu Appa Mali's case. In *C. Masilamani Mudaliar v. Idol of Sri Swaminathaswami*,[219] the Supreme Court held that personal laws, derived as they are from religious scriptures, 'must be consistent with the Constitution' and can 'become void . . . if they violate fundamental rights'.[220]

Thereafter, in *Shayara Bano v. Union of India*,[221] Justices Nariman and Lalit held that Narasu Appa Mali's case would have to be revisited in a 'suitable case' in the future.[222] The dissenting judges, Chief Justice Khehar and Justice Nazeer, held that personal laws could be tested on the touchstone of Article 25 of the Constitution, and struck down if they were contrary to public order, morality and health.[223]

In that case, the Supreme Court invalidated the practice of 'triple talaq' or 'talaq-e-Biddat' by which a Muslim husband could divorce his wife by saying the word 'talaq' to his wife three times.[224] Justices Nariman and Lalit found that this practice violated the right to equality contained in Article 14 of the Constitution because it allowed the husband to arbitrarily divorce his wife without exploring any possibility of reconciliation.[225] They got over the Bombay High Court's judgment in Narasu Appa Mali's case by holding that 'all forms of talaq recognised and enforced by Muslim Personal Law are recognised and enforced by the 1937 Act'.[226] In other words, since the practice of triple talaq was, according to them, sanctioned by the 1937 Act, it could be challenged for violating the Constitution. What they considered unconstitutional, therefore, was not the practice of triple talaq under Muslim personal law itself, but the practice of triple talaq as sanctioned by the 1937 Act.

However, Justices Nariman and Lalit were in the minority on this point. Justice Kurian Joseph, on the other hand, found that the practice of triple talaq violated the Quran itself and was void.[227] However, Justice Joseph agreed with the minority (Chief Justice Khehar and Justice Nazeer) and held that the 1937 Act did not regulate the practice of talaq and as such, triple talaq could not be examined under Article 14 of the Constitution.[228] Justice Joseph found that triple talaq was 'against the basic tenets of the Holy Quran' and that it violated the Shariat.[229] Justices Nariman and Lalit too found that the practice of triple talaq was frowned upon under Islamic law.[230]

Following this decision, the President of India under the BJP administration promulgated and re-promulgated the Muslim Women (Protection of Rights on Marriage) Ordinance, 2018.[231] The ordinance made it a cognizable[232] and non-bailable[233] criminal offence for a Muslim man to divorce his wife by triple talaq,[234] punishable by up to three years' imprisonment.[235] Thereafter, Parliament replaced the ordinance with a statute.[236] This is a rare instance of legislative interference in Muslim personal law after Indian independence.

Thereafter, in the Sabarimala case,[237] one judge held that Narasu Appa Mali's case was decided on 'flawed premises'[238] and required 'detailed reconsideration in an appropriate case in the future'[239] because it 'immunize(d) [personal laws] from constitutional scrutiny', thereby 'deny[ing] the primacy of the Constitution'.[240] However, the remaining four judges who decided that case did not express any opinion on Narasu Appa Mali's case.

Conclusion

In short, in British India, the colonial government adopted a formal policy whereby it would not interfere with religious laws unless they were contrary to fundamental notions of British morality and justice. In practice, however, the colonial government, whether deliberately or otherwise, repeatedly violated its own policy and altered religious laws. Religious laws in the public sphere were modified without much of an outcry, which was not so when religious laws in the private sphere were tampered with. When Indian leaders came to power in colonial legislatures, they abandoned the formal policy of non-interference in religious matters, which was one of the hallmarks of colonial secularism.

Thereafter, something interesting happened after India became independent. In Article 44, which spoke of the ideal of a uniform civil code, the Constitution formally repudiated the British-era principle of non-interference in personal religious laws. However, while India's Parliament enacted a code interfering with and modifying Hindu personal law, it informally retained the colonial policy advocated by Hastings, Macaulay and Queen Victoria, of non-interference in the personal religious laws of Muslims. While Hindus, Jains, Buddhists, Sikhs, Christians and Parsis are all regulated by statutes that deal with marriage, divorce and succession,[241] the subjects of Muslim marriage and succession are still governed by personal law.[242]

Apart from the Hindu Code, some steps have been taken by India's Parliament towards formulating a uniform civil code.[243] One of these was the enactment of the Special Marriage Act, 1954,[244] which sought to bring about a uniform law of marriage, divorce, succession and alimony, regardless of the religion of the married couple. When parties marry under that Act, unless both are Hindu, Buddhist, Sikh or Jain,[245] the Indian Succession Act, not personal law, applies to their property and the property of their children upon their demise.[246] Similarly, if only one of the parties to the special marriage is a Hindu, Buddhist, Sikh or Jain, he or she is deemed to have severed ties from his or her undivided family.[247] However, the Special Marriage Act is hardly the uniform civil code contemplated by Article 44 of the Constitution. It applies only when the parties consent to be bound by it,[248] and very few marriages have been registered under that statute.[249]

Another such step was taken with the enactment of Section 125 of the Code of Criminal Procedure, 1973. The previous law, dating back to 1898, had a provision which required husbands to maintain their wives, but not their divorced wives.[250] In the 1973 statute, husbands of sufficient means were, for the first time, required to pay alimony to wives they had divorced, who were unable to maintain themselves and who had not remarried.[251] This provision applied regardless of the religion of the couple, and caused considerable controversy when applied to Muslims, as we have seen above.

Later, in 2000, India's Parliament enacted a statute that allowed children to be given in adoption regardless of the religion of the parent or parents.[252] In *Shabnam Hashmi v. Union of India*,[253] the Supreme Court held that this statute constituted 'a small step in reaching the goal enshrined by Article 44 of the Constitution'. Until then, adoptions were not recognized under the personal laws of Muslims,[254] Parsis[255] and Christians.[256] However, the scope of adoptions was limited to children who had been 'orphaned, abandoned or surrendered'.[257] Though the scope of adoptions was broadened by a subsequent statute in 2015,[258] the new law took adoption by Hindus, Buddhists, Sikhs and Jains out of its ambit.[259] That apart, the Protection of Women from Domestic Violence Act, 2005, protects women, regardless of their religion, from 'domestic violence', which includes 'economic abuse',[260] and among other things, gives them the right to reside in a shared household.[261] These are not the only such legislative measures which have been taken towards enacting a uniform civil code.[262] Further, in 2006, the Supreme Court issued directions to the Central and state governments to mandatorily register marriages, regardless of the couple's religion.[263]

There may be several reasons why a uniform civil code has not yet been enacted in India. As one scholar points out, the demand for a uniform civil code carries with it a 'certain subtext'.[264] Those who ask for it ostensibly do so to promote gender justice and national unity. However, a uniform civil code is often intertwined with Hindu nationalism,[265] especially because Muslims identify very strongly with their personal laws.[266] Several scholars instead argue that the uniform civil code debate has become socially irrelevant—that the existing personal law regime is now modernizing and becoming separate but equal through judicial and legislative interventions.[267]

6

Secularly Swearing

One of the hallmarks of a secular state is that its citizens are not required to satisfy any religious tests in order to exercise rights of citizenship or to hold public office. At variance with this principle, public officials in seventeenth-century England, for instance, had to make a declaration that they did not believe in the Roman Catholic doctrine of transubstantiation (the idea that bread and wine in the Eucharist ceremony performed in church become the body and blood of Jesus Christ).[1]

This chapter examines the religious oath that citizens and constitutional office-bearers are required to take, by law, in India. Through the lens of these oaths, we will see that there are no overt religious tests for citizenship or public office in India. Witnesses are considered competent to give their testimony in Indian courts whether or not they affirm their belief in God, and public officials need not swear by any particular God or religious belief in order to hold office in India. Unlike seventeenth-century England, neither witnesses nor public officials in India have to declare their belief system in any particular theory of Hinduism or affirm a lack of belief in any particular idea of Islam.

At the same time, this chapter explores how India's founding fathers rejected the notion of secularism that was imposed on them

144

in British colonial India. The colonial administration found Indian religions to be 'heathen' and 'false'. At the same time, it did not want to impose Christian beliefs on its native subjects. The result was that the administration tried to remove God from public life. After 1840, Hindu and Muslim witnesses were forced to secularly affirm their testimony like Quakers, even if they might have had no conscientious objection to the erstwhile Ganga Jal and Quran religious oaths. Public officials who took office under the Government of India Act, 1935, had to swear an oath which had no mention of God in it. However, India's founding fathers rejected this conception of secularism and brought God back into the Constitution by giving office-holders an option of swearing in God's name if they so wished. Hindu and Muslim witnesses are today no longer forced to subscribe to the Quaker affirmation before giving their testimony. We will therefore see that secularism in independent India does not mean the absence or negation of religion in public life—it merely means state neutrality towards religious practice.

Promissory Oath

Some constitutional office bearers in India are required to take an oath or affirmation before they assume office. The Constitution of India gives these office bearers the option of either taking an oath in the name of God (but not any particular God or religious belief) or of making a secular affirmation. This section examines how the oath of office, sometimes called the 'promissory oath', evolved from British India to the present day. We will see that from the colonial period onwards, no religious test was prescribed for holding public office in India. In other words, though there was an established religion in England (Protestant Christianity through the Church of England), those who held positions in British India, officials like magistrates, judges and even members of the Governor General's Executive Council, were not required to subscribe to that established religion or to even take an oath to abide by the principles of that religious belief system. As nineteenth-century England reformed itself, and impediments that were placed there on Roman Catholics, Jews, Protestant Dissenters and even atheists began to be removed, laws were enacted in colonial India that allowed persons of all religious persuasions to hold public office. In fact, atheists got rights to hold public office in British India even before they did in England. We will also see that Indian independence brought about an important change in the secular identity of the state. While there were no religious oaths of office, only affirmations, during much of British rule in India, the Constitution of independent India gave officials the option of expressly declaring their belief in God or a Supreme Being while assuming office. India's founding fathers rejected colonial secularism and brought God back into the Constitution.

Religious tests in Britain

For a long time in England, those who did not subscribe to the established state religion, Roman Catholics, Jews, and Protestant Dissenters, faced criminal sanctions and were not able to hold public office. For example, in 1559, Queen Elizabeth I's *Act of Supremacy*[2] required officials like judges to take an oath '[renouncing] and [forsaking] all foreign jurisdictions, powers, superiorities, and authorities', which essentially excluded Roman Catholics, on account of their loyalty to the Pope in Rome.[3] The oath had to be taken 'upon the Evangelist'[4] and ended with the line 'so help me God and by the contents of this Book' which excluded Jews and Protestant Dissenters. In 1661, the *Corporations Act* required all officers of municipal corporations to swear oaths of office and take sacraments according to the rites of the Church of England,[5] which excluded Roman Catholics from office. Under the Test Act of 1673, all public officials were required to receive Anglican sacraments and make a declaration against transubstantiation.[6] The Act of Toleration of 1689 relieved Protestant Dissenters from the criminal sanctions that were otherwise imposed on non-Anglicans on account of their belief system, but Roman Catholics were not given any relief under it.[7] Laws enacted in 1778 and 1791 gave Roman Catholics some protection against legal disabilities faced by them and allowed them to hold minor public offices respectively.[8] In 1813, the Act of Toleration was extended to Roman Catholics, but they still could not hold major public offices.[9] In his classical treatise, *Commentaries on the Laws of England* (first published between 1765 and 1769[10]), the jurist William Blackstone defended the impediments suffered by Roman Catholics by arguing that 'while they acknowledge a foreign power, superior to the sovereignty of the kingdom, they cannot complain if the laws of that kingdom will not treat them upon the footing of good subjects'.[11]

However, nearly all religious tests to hold public office in England were done away with during the course of the nineteenth century.[12] In 1828, the sacramental tests imposed under the Corporations Act and Test Act of 1673 were abolished, though office holders had to swear an oath that they would not 'injure or weaken the Protestant church as it is by law established in England'.[13] The Roman Catholic Relief Act, 1829, removed impediments that prevented Roman Catholics from holding public office, provided that they took an oath that if a king was excommunicated by the Pope, that king could not be murdered or deposed by his subjects.[14] In 1833, a law was enacted that was considered as having allowed Quakers to join the House of Commons.[15] As a result of laws enacted in 1845 and 1858, Jews could hold public office as well.[16] Benjamin Disraeli, who became the prime minister of the country in 1868, was born a Jew, and was baptized in 1817 because of a quarrel which his father had with the synagogue. Had it not been for his baptism, Disraeli would never have become prime minister.[17]

After the Parliamentary Oaths Act of 1866 and Promissory Oaths Act of 1868,[18] members of Parliament had to swear an oath that did not require any declaration against transubstantiation or oath takers to take sacraments according to Church of England rites. While the oath which was prescribed ended with the line

'So Help Me God', Quakers and others who were allowed to make affirmations could do so instead.[19] In 1871, the Universities Tests Act ensured that professors and students at Oxford and Cambridge did not have to take religious oaths in order to hold their posts or earn their degrees.[20]

Atheists were only allowed to make the affirmation while assuming public office under the Oaths Act of 1888.[21] Under the Act, any person who objected to taking an oath either on the grounds that it was contrary to his religious beliefs or 'that he has no religious belief' could make the following affirmation instead: 'I, A.B., do solemnly, sincerely, and truly declare and affirm . . .' This law was enacted thanks to Charles Bradlaugh, an atheist, who was elected to the House of Commons in 1880, but who was not permitted to take office until 1886, despite several successful re-elections, because he was an atheist.[22]

However, the head of state (i.e. the King or Queen of England) still has to be a Protestant Christian. The Act of Settlement, 1701, says that whoever gets the crown 'shall join in communion with the Church of England as by law established'.[23] The Accession Declaration Act, 1910, requires the sovereign to make the following declaration: 'I . . . do solemnly and sincerely in the presence of God profess, testify and declare that I am a faithful Protestant, and that I will, according to the true enactments which secure the Protestant succession to the Throne of my Realm, uphold the said enactments [the Bill of Rights and the Act of Settlement] to the best of my power according to law.'[24]

In this respect, England is much like its colonial stepchild, Pakistan, whose Constitution requires the President to solemnly swear, 'In the name of Allah, the most Beneficent, the most Merciful' that he is a Muslim and that he believes 'in the Unity and Oneness of Almighty Allah, the Books of Allah, the Holy Quran being the last of them, the Prophethood of Muhammad (peace be upon him) as the last of the Prophets and that there can be no Prophet after him, the Day of Judgement, and all the requirements and teachings of the Holy Quran and Sunnah'.[25]

Promissory Oaths in British India

Officials who assumed office in British India in the eighteenth century had to take oaths similar to those in the metropole, which excluded Roman Catholics, Protestant Dissenters and Jews. For instance, the Letters Patent,[26] which established the Supreme Court in Calcutta in 1774, required the chief justice to make a 'Declaration against Transubstantiation' in the 'Manner and Form' prescribed in Great Britain.[27]

However, in the nineteenth century, as oaths in England were being reformed, religious tests for holding office were done away with in British India as well. In 1828,[28] a statute was enacted that allowed officials who had to take an oath in order to sit as members of a court or 'for any other purpose whatsoever' to instead 'be sworn according to the forms of their respective religions'.[29] In 1833, the Charter Act enacted by Britain's Parliament said that no person would 'by reason only of his Religion, Place of Birth, Descent, [or] Colour . . . be disabled from holding' office in India.[30] In 1843[31] and 1856,[32] laws were enacted which exempted judges or staff members of the subordinate judiciary (deputy magistrates and civil court amins[33]) from taking oaths. In 1866, judges appointed to the Chief Court of Judicature in Punjab had to make the following secular declaration: 'I, A.B., appointed Judge of the Chief Court of the Punjab, do solemnly declare that I will faithfully perform the duties of my office to the best of my ability, knowledge, and judgment.'[34] In 1869[35] and 1871,[36] similar laws were enacted which required justices of the peace, coroners and district judges to make secular declarations that contained no mention of God or religion.

Interestingly, atheists got the right to hold public office in British India before they did in England. In 1872,[37] a statute was enacted that allowed a person who, by law, was required to be sworn or to make a solemn affirmation, 'in any capacity whatever', to omit phrases like 'so help me God', 'in the presence of Almighty God', or 'other expressions of the same nature'. Under the Indian Oaths Act of 1873, promissory oaths (including affirmations and declarations) were altogether abolished.[38]

The Government of India Act of 1935 prescribed a format for an oath that was to be taken by certain officials, like judges of high courts or members of the legislature. However, this oath did not contain any mention of God. The format of the oath for judges was as follows: 'I, A.B., having been appointed Chief Justice [or a judge] of the Court do solemnly swear [or affirm] that I will be faithful and bear true allegiance to His Majesty the King, Emperor of India, His heirs and successors and that I will faithfully perform the duties of my office to the best of my ability, knowledge and judgment.'[39]

This was the quintessence of British colonial secularism in India. The colonial administration found Indian religions to be 'heathen' and 'false', but it could not impose Christian beliefs on its native subjects. It therefore decided to remove God from public life as far as possible.

Let Grammar Not Stand in the Way of God

The secular identity of the state in British India was defined by an absence of religion in public life. Not merely were there no religious tests for holding public office, but officials had to make secular declarations which contained no reference to God, and were not given any option to refer to God in their oaths of office. Most promissory oaths were altogether abolished in 1873. However, the Constitution of independent India, enacted in 1950, brought about an important change. It gave constitutional officials who had to take an oath the option of either swearing their oaths of office in the name of God or making a secular affirmation, an option which was not given to them in British India. The debates of the Constituent Assembly on the promissory oath of constitutional office-bearers reveal that the framers of India's Constitution did not understand secularism as the negation of religion or the absence of religion from public life. Secularism, to them, meant that officials could expressly declare their religious beliefs, but that the state had to be neutral in its attitude towards different religions.

On 27 December 1948, H.V. Kamath moved an amendment which sought to give the President (who had to take an oath under the Constitution) the option of either swearing his oath in the name of God or making a solemn affirmation.[40] In other words, Kamath tried to introduce 'God' into the Indian Constitution, as the draft which had been circulated to members of the Assembly did not give the President the option of swearing in the name of God.[41] While introducing his amendment in the House, Kamath remarked that there was a 'void' and 'vacuum' in the Constitution, that the framers 'had forgotten . . . to invoke the grace and blessing of God', and that it fell to him to 'plead that God may find a place in our Constitution'. 'Perhaps', he wondered, 'it was the will of God that the Constitution should be barren of His name and that later on the name of God should be invoked in the course of a discussion on the Constitution.' 'Do [the framers of India's Constitution] think that it is possible to legislate God out of existence?' he asked. 'The more, Sir, we avoid God,' he said, 'the more we try to flee from Him, the more He pursues us.' He referred to different religious texts and said, 'if eating and drinking is to be an offering to God, then this Constitution which is a sacred task, must be an offering to God also.'

Another member of the Assembly, Mahavir Tyagi,[42] who later became a Union minister, moved a similar amendment, and said that the resolution passed by the Assembly that 'the State will be a secular State' had caused 'a lot of misunderstandings'. It was, in his opinion, perfectly fine for the President of India to believe in the existence of God. Secularism, he said, did not mean that the Government had 'banished God altogether', and God was not 'taboo' in a secular state. 'A secular State means the state of Truth and God and eternity without prejudice to any particular religion', he said. Real freedom, according to Tyagi, meant 'Ram Raj'. 'If secular State means that our children will not know about the Ramayana or listen to the Gita or the Koran or the Granth what is political freedom worth?' he asked.

If God were banished from India, he said, then India would become 'Ayodhya without Ram'. He submitted, evoking peals of laughter, that by 'Ram' he meant 'Hindu God and also Christian God'. He concluded by saying that 'India believes in God and therefore the Indian State must remain a State of God', that India 'must be a godly State and not a godless State', and that this was 'our meaning of secularity'.[43]

K.M. Munshi rose to support the insertion of God into the oath of office. He felt that members of the Assembly were 'emphasising the absence of God in this Constitution too much'. He did not think that the insertion of an option to swear in the name of God offended 'against the conception of a secular State'. In an eloquent speech, he outlined what he meant by secularism:

A secular State is used in contrast with a theocratic Government or a religious State. It implies that citizenship is irrespective of religious belief, that every citizen, to whatever religion he may belong, is equal before the law, that he has equal civil rights, and equal opportunities to derive benefit from the State and to lead his own life; and nothing more. A secular State is not a Godless State. It is not a State which is pledged to eradicate or ignore religion. It is not a State which refuses to take notice of religious belief in this country . . . Religion is the richest possession of man and even under this secular State, a person having a religious belief will be fully entitled to it in the way that he likes. Any State that seeks to outlaw God, will very soon come to an end . . . [I]t will be a day of disaster for India if, by some legislative trick, our State is converted into an irreligious, Godless State. We need not fear that a secular State is inconsistent with a religious mind among the people.

Jerome D'Souza, a Roman Catholic priest,[44] supported the amendment. He said that all it did was to 'accept the fact that in our country the vast majority of men are believers in God and that almost certainly, anyone who would come to this exalted office would be moved to fulfil the functions of that office most faithfully if he promised to do so in the name of Almighty God'. He agreed that a secular Constitution was 'not a Godless Constitution' and was 'not in opposition to the very notion of God'. A secular Constitution made 'no choice as between this or that particular profession, or religious section', but looked 'with sympathy upon the convictions, the feelings, the desires, the hopes and aspirations of the entire people'. He said that by allowing the President the option of swearing in the name of God, the framers were 'not cheapening the concept of God' nor 'imposing it upon all and sundry', but merely asking the President of India, 'if he is a believer, to promise in His sacred Name'.

Tajamul Husain proved to be the lone voice of dissent on that day. He asked how the word 'God' would be translated into an Indian language. 'Whose God are you going to have?' he asked. 'Supposing it is translated and the word "Bhagwan" is there,' he asked, 'can you compel the Parsee or Christian or a non-Hindu to say that when he becomes a President?' 'Either you do not want him to become the President or if he does, he cannot swear that', he answered. Husain's objection was an interesting and prescient one. In the official Hindi version of the Indian Constitution, the word 'God' has been translated as 'Ishwar',[45] not Allah. In 2006, eleven members of the legislative assembly of Kerala took their oaths of office in the name of Allah instead of God. The Kerala High Court held that 'Allah is a synonym for God', that '[o]ath taking' was a 'purely personal' act whose only purpose was to 'give sanctity to the pledge by which the oath-taker binds himself'. 'To insist', said the court, 'that a person who takes oath in the name of God should take the oath not only in the name of God in whom he believes, but also in the names of the Gods in whom the members of the constituency believe is clearly illegal and unconstitutional.'[46] A similar view was taken by the Jharkhand High Court. In 2011, the Muslim governor of Jharkhand,

Syed Ahmad, took his oath in the name of 'Allah' instead of Ishwar. A PIL was filed saying that this was illegal. The case was dismissed by the Jharkhand High Court, which found, relying on dictionaries, that God was known by the word 'Allah' by Muslims.[47]

Ambedkar accepted the proposed amendments of Kamath and Tyagi, and said that the Drafting Committee had not considered this question fully. He said that the word 'God' had a 'different significance in different religions'. To Christians and Muslims, God was 'not merely . . . a concept, but . . . a force which governs the world', whereas to Hindus, God was 'merely a summation of an idea, of a concept'. It was therefore 'very difficult for the Drafting Committee . . . to have introduced phraseology which would have required several underlinings'. He referred to Charles Bradlaugh in England, and said:

> If the President thinks that God is a mentor and that unless he takes an oath in the name of God he will not be true to the duties he assumes I think we ought to give him the liberty to swear in the name of God. If there is another person with whom God is not his mentor, we ought to give him the liberty to affirm and carry on the duties on the basis of that affirmation.

On 26 August 1949, this provision was debated again.[48] Some more voices of opposition to the insertion of the word God into the Constitution were heard on that day. Sardar Bhopinder Singh Man argued that it was 'beneath one's dignity to be asked to swear by God', that this amounted to 'showing disrespect to God Himself that we should use His name for swearing purposes'.[49] Brajeshwar Prasad[50] said that constitutional officials like governors, ministers and Presidents had to perform 'a secular function', which required a study of the provisions of the Constitution, for which there was no question of swearing an oath in the name of God. He also felt 'quite clear in [his] own mind that secularism is the negation of all

religion', and that '[w]hatever statesmen and politicians may say on
the ground of expediency . . . the concept of religion and the concept
of secularism are poles asunder. There is no meeting ground between
these two.' Brajeshwar Prasad's understanding of secularism, which
was part of the secular identity of the colonial state in British India,
was rejected by the framers of India's Constitution.

Ambedkar tried to make the affirmation the first option
for the President, and the oath in the name of God the second
option, but Tyagi responded by saying: 'Let grammar not stand
in the way of God!' Thus, the Constitution of India gives oath
takers like the President and judges of the Supreme Court and high
courts the option of saying that they either 'swear in the name of
God' or 'solemnly affirm' to 'bear true faith and allegiance to the
Constitution of India' etc.[51]

However, the word 'God' in the Constitution does not refer
to the God of any particular religion or religious belief. Several
speeches made by members of the Constituent Assembly suggest
that the word 'God' was used in the assembly in a general sense,
and not with reference to any particular religion. On the eve of
Indian independence, President Rajendra Prasad, a devout Hindu,
said 'The country, which was made by God and Nature to be one,
stands divided today.'[52] In May 1949, Sardar Vallabhbhai Patel said,
'Let God give us the wisdom and the courage to do the right thing
to all manner of people.'[53] In December 1948, one member of the
Assembly, L. Krishnaswami Bharati,[54] said, 'all religions are one and
the same. It is all God, though under different names.'[55]

However, the framers of India's Constitution refused to put the
word 'God' into the preamble to the Constitution. Some members of
the Assembly complained that the word 'God' was missing from the
preamble.[56] On 17 October 1949, Kamath moved an amendment
to introduce the words 'In the name of God' at the beginning of the
Constitution, before the words 'We, the people of India'. Several
members, however, objected to this amendment. M. Thirumala
Rao,[57] for instance, said that 'it should not be subjected to the vote

of a House of three hundred people whether India wants God or not'. He made an important point when he argued that while the President was given the option to either swear in the name of God or solemnly affirm his oath of office, the proposed insertion of the word 'God' in the preamble gave no such option to the Indian people. A. Thanu Pillai, who later became the chief minister of Kerala,[58] said that this would result in compulsion in a matter of faith. Though he himself made it a point to let it be known that he believed in God, '[a] man has a right to believe in God or not, according to the Constitution', he said. Pandit Kunzru[59] too objected and said that these were personal matters. Kamath's amendment was defeated. In response, Kamath said, 'This, Sir, is a black day in our annals. God save India.'[60] God, then, was not to be forced on everyone in India's soft secular State—but public officials who wished to take their oaths in his name had the option of doing so.

Many years later, in his concurring judgment in the case of *S.R. Bommai v. Union of India*,[61] Justice K. Ramaswamy noticed the connection between the oath of office prescribed under the Third Schedule to the Constitution of India and the nature of the secularism of the Indian state. The word 'God' in the presidential oath, said Justice Ramaswamy, was not a 'recognition' that the President 'has his religion or religious belief in God of a particular religion' but an expression that he must be bound by his oath 'as a moral being'.

By contrast, the US Constitution contains no reference to God, though the Declaration of Independence and the Articles of Confederation referred to God's blessing.[62] While it is customary for the US President to utter the words 'so help me God' at the end of the oath, the Constitution does not require it. The first US President, George Washington, is said to have uttered these words, though there is no evidence that he did so—it seems to have become customary after Chester A. Arthur did so in 1884.[63] Similarly, Article VI of the US Constitution says that 'no religious Test shall ever be required as a Qualification to any Office or public Trust under the United States'.[64] Prior to the Constitution, some states prescribed religious tests for public office. For instance, the state of Delaware, in its Constitution of 1776, required members of the legislature to take the following oath: 'I, A.B., do profess faith in God, the Father, and in Jesus Christ his only Son, and in the Holy Ghost, one God, blessed for evermore; and I do acknowledge the holy scriptures of the Old and New Testament to be given by divine inspiration.'[65] Even after the US Constitution came into force, several states there had established religions—the last of these being Massachusetts until 1833.[66]

Judicial Oath

When a person steps into a witness box in a court of law for testifying in a case, how does the court ensure that he will tell the truth? Self-interested witnesses may sometimes lie, and British officials in colonial India believed that Indian witnesses were especially untruthful. Thomas Babington Macaulay, a British official responsible for drafting the Indian Penal Code, and notorious for his anti-Indian views, once said:

> What the horns are to the buffalo, what the paw is to the tiger, what the sting is to the bee, what beauty, according to the old Greek song, is to woman, deceit is to the Bengalee. Large promises, smooth excuses, elaborate tissues of circumstantial falsehood, chicanery, perjury, forgery, are the weapons, offensive and defensive, of the people of the Lower Ganges.[67]

The law has devised many mechanisms for ensuring that witnesses tell the truth.[68] The law of perjury, for instance, punishes witnesses who lie. Witnesses are subjected by the opponent's lawyers to cross-examination, a rigorous process designed to ascertain whether the witness's testimony holds up to careful scrutiny. However, in India, as in many other countries, the law also sometimes seeks to enlist the help of a divine being in ensuring that the witness sticks to the truth. A witness in India is required to give his testimony on oath or solemn affirmation. In other words, an Indian witness has to either 'swear in the name of God' or 'solemnly affirm' that what he says will be 'the truth, the whole truth and nothing but the truth'.[69]

This 'judicial oath',[70] given by a witness in a court of law, is sometimes a religious one—it invokes the name of God and exposes the witness to the fear of 'temporal and . . . eternal punishment'[71] if he were to tell a lie. However, the religious nature of the judicial oath raises some questions: Can an 'infidel' or a person who does not subscribe to the state's established religion or to the religion of the majority of the populace take an oath in the name of a God or a divine being in whom the State or the majority of its people have no faith? What about an atheist, who does not fear God because he doesn't believe in one—can he be considered a competent witness in a court of law? At a broader level, does the religious judicial oath alter the secular character of the Indian state?

In this section we will see that though England had an established state religion (Protestant Christianity through the Church of England) and though British missionaries considered Indian religions to be 'heathen', non-Christian witnesses in British India were nonetheless considered perfectly competent[72] witnesses, and the testimony of 'infidels' was not formally given any second-class treatment in colonial courts. Hindus and Muslims were, however, required to testify as witnesses by subscribing to a secular affirmation, like Quakers back in the metropole. The secularism of the colonial courtroom of British India was born out of the desire of Britons to engage in international trade and commerce with people of diverse faiths and deep pockets. Though there is now a religious judicial oath in India today, it is optional, as witnesses can make a secular solemn affirmation instead. Further, the religious judicial oath does not insist on the primacy of any particular idea of divinity or dogma. As such, it cannot be considered to conflict with the secular nature of India's constitution.

Infidels

Sometime between 1628 and 1644, a famous English judge, Sir Edward Coke, published a four-volume treatise known as the 'Institutes of the Lawes of England'.[73] In it, Coke, who was the first person to be referred to as the 'Lord Chief Justice of England',[74] wrote that infidels, that is non-Christians, could not be witnesses in courts of law. This is because witnesses had to swear an oath in court, and Coke thought that only the sworn testimony of Christians could be believed. 'An oath is an affirmation or denial by any *Christian* of any thing lawful and honest . . . calling Almighty God to witness, that his testimony is true',[75] he wrote. A witness's oath in court was 'sacred', he thought, and deeply concerned with the 'consciences of Christian men'. It was called a 'corporal oath', because the witness had to touch 'with his hand some part of the holy scripture'.[76] Quoting from a leading thirteenth-century medieval English jurist, Henry de Bracton,[77] Coke opined that 'an alien born cannot be a witness', that is 'an alien Infidel'.[78]

Over the years, the 'general received opinion' in England was that 'infidels' could not be witnesses.[79] Jews, however, were admitted as witnesses in English courts since they swore their testimony on the Old Testament which was a part of Christian belief, but the evidentiary value of their statements in court was still left to be determined by the jury.[80]

In 1726, however, King George I of England issued a charter to the East India Company for setting up courts called 'Mayor's Courts' in India. The charter provided that these company-run Mayor's Courts would have the authority to administer oaths to witnesses, but no format was prescribed for the oath. Two lawyers, John Hungerford and Thomas Woodford, were hired by the East India Company to write an instruction manual on how these courts would be administered. Hungerford and Woodford wondered what to make of the testimony of 'native' witnesses in these courts. Contrary to Coke's view from a century before, in their manual of around 200 pages, they wrote that non-Christians could be accepted as witnesses in courts in India, and that their testimonies would have to be sworn 'in such manner as to suit such witnesses and the solemnity of the occasion and thing to be done'.[81] They wrote that new oaths could be 'formed and administered' to non-Christians as long as they suited the 'solemnity of the occasion'.[82] In other words, if Hindus, Muslims, Sikhs, Parsis, Jains, or Buddhists were to be witnesses in company courts in colonial India, they would not have to swear their testimony by laying their right hand on or kissing the Bible, but they would have to swear an oath in the manner that the judge found most fitting for the occasion.

In practice, the Mayor's Courts allowed 'native' Indian witnesses to swear their testimonies by all kinds of oaths. For example, Hindu witnesses were sometimes asked to swear an oath by touching the head of a cow, the feet of a Brahmin, or the Bhagavad Gita.[83] The most common form of swearing oaths by Hindus was the *Ganga Jal* oath. A Hindu witness would have to hold a copper vessel containing a *tulsi* (basil) leaf and water from the holy Ganga River, and swear that the testimony he was about to give in court was true.[84] Muslims, on the other hand, were usually asked to swear an oath on the Quran.[85] For administering oaths to Hindus and Muslims, colonial courts hired local officials called the 'Gunga Jullee' and the 'Moolah Kooranee'.[86] A company court in Calcutta purchased a copy of the Quran for six rupees for its use in the oath ceremony.[87]

However, the formal law of England at that time still insisted that infidels were not competent witnesses. This changed because of a case decided in England in 1744, the case of *Omychund v. Barker*.[88] The plaintiff Omychund was a wealthy Sikh[89] merchant in Calcutta. He lent a sum of money to an East India Company official by the name of Hugh Barker, at 12 per cent interest. When Barker refused to repay the sum of Rs 67,955, which was £7,600 in English money, Omychund filed a suit against him in the Mayor's Court at Calcutta in 1736. Barker fled Calcutta, and boarded a French ship to leave for Europe. The Mayor's Court, considering this a flight from justice, decreed the suit in favour of Omychund. Omychund then filed proceedings in the Chancery Court in England against Barker's estate (Barker had died during the voyage) for execution and enforcement of the decree.

The Attorney General of England, Sir Dudley Rider, represented Omychund in court. When he attempted to read the evidence of one of the witnesses who had deposed for Omychund in the Mayor's Court, Barker's lawyers objected on the grounds that the witness was a non-Christian who had sworn an oath to tell the truth by touching a Brahmin's feet—an oath not recognized under English law. They submitted that the 'natives' in India were 'extremely ignorant', that their 'notions of religion' were so 'absurd and ridiculous' and their 'ideas of the Deity so gross' that 'it would be shocking even to mention' them. 'How then can they be said to perform such a ceremony with a sacred and religious mind' as taking a testimonial oath as a witness in a court of law, they asked. Barker's lawyers argued that '[a]n oath ought to be accompanied with the fear of God and service of God, for advancement of truth'. They said that Omychund and his witnesses were 'Gentoos', i.e. Hindus, though the term in this case was used to describe even the Sikh Omychund.

Attorney General Rider, on the other hand, argued that Omychund and his witnesses did 'believe in a Deity' and by touching the Brahmin's feet, they had shown 'great humility', which was akin to a Christian kissing the holy Bible. He also argued that it would be good public policy to allow non-Christians to become witnesses in English courts, as this would be in the interests of trade and commerce. In his words:

> It is of the greatest moment, that we should have commerce and correspondence with all mankind; trade requires it, policy requires it, and in dealings of this kind it is of infinite consequence, there should not be a failure of justice . . . *Gentoos* are the common brokers in this country, and the necessity of the case will work strongly for us.

To resolve this debate, the Chancery court sent commissioners to India to investigate whether the witnesses who had testified in favour of Omychund believed in the existence of God. They were asked questions like: 'Of what religion are you?', 'Do you or do you not believe in the Supreme Being that made the heavens and the earth?', and if a witness lies on oath, would he 'be subject to any punishment and what in this life or the next from any and what being?'[90] The witnesses answered by saying that they believed in the existence of God, and that God rewards good men and punishes evil men.

Though the case came before the Chancery Court in England, it was decided by the chief justices of all four of the major English courts at the time: the Chancery Court, King's Bench, Common Pleas, and the Court of Exchequer. The judges decided *Omychund v. Barker* by holding that so long as a witness believes in the existence of God and in divine retribution for falsehood on earth, he was competent to testify as a witness. The form of the oath did not matter. In the words of Lord Chief Justice Willes:

> Though I have shewn that an Infidel in general cannot be excluded from being a witness, and though I am of opinion that infidels who believe a God, and future rewards and punishments in the other world, may be witnesses; yet I am as clearly of opinion, that if they do not believe a God, or future rewards and punishments, they ought not to be admitted as witnesses.[91]

Willes said that the medieval jurist Bracton 'lived in popish times, when no other trade was carried on except the trade of religion'. Secularism in the courtroom was essential for a country now interested in international trade and commerce. Consequently, in 1753, when the Charter of the East India Company was revised by George II, it empowered colonial courts to examine 'native' witnesses on '[o]ath or solemn [a]ffirmation', 'in such [m]anner as they, according to their several [castes], shall esteem to be most binding on their

[c]onsciences, to oblige them to speak the [t]ruth'. Similarly, when the Supreme Court was set up in Calcutta in 1774, it was authorized to examine non-Christians on oaths administered 'in such [m]anner and [f]orm as the Supreme Court . . . shall esteem most binding upon their [c]onsciences'.[92]

Quakers

However, it was contrary to the religious scruples of the members of certain sects of Christianity in England to take an oath in the name of God. Foremost among these were the Quakers, or members of the Religious Society of Friends,[93] who believed that oaths were blasphemous. Quakers lived their lives according to an 'inward light', and believed in a direct connection with God, without mediation by clergy or other ecclesiastical forms.[94] According to one story, the name 'Quakers' came from the trembling which members of the sect underwent during their religious experiences.[95] According to the Utilitarian philosopher Jeremy Bentham, the Biblical injunction against swearing, 'Swear not at all', uttered by Jesus Christ and recorded by his biographer Matthew, author of one of the gospels, was one which a 'Quaker refuses to disobey'.[96] In 1678, a man called William Brayne was accused of stealing a horse from a Quaker, Ambros Gallaway.[97] Though Brayne stood trial for the crime, he was acquitted because Gallaway refused to swear his testimony on oath. Instead, Gallaway himself was punished for refusing to take an oath,[98] while Brayne went scot-free.

In 1696, a law was passed in England which allowed Quakers to testify as witnesses in civil cases by subscribing to a secular affirmation instead of a religious oath.[99] Thereafter, Quaker witnesses had to say the following words before giving their testimony: 'I A.B. do declare in the Presence of Almighty God, the Witness of the Truth of what I say'. This form of affirmation was not entirely acceptable to Quakers since it still contained a reference to God—an objection that was accommodated by legislation enacted in 1721, after which the Quaker affirmation was to be in the following form: 'I A.B. do solemnly, sincerely and truly declare and affirm . . . '[100] The colonial legislative assemblies of Pennsylvania and New York in the US in fact enacted such a law even earlier, in 1682 and 1691 respectively (affirmation was made universal in Pennsylvania).[101] Over the years, other sects of Christianity, like Moravians and Separatists, were allowed to testify on solemn affirmation instead of the religious oath.[102] Quakers, Moravians and Separatists could make such affirmations even in the courts of colonial India.

Hindus and Muslims

Like the Quakers, many Hindu witnesses in British India began to object, on religious grounds, to the manner in which they were being forced to take oaths in colonial courts. Some of them believed that oaths like the Ganga Jal oath were far too solemn, that if they even inadvertently or unwittingly uttered a lie, then that would be enough to send their souls to eternal damnation. 'People who went to a British court of justice ran the risk of losing their souls', wrote Bipin Chandra Pal, an Indian nationalist leader. According to him:

> People with the fear of religion in their heart, would never agree to go to the witness box in a British court of law. They were mortally afraid of telling a falsehood, however, unwittingly it might be, upon their oath . . . there might be confusion of thought, many things beyond the control of the individual deponent might happen to mislead him and make him bear false witness against his neighbour. All these thoughts and sentiments very powerfully disuaded (sic) good people, in those days, from going to a British court of justice.[103]

Hindu witnesses gave one inquirer the following reasons for refusing to take an oath: 'if I put my hand into the Gunga Jul, I put my hand into the fire of hell', 'should I happen to say one word which is not true, I shall be tormented during an hundred transmigrations', 'I shall sink my ancestors into places of torment', or 'this is a very solemn mode of swearing'. For instance, a Hindu witness called Hulladar Doss refused to take the Ganga Jal oath in one case and pleaded that he was his father's only son, thereby implying that if he took the oath, he would lose his caste and would not be able to perform the last rites of his father.[104] In another case, in Bombay, a Hindu witness was asked to take an oath on the head of a cow. He refused, and many Hindu merchants supported him on the grounds that they would be declared outcastes if they took such an oath. Eventually, the Bombay Mayor's Court relented, and allowed the witness to take an oath on the Bhagavad Gita instead.[105]

Something therefore had to be done in order to encourage Hindu witnesses to give testimony in colonial courts. Consequently, in 1793, regulations were enacted in Bengal by which courts were given the authority to dispense with an oath 'if a witness shall be of rank or caste which, according to the prejudices of the country, would render it improper to compel him to take an oath'.[106] In other words, if a judge felt that a Hindu witness would lose his caste, status or position in society by taking the Ganga Jal oath, the cow oath, or any similar oath, he could ask the witness to make a secular declaration, which merely contained a reference to a supreme being.

Thereafter, in 1828, Britain's Parliament enacted a law[107] which allowed any 'native' who objected 'on the ground of any religious scruple to take an oath in the usual form' to, at the discretion of the court, make a solemn affirmation or declaration akin to that made by Quakers and Moravians.[108] This law only applied to 'King's Courts', i.e. to the Supreme Courts which were set up in the presidency towns of Calcutta, Madras and Bombay by this time. As far as the company courts were concerned[109] (these courts were typically mofussil courts, or courts in the rural districts of British India, with an appellate court in the presidency towns), a law[110] was enacted in 1840 according to which all Hindus and Muslims were now required to make a solemn affirmation instead of taking an oath in court, whether they had an objection to taking the oath or not. In other words, it was presumed by the 1840 law that Hindus and Muslims have a conscientious objection to taking a judicial oath, akin to the objection of Quakers. It is not entirely clear why Muslims were forced to make the affirmation as well, since most of the complaints against judicial oaths came from Hindus. In fact, in a legislative debate held in 1873, the lieutenant governor of Bengal said, 'Muhammadans had no religious repugnance to taking oaths.'[111]

The affirmation was to be in the following form: 'I solemnly affirm, in the presence of Almighty God, that what I shall state shall be the truth, the whole truth, and nothing but the truth.' Though the Hindu and Muslim affirmation was required to be made 'in the presence of Almighty God' like the early Quaker affirmation, after 1872, any person who objected to these words could omit them.[112] When the East India Company's rule was abolished by Queen Victoria after the Mutiny, the 1840 law was made applicable to all courts in British India in 1863.[113]

In Omychand's case, the Chancery Court in England had held that belief in God and in a divine system of retribution was essential for an infidel witness's testimony to be considered admissible in evidence. However, this meant that atheists, i.e. those who did not believe in God, were not competent witnesses. The political philosopher John Locke believed that atheists were 'not at all to be tolerated' since they 'deny the being of a God', and since '[p]romises, covenants, and oaths, which are the bonds of human society, can have no hold upon an atheist'.[114] This changed in 1869 in England,[115] when a law[116] was enacted which allowed atheists to give evidence by subscribing to the following affirmation: 'I solemnly promise and declare that the evidence given by me to the court shall be the truth, the whole truth, and nothing but the truth'.[117] Likewise, in India, laws enacted in 1872 and 1873 gave any person who had a conscientious objection to taking an oath the right to make a solemn affirmation instead.[118] In other words, it was not only those who refused to take an oath on religious scruples, like Quakers, who were competent witnesses allowed to make the secular affirmation, but even atheists, who did not believe in the existence of God at all.

After the Indian Oaths Act, 1873, if any witness other than a Hindu or a Muslim had an objection to taking an oath, he could make a solemn affirmation instead. However, this law presumed that all Hindus and Muslims had a conscientious objection to taking a religious oath. Thus, all Hindu and Muslim witnesses, by default, were required to make a secular affirmation like atheists instead of taking a religious oath.[119] In 1897, the General Clauses Act, which contained definitions applicable to all statutes in British India, defined an 'oath' as including an 'affirmation and declaration' wherever permitted by law. In other words, whenever any law required a person to take an oath, it was implied that a person could also make an affirmation or declaration instead of taking an oath.

Post-Independence

In short, witnesses in British India, apart from Hindu and Muslim witnesses, had the option either of taking a religious oath or making a secular affirmation. Even the religious oath did not insist on the supremacy of any particular system of religious practice or belief. Parsi witnesses, for instance, who took the religious judicial oath, did not have to kiss the holy Bible. The religious judicial oath which was prescribed by most High Courts was: 'I do swear in the name of God that what I shall state shall be the truth, the whole truth and nothing but the truth.'[120] The word 'God' in the religious judicial oath did not refer to the God of any particular religion or religious practice. In fact, the following were the definitions of the word 'God' in an edition of the Oxford dictionary of the English language published in 1919: 'Superhuman being worshipped as having power over nature & human fortunes, deity', 'image, animal, or other object, worshipped as symbolizing, being the visible habitation of, or itself possessing, divine power, an idol'.[121] In other words, the word 'God' did not mean only a Christian God.

Under the 1873 law, courts in British India retained the discretion to administer an oath to a witness in a 'form common amongst, or held binding by' persons of his community, so long as the oath was 'not repugnant to justice or decency'.[122] Relying on this provision, some colonial judges overstepped their boundaries while administering judicial oaths. For example, a district judge in Bombay, Frank Beaman, used to make witnesses hold the tail of a cow while taking an oath, a practice which was deprecated by the Bombay High Court.[123] In 1903, one American author referred to 'a mendacious Hindoo swinging the tail of a cow in his hand', and 'a Chinaman burning a joss stick or cracking a saucer and invariably grinning as he did it', while comparing them to the 'simple, straightforward Friend', i.e. Quaker.[124] Additionally, the judicial oath itself was a mere formality—any irregularity in its administration did not render the evidence inadmissible, make the proceedings void, or affect the obligation of the witness to state the truth.[125] Even in England, since the late eighteenth century, the judicial oath had become 'largely ritualistic',[126] and in the US, one commentator in 1903 called it 'a religious ceremonial which appears to have become but an idle form'.[127]

In 1856, the Indian Law Commission suggested that both the oath and affirmation be abolished in British India,[128] but their recommendation was not accepted. After India became independent, the Law Commission concluded that judicial oaths still served a useful purpose and should not be abolished.[129] The law relating to judicial oaths was recast in 1969.[130] The only major difference between this law and the law prevalent during the colonial period was that Hindus and Muslims were no longer forced to make a solemn affirmation. However, the basic premises of the law of judicial oaths remained the same after Independence. Today, witnesses are given the option of either swearing an oath in the name of 'God' (but not the God of any particular religion or religious belief), or of making a secular affirmation.[131] Courts continue to have the discretion to administer a customary oath which is not repugnant to justice or decency.[132] The oath itself remains a formality.[133]

Christian missionaries in British India saw Indian religious practices as 'heathen'. For instance, a manual published for the instruction of Christian missionaries in 1864 advised readers to hire native Christian servants, and warned that '[h]eathen servants' were to be preferred only to 'bad Christians'.[134] According to this manual, Hindus were unscrupulous litigants:

> The Hindus are notorious for their litigiousness . . . Strange as it may seem, one mode of frightening their opponents is to threaten to become Christians! . . . As the Missionary belongs to the same 'caste' as the judge, and may perhaps be on friendly terms with him, they hope through him to be successful. Their case may be good or bad; but in India few native suitors look for mere justice in law-courts.[135]

Despite this Christian missionary view of the 'heathen' infidels of British India, the judicial system was not designed in a manner that made it necessary for witnesses to satisfy any Christian religious test for their testimony to be considered admissible or especially worthy of evidentiary or probative value. According to the Indian Evidence Act, enacted in 1872,[136] the competence of a witness to testify in court had nothing to do with his religious beliefs. This is contrary, for instance, to the Qanun-e-Shahadat Order,[137] enacted in Pakistan in 1984, which requires courts to determine the competence of a witness in accordance with 'the qualifications prescribed by the Injunctions of Islam as laid down in the Holy Quran and Sunnah for a witness'. In order to attract certain punishments for some offences in Pakistan, the evidence of a prescribed number of male Muslim witnesses is required.[138] In pre-colonial Bengal, the testimony of two male eyewitnesses was required to establish a charge of murder, and the testimony of non-Muslims was insufficient to establish the guilt of a Muslim accused.[139] This was never a part of the codified evidentiary rules in British India, and continues not to be so in independent, secular India.

Acknowledgements

I am grateful to Tarunabh Khaitan, Farrah Ahmed, Lawrence Friedman, Stefan Vogenauer and Rohit De for going through and commenting on this manuscript. Many thanks to Fernan Restrepo, Shreyas Narla, Chetan Arora and Uma Narayan for helping me find reading materials that were out of my reach. I must thank my interns Geethanjali Jujjivarapu, Anant Sangal and Anirban Chanda who helped me find a few sources for this book. Thanks are also due to Shreyas Narla for painstakingly reviewing the manuscript for errors. I am also grateful to Menaka Doshi and the team at Bloomberg Quint. My column in Bloomberg Quint was an incubator for some of the ideas that are presented here.

This book would not have been possible without Meru Gokhale's unfaltering encouragement over these past few years. Thank you, Premanka Goswami, my editor, for the unwavering faith that you have had in me. Many thanks also to the entire team at Penguin.

Finally, none of this would have been possible without the love and support of my family. Many thanks, Dad, Kalpana, Aai, Baba, Radha and Uday, for being my pillars of strength. And thank you, Chintan, Jayati, Madhav, Pranay and Vinayak, for being buddies as much as brethren.

Notes

Introduction

1.   Blasphemy as an offence was abolished in England in 2008. However, before it was abolished, the test for blasphemy was modified to penalize only those attacks on the Church of England (or its doctrines) that were scurrilous. This is discussed in Chapter 2.

2.   Todd M. Endelman, *The Jews of Britain, 1656 to 2000* (Berkeley: University of California Press, 2002) (available on Google Books), at p. 98; H.S.Q. Henriques, *The Jews and the English Law* (Clark: The Lawbook Exchange, 2006) (available on Google Books), at p. 209. See, sections 43–44, Oxford University Act, 1854, available at: https://www.legislation.gov.uk/ukpga/1854/81/pdfs/ukpga_18540081_en.pdf (last visited 12 May 2019); section 45, Cambridge University Act, 1856, available at: https://www.legislation.gov.uk/ukpga/1856/88/pdfs/ukpga_18560088_en.pdf (last visited 12 May 2019); James W. Torke, 'The English Religious Establishment', *Journal of Law and Religion*, vol. 12, p. 399 (1995–96), at p. 423. Further, it was only after 1871 that religious tests at those universities were abolished for professors. Robert Ivermee, *Secularism, Islam and Education in India, 1830–1910* (New York: Routledge, 2016), pp. 34, 133; 'Catholic Emancipation', *Encyclopaedia Britannica*, available at: https://www.britannica.

com/event/Catholic-Emancipation#ref174217 (last visited 12 May 2019). The Universities Tests Act was enacted in 1871.

3. Section 2(1), Succession to the Crown Act, 2013. Available at: http://www.legislation.gov.uk/ukpga/2013/20/pdfs/ukpga_20130020_en.pdf (last visited 16 April 2019). See further, 'New Rules on Royal Succession Come into Force', BBC News, 26 March 2015, available at: https://www.bbc.com/news/uk-32073399 (last visited 16 April 2019). The Act came into force in 2015. The statute ensured that Prince Harry would not be disqualified from succeeding to the Crown upon marrying Meghan Markle, who had been raised a Catholic. See, Kate Samuelson, 'Here's How Kate Middleton . . .', *Time*, 23 April 2018, available at: http://time.com/5218422/royal-baby-succession-british-throne/ (last visited 16 April 2019).

4. See, Peter van der Veer, *Imperial Encounters: Religion and Modernity in India and Britain* (Princeton: Princeton University Press, 2001) (Kindle edition), p. 230. According to this author, the British state in India was more secular than in Britain itself. Ibid., p. 318.

5. 'The Queen, the Church and Other Faiths', available at: https://www.royal.uk/queens-relationship-churches-england-and-scotland-and-other-faiths#na (last visited 21 May 2019).

6. 'Lords Spiritual and Temporal', website of the UK Parliament, https://www.parliament.uk/site-information/glossary/lords-spiritual-and-temporal/ (last visited 11 May 2018).

7. The first amendment to the US Constitution says that Congress can make no law 'respecting an establishment of religion' or 'prohibiting the free exercise thereof'.

8. However, as we shall see in Chapter 4, until 1927, the Church of England in India was established, and even thereafter, churches and clergy members in India received funding from the government.

9. The term 'secularism' itself was coined in England in the 1850s. Julia Stephens, *Governing Islam: Law, Empire, and Secularism in South Asia* (Cambridge: Cambridge University Press, 2018), p. 10. Stephens argues that in colonial India, Hindu leaders used the word 'secular' in juxtaposition to Muslim leaders whom they considered to be overtly religious or 'communal'. Ibid., at p. 16–17. According to Tejani, secularism does not have a fixed meaning but one which is 'particular

to its historical context.' She argues that the word 'nationalism' used in pre-colonial India (as distinguished from 'communalism') was replaced by 'secularism' in independent India. Shabnum Tejani, *Indian Secularism: A Social and Intellectual History, 1890–1950* (Ranikhet: Permanent Black, 2016), pp. 4–5, 13. The word 'secular' was coined in England in the middle of the nineteenth century and was commonly used in India in the twentieth century. Ivermee, *Secularism, Islam and Education in India, 1830–1910*, p. 4.

10. For instance, according to Donald Smith, a secular state has three features: (i) it grants freedom of religion to all; (ii) citizenship is not determined by religion; and (iii) it is unconnected with and does not promote or interfere with religion. Donald Eugene Smith, *India as a Secular State* (Princeton: Princeton University Press, 1963), p. 4. Galanter says that there is a disagreement over whether a secular state is one which is severely aloof from religion, benignly impartial towards it, engages in 'corrective oversight' of it, or fondly and equally indulges all religions. Marc Galanter, *Law and Society in Modern India* (Delhi: Oxford University Press, 1989), p. 237. Nandy says that secularism could either mean the absence of religion in public life or accommodative secularism. Ashis Nandy, 'The Politics of Secularism and the Recovery of Religious Tolerance', *Alternatives*, vol. 13, p. 177, at p. 181 (1988). Gary Jacobsohn identifies three models of secularism: 'assimilative' (the US model), 'visionary' (the Israeli model), and 'ameliorative' (the Indian model), based on such factors as the 'official cognizance' each of these systems takes of religion. Gary Jeffrey Jacobsohn, *The Wheel of Law: India's Secularism in Comparative Constitutional Context* (Princeton: Princeton University Press, 2003), p. 29. Ronojoy Sen identifies three models of secularism: the American model of a wall of separation between church and state which is hard to implement in practice, the European model where one religion is preferred but others are not discriminated against, and the French model of laicite or hard secularism. Ronojoy Sen, *Articles of Faith: Religion, Secularism, and the Indian Supreme Court* (New Delhi: Oxford University Press, 2010), pp. xvii–xx.

11. Stephens, *Governing Islam*, p. 10.

12. However, in practice, the colonial encounter altered personal law.
     Colonial administrators sanctioned translations of Hindu and Muslim
     law which were 'fraught with errors, reified textual sources of authority
     over oral traditions, and discounted the diversity of everyday religious
     practice'. Stephens, *Governing Islam*, p. 24. Even thereafter, colonial
     courts covertly reformed religious personal laws. Stephens, ibid., p.
     53; Mitra Sharafi, 'The Semi-Autonomous Judge in Colonial India:
     Chivalric Imperialism Meets Anglo-Islamic Dower and Divorce Law',
     Indian Economic and Social History Review, vol. 46(1), pp. 57–81
     (2009).

13. According to Rajeev Dhavan, personal laws were not codified in
     British India because this would have generated opposition and
     because personal laws dealing with joint family properties suited the
     state's revenue interests. Rajeev Dhavan, 'Codifying Personal Laws',
     The Hindu, 1 August 2003, available at: https://www.thehindu.
     com/2003/08/01/stories/2003080100521000.htm (last visited 12 April
     2019).

14. The full text of the minute dated 2 February 1835 is available here:
     https://babel.hathitrust.org/cgi/pt?id=mdp.39015030689569;view=
     1up;seq=20 (last visited 6 May 2019). Macaulay struck the decisive
     blow in favour of the 'Anglicists' against the 'Orientalists' over the
     question of whether education in India should be in English or local
     languages. Evangelicals sided with the Anglicists in this debate. Peter
     van der Veer, *Imperial Encounters*, p. 574.

15. Macaulay's minute, ibid., at p. 6.

16. Ibid., p. 7.

17. Peter van der Veer, *Imperial Encounters*, p. 89.

18. Ibid., p. 87.

19. Charles Wood was the president of the Board of Control of the East
     India Company in 1852–55. He later became the secretary of state
     for India in 1859. See, 'Mr. Charles Wood', *Hansard, 1803–2005*,
     available at: https://api.parliament.uk/historic-hansard/people/mr-
     charles-wood/index.html (last visited 18 May 2019).

20. 'Despatch to the Government of India, on the Subject of General
     Education in India', 19 July 1854, available at: https://babel.
     hathitrust.org/cgi/pt?id=hvd.32044106500515;view=1up;seq=161

(last visited 6 May 2019), p. 16, paragraph 84. Prior to this, in 1780, the government had established a madrasa in Calcutta at which Muslim religious instruction was provided to students. Similarly, in 1791, a Sanskrit college at Benares was established which provided Hindu religious instructions. After 1835, religious instruction at the Madrasa was stopped. Ivermee, *Secularism, Islam and Education in India, 1830–1910*, pp. 22, 60, 61, 65. However, Ivermee argues that many British officials felt that the secular educational policy deprived Indian students of a moral education, which partly contributed to disaffection among them. Religious instruction was partially allowed in government institutions in 1887, subject to several conditions. Ibid., pp. 114, 119–20.

21. Ivermee, *Secularism, Islam and Education in India, 1830–1910*, pp. 19, 102. Even now, state maintained schools in England are required to provide religious instructions to their pupils, though parents can have their children excused from those lessons. Sections 69 and 71, School Standards and Framework Act, 1998, available at: https://www.legislation.gov.uk/ukpga/1998/31/contents (last visited 12 May 2019). Neville Harris, 'Equal Rights in Education in the UK (England)', *International Journal for Education Law and Policy*, vol. 4, p. 4 (2008), at p. 11.

22. Ivermee, ibid., pp. 23–26. From 1844 onwards, the colonial government preferred candidates in public employment who were conversant with English. Ibid., p. 28.

23. Ivermee, *Secularism, Islam and Education in India, 1830–1910*, pp. 65–66, 70.

24. Peter van der Veer, *Imperial Encounters*, p. 370; J.E. Riddle, Latin-English Dictionary (Oxford: Oxford University Press, 1839), 2nd edition, available at: https://catalog.hathitrust.org/Record/100025721 (last visited 2 December 2019), at p. 256; Anthony Xavier Soares, Portuguese Vocables in Asiatic Languages (New Delhi: Asian Educational Services, 1988) (available on Google Books), at p. 167.

25. 'Despatch to the Government of India, on the Subject of General Education in India', 19 July 1854, paragraph 84, p. 16. Wood's despatch also provided that religious subjects would not be mandatory for obtaining a degree at a university. Ibid., paragraph 28, p. 6.

However, private colleges affiliated with universities were permitted to teach religious subjects. Ibid., paragraph 28, p. 6.

26. Ibid., paragraph 53, p. 10.
27. Section 4(1), Banaras Hindu University Act, 1915.
28. Section 5, ibid.
29. Section 6(1), ibid.
30. Section 5(2), Aligarh Muslim University Act, 1920.
31. See, Leah Renold, *A Hindu Education: Early Years of the Banaras Hindu University* (New Delhi: Oxford University Press, 2005) (Kindle Edition), at pp. 769–80; Jürgen Lütt, 'The Movement for the Foundation of the Benares Hindu University', in Cultural Department of the Embassy of the Federal Republic of Germany (ed.), *German Scholars on India: Contributions to Indian Studies* (Bombay: Nachiketa Publications Ltd, 1976), vol. 2, pp. 160–95 available at: https://archive.org/details/GermanScholarsOnIndiaVolume2NachiketaPublications/page/n221 (last visited 13 May 2019), at p. 162. See further, Ivermee, *Secularism, Islam and Education in India*, pp. 111, 119.
32. This was on 22 March 1915.
33. For instance, Sir Gangadhar Chitnavis said that imparting 'sound religious instruction' would 'inculcate in the youthful mind a due sense of proportion, of duty and responsibility, and respect for authority which will make the graduates useful, virtuous, loyal and contented citizens'. *Abstract of the Proceedings of the Council of the Governor General of India Assembled for the Purpose of Making Laws and Regulations, 1915*, vol. 53, (Superintendent of Government Printing, 1915), at p. 529. Sir Fazulbhoy Currimbhoy said that 'the vitalising force of the Hindu University will be religion, which ought to mould the plastic mind of the graduates into a different and more agreeable shape'. Ibid., at p. 535. Even on 1 October 1915, when the bill was eventually passed, Mr Dadabhoy, a member of the Imperial Legislative Council, said: 'Let us hope that the Hindu University, by a wide dissemination of the high principles of Hindu religion, will inculcate in the students sober and loyal ideas of citizenship . . .' *Proceedings of the Council of the Governor General of India assembled for the purpose of making Laws and Regulations from April 1915 to March 1916*, vol. 54 (Calcutta: Superintendent of Government Printing, 1916), at p. 92.
34. *Abstract of the Proceedings*, ibid., p. 537.

35. Speech of Rai Bahadur Sita Nath Ray, ibid., p. 534. He also said that 'education dissociated from religion . . . is at the root of all anarchy and disregard for constituted authority'.

36. Both Ghaznavi and Chimanlal Setalvad made this point. Ibid., pp. 531, 536. Lütt makes the argument that Benares Hindu University was founded because the government wanted to establish a Muslim university in order to appease Muslims on account of their dissatisfaction with the Minto–Morley reforms. Lütt, 'The Movement for the Foundation of the Banaras Hindu University', at p. 175.

37. Much of the secular educational policy of the colonial government was later carried forward in the Constitution of independent India. After Macaulay's minute of 1835 and Charles Wood's dispatch of 1854, the principle was that religious instruction could not be provided in the government's educational institutions, though it could be provided in institutions which were aided by the government. See, Ivermee, *Secularism, Islam and Education in India, 1830–1910*, pp. 33, 41, 54, 88–89. This policy was continued after the Constitution came into being. Article 28(1) of the Constitution says that no religious instruction can be provided in educational institutions maintained wholly out of state funds. However, this implies that religious instruction can be provided if the institution is maintained partly out of state funds, i.e. if the institution receives government aid. In the colonial period, two universities which were established by statute, Banaras Hindu University (1915) and Aligarh Muslim University (1920) permitted religious instruction to be provided to students. However, a speech delivered by Kazi Syed Karimuddin on 7 December 1948 in the Constituent Assembly suggests that these universities were considered to be aided universities and not universities wholly maintained out of state funds. Karimuddin opposed an amendment proposed by K.T. Shah which would have required no religious instruction to be provided in any educational institution maintained even partly out of state funds. To this, Karimuddin said: 'Today as things stand in India there is Aligarh University, there is Banaras University and there are several colleges run by the Christian Missionaries which are aided by the Government. If [Shah's] amendment is accepted today there will be hundreds and thousands of institutions which will be closed down

immediately.' Sir Harcourt Butler's speech made on 22 March 1915 in the Imperial Legislative Council introducing the Banaras Hindu University bill confirms the fact that the university was funded through private contributions made by princes. *Abstract of the Proceedings of the Council of the Governor General of India Assembled for the Purpose of Making Laws and Regulations, 1915*, at p. 526. Further, according to Smith, Banaras Hindu University and Aligarh Muslim University are saved by Article 28(2), since these institutions were established under endowments which require instruction in Hinduism and Islam. Smith, *India as a Secular State*, p. 132.

As such, even today, the statutes under which these universities are established provide that they can instruct students in Hinduism and Muslim theology. Section 4A(2), Banaras Hindu University Act, 1915; Section 5(2)(a), Aligarh Muslim University Act, 1920.

However, Article 28(3) of the Constitution provides that no student in any aided or government recognized institution can be compelled to take part in any religious instruction or worship. Article 29(2) of the Constitution provides that no citizen can be denied admission into any aided institution on grounds inter alia of religion. What constitutes 'religious' instruction has more recently been diluted by the Supreme Court in *Aruna Roy v. Union of India*, (2002) 7 SCC 368.

38. Ajay Verghese argues that the construction of Hindu and Muslim identities was a pre-colonial, 17th century phenomenon, and that religious riots occurred even in pre-colonial times. Ajay Verghese, 'Did Hindu–Muslim Conflicts in India Really Start with British Rule?', Scroll.in, 5 June 2018, available at: https://scroll.in/article/880832/did-hindu-muslim-conflicts-in-india-really-start-with-british-rule (last visited 5 May 2019). However, scholars disagree about whether the British invented religious identities in India. For instance, Peter van der Veer takes the view that European orientalists made Hindus members of an integrated, coherent religion, by attempting to learn about Hindus and Hinduism. *Imperial Encounters*, p. 370. According to Dirks, '[c]olonial knowledge both enabled conquest and was produced by it'. Nicholas B. Dirks, 'Foreword', in, Bernard S. Cohn, *Colonialism and Its Forms of Knowledge: The British in India* (Princeton: Princeton University Press, 1996), p. ix.

39. Thomas R. Metcalf, *Ideologies of the Raj* (Cambridge: Cambridge University Press, 1995), p. 134. According to Thapar, there was no monolithic Hindu community in pre-colonial India. Instead, those whom we would now consider to be 'Hindus' saw themselves as belonging to different sects and castes. Romila Thapar, 'Imagined Religious Communities? Ancient History and the Modern Search for a Hindu Identity', *Modern Asian Studies*, vol. 23(2), pp. 209–31 (1989), at p. 222, 225, 228. The 'need for postulating a Hindu community' arose because of 'political mobilization in the nineteenth century'. Ibid., at p. 229. However, scholars of pre-colonial India disagree over the extent to which Hinduism could have been considered a religion at that time.

40. Even today, who is a Hindu? A person who eats beef, visits the Haji Ali Dargah, denies the authority of the Vedas, or even denies that he is a Hindu, might still be considered to be one. See, Galanter, *Law and Society in Modern India*, p. 121. According to Galanter, a Hindu is a person who willingly refrains from calling himself anything else. This 'no conversion test' sometimes did not apply to Muslims in the colonial period, and if a person did not adhere to Islam's minimum beliefs (e.g., the authority of the Quran), he was not considered a Muslim, despite the fact that he had not converted to another religion. Galanter, ibid., p. 166–68. Dhavan and Nariman argue that the Supreme Court has adopted a doctrine which is 'over-assimilationist' in its approach towards Hinduism, for instance, in its rejection of the claims of Swami Narayans that they are not Hindus. Rajeev Dhavan and Fali S. Nariman, 'The Supreme Court and Group Life: Religious Freedom, Minority Groups, and Disadvantaged Communities', in B.N. Kirpal et al. (eds.), *Supreme but Not Infallible: Essays in Honour of the Supreme Court of India* (New Delhi: Oxford University Press, 2000), p. 280, note 35. Further, Buddhists, Sikhs and Jains are governed by the statutes that constitute the Hindu Code in India. Flavia Agnes calls this 'legal Hinduism', i.e. groups that are not Hindu are, by a deeming fiction in law, considered to be Hindus for the application of the statute. Flavia Agnes, 'Personal Laws', in, Sujit Choudhry et al. (eds.), *The Oxford Handbook of the Indian Constitution* (Oxford: Oxford University Press, 2016), pp. 903–20, at p. 917.

41. Metcalf, *Ideologies of the Raj*, p. 137.

42. Gauri Viswanathan, *Outside the Fold: Conversion, Modernity, and Belief* (Princeton: Princeton University Press, 1998), p. xii; Nandy, 'The Politics of Secularism and the Recovery of Religious Tolerance', p. 178.

43. Nandy, ibid.

44. According to Freitag, colonial officials applied labels like 'Hindu' and 'Muslim' to communities that were 'far from homogenous'. Sandria B. Freitag, 'Sacred Symbol as Mobilizing Ideology: The North Indian Search for a 'Hindu' Community', *Comparative Studies in Society and History*, vol. 22(4), pp. 597–625 (1980), at p. 597.

45. Metcalf, *Ideologies of the Raj*, p. 134.

46. Stephens, *Governing Islam*, at p. 8.

47. Stephens, *Governing Islam*, at p. 8.

48. C.A. Bayly, 'The Pre-History of "Communalism"? Religious Conflict in India, 1700–1860', *Modern Asian Studies*, vol. 19(2), pp. 177–203, at pp. 201–02 (1985).

49. See, Bayly, ibid., at pp. 177–78. According to John McLane, religious reform movements during British colonial rule in India gave rise to counter-reform movements among traditional and orthodox elements in Indian society, which, in turn, gave rise to a heightened religious consciousness. This resulted in communal violence. John R. McLane, *Indian Nationalism and the Early Congress* (Princeton: Princeton University Press, 1977), pp. 271–72. For instance, the cow protection agitation was a reaction to the age of consent controversy. McLane, ibid., p. 298.

50. Matthew Groves, 'Law, Religion and Public Order in Colonial India: Contextualising the 1887 Allahabad High Court Case on "Sacred" Cows', *Journal of South Asian Studies*, vol. 33(1), pp. 87–121 (2010), at pp. 88–90.

51. Peter Robb, 'The Challenge of Gau Mata: British Policy and Religious Change in India, 1880–1916', *Modern Asian Studies*, vol. 20(2), pp. 285–319, at p. 317 (1986).

52. He held this position during 1884–88. See, 'Frederick Temple Hamilton-Temple-Blackwood, 1st Marquess of Dufferin and Ava', *Encyclopaedia Britannica*, available at: https://www.britannica.com/biography/Frederick-Temple-Hamilton-Temple-Blackwood-1st-Marquess-of-Dufferin-and-Ava (last visited 21 April 2019).

53. Francis Robinson, *Separatism among Indian Muslims: The Politics of the United Provinces' Muslims, 1860–1923* (Cambridge: Cambridge University Press, 1974), p. 131 (note 2); Groves, 'Law, Religion and Public Order in Colonial India', p. 99. However, Dufferin added: 'but these circumstances we found and did not create, nor, had they been non-existent, would we have been justified in establishing them by artificial means. It would have been a diabolical policy on the part of my Government to endeavour to emphasize or exacerbate race hatreds among the Queen's Indian subjects for a political object.' Robinson, ibid.

54. Matthew Groves notes that there is a debate in the scholarly literature over whether the British really manufactured Hindu–Muslim tensions. He concludes that 'communalism before the nineteenth century was uncommon' and that there is 'clear statistical evidence of an acceleration in the intensity of communal conflict from the 1870s'. Groves, 'Law, Religion and Public Order in Colonial India', at pp. 88–90. Though he believes that 'the notion that Indians were oblivious to religious differences until otherwise instructed by their British rulers is simply untenable', the British certainly used religious divisions in India to their advantage though they may not have manufactured religious identities. Ibid., at pp. 98–99. See further, Mitra Sharafi, *Law and Identity in Colonial South Asia: Parsi Legal Culture, 1772–1947* (Ranikhet: Permanent Black, 2017), p. 179. The British tried to get Parsis to think that child marriage within their community was a Hindu influence. Muslims were told that their uncivilized practices were actually Hindu practices, while regressive Hindu practices were blamed on Muslim pre-colonial influence. However, scholars disagree about whether divide and rule was a conscious policy or if Muslim separatism was an unintended consequence of colonialism. Francis Robinson writes, for instance, that it was the latter. Robinson, *Separatism among Indian Muslims*, at pp. 131–32, 164 (citing Stanley Wolpert), 348–49.

55. Robinson, *Separatism among Indian Muslims*, p. 131.

56. Stephens, *Governing Islam*, pp. 39–40. Stephens points out that Christian missionaries felt that 'Indians required prior training in rational modes of analysis before they would embrace Christianity.' Ibid., p. 39. She writes that in the 1830s and 1840s, Alexander Duff set

up missionary schools in Calcutta which offered an English education to Indian students, with the idea that this would facilitate the spread of the gospel. Ibid., p. 39. She also speaks of how C.H. Cameron, the president of the Law Commission, praised 'instruction of the Natives in the Science, Literature and Morality of Europe' as 'the only safe and effectual road to conversion'. Ibid., p. 47.

57. Dhavan and Nariman, 'The Supreme Court and Group Life', pp. 262–63. Dhavan and Nariman argue that the government takeover of the Vaishno Devi shrine in Jammu and Kashmir is the starkest example of this phenomenon. According to them, 'under the guise of regulatory control, religious endowments are . . . nationalized on a mass scale'. See further, Farrah Ahmed, *Religious Freedom under the Personal Law System* (New Delhi: Oxford University Press, 2016), p. 37.

58. According to Sir Harcourt Butler, the education member in the Viceroy's Council, the bill to establish Banaras Hindu University was 'in the nature of a private Bill which has been taken over by Government'. *Proceedings of the Council of the Governor General of India assembled for the purpose of making Laws and Regulations from April 1915 to March 1916*, at p. 15 (8 September 1915). Butler repeated this point on 1 October 1915, when he said that the bill had 'a mixed parentage'. Ibid., p. 79. On 1 October 1915, Mr Dadabhoy, a member of the Imperial Legislative Council, also concurred that the bill was 'to all intents and purposes, a private Member's Bill'. Ibid., p. 90.

59. Marc Galanter, 'Caste Disabilities and Indian Federalism', *Journal of the Indian Law Institute*, vol. 3, pp. 205–34, at p. 209 (1961).

60. Galanter, *Law and Society in Modern India*, pp. 147–48.

61. The first such comprehensive law was enacted in 1938 in Madras, i.e. the Madras Removal of Civil Disabilities Act, 1938. Galanter, 'Caste Disabilities and Indian Federalism', p. 211. Most of the other provinces followed suit (e.g., in Bombay, the statute was known as the Bombay Harijan (Removal of Social Disabilities) Act, 1946). Galanter, ibid., p. 212 (note 36).

62. Articles 15(2), 17 and 25(2)(b). The first provincial law which made it a criminal offence to prevent 'untouchables' from entering Hindu temples was enacted in Madras in 1947, the Madras Temple Entry Authorization Act, 1947. Most other provinces followed suit. Galanter,

'Caste Disabilities and Indian Federalism', p. 214 (notes 48–49). For instance, the statute in Bombay was known as the Bombay Harijan Temple Entry Act, 1947. After the Constitution was enacted, Section 3 of the central Untouchability (Offences) Act, 1955 and Section 3 of the Protection of Civil Rights Act, 1955, made it a crime to prevent a person, on the grounds of 'untouchability', from entering a temple. See further, Marc Galanter, 'Temple-Entry and the Untouchability (Offences) Act, 1955', *Journal of the Indian Law Institute*, vol. 6, p. 185–95 (1964), available at: http://14.139.60.114:8080/jspui/bitstream/123456789/15101/1/018_Temple-Entry%20and%20the%20Untouchability%20(Offences)%20Act,%201955%20(185-195).pdf (last visited 24 November 2018). Section 3 of the central Scheduled Castes and the Scheduled Tribes (Prevention of Atrocities) Act, 1989, goes even further, and criminalizes several kinds of conduct towards Scheduled Castes and Scheduled Tribes, including the filing of a 'malicious or vexatious suit' against their members, or insulting or intimidating their members, with intent to humiliate them, in any place within public view.

63. Galater, *Law and Society in Modern India*, p. 156.
64. Dhavan and Nariman, 'The Supreme Court and Group Life', p. 275. According to these authors, a comparison between secularism in India and the US or other countries might be 'misleading'. Dhavan and Nariman, 'The Supreme Court and Group Life', p. 286, note 131, and accompanying text.
65. *Rajesh Himmatlal Solanki v. Union of India*, (2011) SCC Online Guj 1079. The special leave petition against this judgment was dismissed by the Supreme Court in SLP(C) 7283/2011 through the order dated 28 March 2011.
66. Other scholars have argued that secularism in India was foreign. Madan has argued that secularism was a Christian idea which could not simply be transferred to South Asian societies without translation. T.N. Madan, 'Secularism in its Place', *Journal of Asian Studies*, vol. 46, p. 747, at pp. 753–54 (1987), available at: https://ael.eui.eu/wp-content/uploads/sites/18/2014/05/Bhargava-01-Madan.pdf (last visited 16 November 2018). He also calls secularism an 'alien cultural ideology'. Ibid., p. 757. Nandy says tolerance in India will have to

be derived from the principles of non-modern India. He gives the example that Ashoka, Akbar and Gandhi derived their notions of secularism from Buddhism, Islam and Hinduism respectively. Nandy, 'The Politics of Secularism and the Recovery of Religious Tolerance', p. 188. However, none of these scholars pays close attention to the colonial difference inherent in the secularism that was imposed on British India.

Of course, one could argue that the entire legal system which is found in India today is a foreign transplant. If this foreign legal system has survived in India, why is it that colonial secularism has not? Galanter provides some possible answers. He says that the foreign legal system in India underwent a process of indigenization, such that it ceased to be an altogether foreign system. It had support from a large body of lawyers and judges who genuinely believed in its virtues. Those who wanted to revive indigenous law could not suggest a viable alternative. Marc Galanter, 'The Aborted Restoration of "Indigenous" Law in India', in, Galanter, *Law and Society in Modern India*, pp. 46, 48, 51. By contrast, born out of Christian revulsion towards heathen religions, secularism remained an unnatural, foreign idea in India. It lacked the large-scale support that lawyers and judges provided to the legal system generally. Unsecular options, like banning cow slaughter or rendering conversion from Hinduism difficult, were easily imagined and executable with relative ease.

67. See, Abhinav Chandrachud, *Republic of Rhetoric: Free Speech and the Constitution of India* (Gurgaon: Penguin Viking, 2017).

68. See, the introductory essay in Sen, *Articles of Faith*, pp. xiv–xxvi; Smith, *India as a Secular State*, p. 499.

69. See, Smith, *India as a Secular State*, pp. 499–500.

70. See, Samira Shackle, 'Imran Khan's Treatment of Asia Bibi Is a Dangerous Betrayal', *The Guardian*, 13 November 2018, available at: https://www.theguardian.com/commentisfree/2018/nov/13/asia-bibi-imran-khan-pakistan-blasphemy-law (last visited 16 November 2018).

71. Third Schedule, Constitution of Pakistan. Available at: http://na.gov.pk/uploads/documents/1333523681_951.pdf (last visited 2 January 2018). The Constitution of Pakistan does not seem to offer any option to the President to make an affirmation instead of swearing an oath.

72. Following the demolition of the Babri Masjid, the Supreme Court, in
     S.R. Bommai v. Union of India, (1994) 3 SCC 1, upheld the imposition
     of President's rule in four BJP-ruled states. See, Dhavan and Nariman,
     'The Supreme Court and Group Life', p. 262.

73. See, *Tehseen S. Poonawalla v. Union of India*, (2018) 9 SCC 501.

74. Of course, one must acknowledge that the British Raj was not 'a single-
     minded and totally cohesive entity', as scholars of the 'Cambridge
     School' of Indian historians would point out. Groves, 'Law, Religion
     and Public Order in Colonial India', p. 116. However, the colonial
     policy of 'neutrality' towards indigenous religions was a formal policy
     which all colonial officials in India had to follow, and there were
     'certain repeated assumptions and tendencies' in enforcing it. Robb,
     'The Challenge of Gau Mata', p. 285.

75. Peter van der Veer borrows Jose Casanova's definition of secularization
     and says that it has three ingredients: (i) the separation of religion from
     politics, etc.; (ii) the privatization of religion; and (iii) the declining
     social significance of religious beliefs. Peter van der Veer, *Imperial
     Encounters*, p. 195.

76. Sen, *Articles of Faith*, p. xv; Smith, *India as a Secular State*, p. 495.
     Ahmed considers this to be 'an important mistake to avoid'. Ahmed,
     Religious Freedom, p. 36.

Chapter 1: Holy Cow

1.   Groves explains that the festival of Idu'l Azhā (or Eid-ul-Adha) is 'held
     on the ninth day of the twelfth month of the Muslim year'. Muslim
     families are supposed to slaughter a large animal to mark Abraham's
     offering of his son, Ishmael, to God. According to Groves, sheep and
     goats are 'perfectly acceptable for this purpose' and are 'commonly
     sacrificed throughout the Islamic Middle East'. However, the sacrifice
     of one larger animal like a cow can 'cover the ritual obligations of
     seven families'. Since cows were relatively abundant and inexpensive
     in India, they were preferred as animals of slaughter. This is why the
     festival of Idu'l Azhā became locally known as Bakr Id. Groves, 'Law,
     Religion and Public Order in Colonial India', p. 94. On cows being

inexpensive in India, see further, McLane, *Indian Nationalism and the Early Congress*, p. 279. See further, Joseph Catafago, An English and Arabic Dictionary (London: Bernard Quaritch, 1873), available at: https://babel.hathitrust.org/cgi/pt?id=hvd.hnjtae&view=1up&seq=5 (last visited 2 December 2019), at p. 59.

2. Rohit De, *A People's Constitution: The Everyday Life of Law in the Indian Republic* (Princeton, New Jersey: Princeton University Press, 2018), p. 125; Groves, ibid., p. 94. See further, Joseph Catafago, *An English and Arabic Dictionary* (London: Bernard Quaritch, 1873), available at: https://babel.hathitrust.org/cgi/pt?id=hvd.hnjtae&view=1up&seq=5 (last visited 2 December 2019), at p. 59.

3. Romila Thapar, *A History of India* (London: Penguin Books, 1990 reprint), vol. 1, at pp. 29–30.

4. Thapar, ibid., at p. 338. According to Groves, cow killing was expressly condemned from the early fourth century onwards. Cow worship started, he says, from the fifteenth century after the Bhagavata Purana was translated into Hindi and with the rise of the worship of Krishna. Ritual cow sacrifice was once prevalent even among Hindus, he says. More recently, chickens are sacrificed to appease 'Poleramma, the goddess of smallpox'. Groves, 'Law, Religion and Public Order in Colonial India', p. 93.

5. Dr B.R. Ambedkar, *The Untouchables: Who Were They and Why They Became Untouchables* (New Delhi: Amrit Book Co., 1948), available at: https://archive.org/details/TheUntouchables_1948/page/n1 (last visited 22 May 2019), at pp. 87, 88 and 120; Smith, *India as a Secular State*, at p. 455, 484. The Supreme Court in *Mohd. Hanif Quareshi v. State of Bihar*, AIR 1958 SC 731 (from SCC Online) (paragraphs 22–23) referred to the works of two scholars, A.G. Das and P.V. Kane, and found that even in Rig Vedic times, 'there seems to have grown up a revulsion of feeling against the custom' of cow killing, though cows were slaughtered for food during that period. Noting the 'high praise' that was bestowed on the cow even in the Rig Veda, the court recorded Kane's argument that 'only barren cows, if at all' were killed in that period.

6. However, during the 'Mutiny' in 1857, the Mughal emperor Bahadur Shah banned cow slaughter during Bakr Id. McLane, *Indian Nationalism and the Early Congress*, p. 278.

7.   Smith, *India as a Secular State*, at p. 222; Gyan Pandey, 'Rallying
     Round the Cow: Sectarian Strife in the Bhojpuri Region, c. 1888–
     1917', Centre for Studies in Social Sciences, Calcutta, Occasional Paper
     No. 39 (1981), available at: https://opendocs.ids.ac.uk/opendocs/
     handle/123456789/3241 (last visited 10 November 2018); Tejani,
     Indian Secularism, p. 43–44; De, *A People's Constitution*, p. 126. One
     of the largest of these was in 1893. McLane, *Indian Nationalism and
     the Early Congress*, p. 272. A cow protection society was set up by the
     Arya Samaj in Punjab under Swami Dayanand Saraswati in 1881.
     De, *A People's Constitution*, p. 126; Groves, 'Law Religion and Public
     Order in Colonial India', p. 95. Hindu processions near mosques were
     also responsible for communal riots. Riots took place in the 1880s and
     1890s on an upsurge in kine killing. Groves, 'Law, Religion and Public
     Order in Colonial India', p. 90. However, after 1920, riots occurred
     over other subjects like playing music in front of mosques, the actions
     of those who celebrated Holi, and insults to the Prophet. Groves, ibid.,
     p. 121. For a narrative of the 1893 riot in Basantpur, see, Anand A.
     Yang, 'Sacred Symbol and Sacred Space in Rural India: Community
     Mobilization in the "Anti-Cow Killing" Riot of 1893', *Comparative
     Studies in Society and History*, vol. 22(4), pp. 576–96 (1980).

8.   There was, however, a ban on cow slaughter for sale in Delhi since
     1849. Robb, 'The Challenge of Gau Mata', p. 301.

9.   This was done after the annexation of Punjab. McLane, *Indian
     Nationalism and the Early Congress*, p. 277. Similarly, in 1882, cow
     slaughter was a crime punishable with life imprisonment in Kashmir.
     McLane, ibid., p. 279.

10. De, *A People's Constitution*, p. 144; McLane, *Indian Nationalism
     and the Early Congress*, p. 292. See further, Memorandum by the
     Honourable Sir Sankaran Nair, Kt., CIE, chairman, the Honourable
     Raja Nawab Ali Khan, and the Honourable Sardar Shivdev Singh
     Uberoi in *East India (Constitutional Reforms): Report of the Indian
     Central Committee, 1928–29* (London: H.M. Stationery Office,
     1929), available at: https://catalog.hathitrust.org/Record/010315381
     (last visited 8 November 2018), at p. 126 ('The Muslims are entitled
     to slaughter cows subject to any municipal regulations or laws.').

11. Smith, *India as a Secular State*, at p. 66.

12. See further, Robb, 'The Challenge of Gau Mata', p. 316.

13. Section 295, Indian Penal Code.

14. 'Note J', *A Copy of the Penal Code, Prepared by the Indian Law Commissioners* (Hertford: S. Austin, 1851), available at: https://catalog.hathitrust.org/Record/011627302 (last visited 12 November 2018), p. 156. See further, W. Morgan and A.G. Macpherson, *The Indian Penal Code (Act XLV of 1860) with Notes* (Calcutta: G.C. Hay, 1861), available at: https://catalog.hathitrust.org/Record/011619848 (last visited 12 November 2018), p. 218.

15. *Queen Empress v. Imam Ali*, (1887) SCC Online All 12. For an interesting discussion of this case, see, Groves, 'Law, Religion and Public Order in Colonial India'. Groves notes that one of the judges who heard the case, Saiyyid Mahmud, was the son of Sir Saiyyid Ahmad Khan, a prominent Muslim anti-Congress leader. Ibid., at p. 102. Justice Mahmud eventually resigned after he delivered a subsequent judgment in an inebriated state. Ibid., p. 115. Groves also wonders why the colonial government did not try and amend Section 295 of the Indian Penal Code after the Allahabad High Court's judgment in the Imam case. Ibid., p. 113. This case 'played a role in stimulating the cow protection agitation'. Groves, ibid. The judgment of the Allahabad High Court in the Imam case was followed by a Division Bench of the Calcutta High Court in *Romesh Chunder Sannyal v. Hiru Mondal*, (1890) ILR 17 Cal 852. See further, Groves, ibid., pp. 92, 109–10.

16. He was the wealthiest landlord in Bihar. Groves, ibid., p. 112.

17. Groves, 'Law, Religion and Public Order in Colonial India', pp. 112–13.

18. *Hajee Mazhur Ali v. Gundownee Sahoo*, (1882) 25 W.R. 72 (as recorded in *Shahbaz Khan v. Umrao Puri*, (1908) SCC Online All 13).

19. *Shahbaz Khan v. Umrao Puri*, (1908) SCC Online All 13.

20. Ibid., paragraph 6.

21. Ibid., paragraph 9.

22. Ibid., paragraph 10.

23. *Muhammad Salim v. Ramkumar Singh*, (1928) SCC Online All 176 (paragraph 20).

24. *Naubahar Singh v. Qadir Bux*, (1930) SCC Online All 171 (paragraph 18).

25. See, *Ibrahim v. Emperor*, (1937) SCC Online Lah 59.

26. Speech dated 24 August 1949 of N.C. Laskar in the Constituent Assembly. Constituent Assembly Debates of India, vol. vii.

27. M.K. Gandhi, 'Speech on Cow Protection, Bettiah', 9 October 1917, in, *The Collected Works of Mahatma Gandhi* (electronic book) (New Delhi: Publications Division, Government of India, 1999) in ninety-eight volumes (*Collected Works*), available at: http://www.gandhiashramsevagram.org/gandhi-literature/collected-works-of-mahatma-gandhi-volume-1-to-98.php (last visited 8 November 2018), vol. 16, at p. 54 onwards. In the late nineteenth century, around 1,00,000 cattle were slaughtered each year in order to feed English soldiers in India. Groves, 'Law, Religion and Public Order in Colonial India', p. 99. Colonial officials were aware that the cow protection agitation was, at some level, an anti-colonial one. Robb, 'The Challenge of Gau Mata', p. 299. Indeed, the 1893 Basantpur riot had distinct 'anti-British overtones'. Yang, 'Sacred Symbol and Sacred Space in Rural India', p. 596.

28. M.K. Gandhi, 'Cow Protection', *Young India*, 4 August 1920, in, *Collected Works*, vol. 21, at p. 118.

29. Letter dated 20 August 1954 from Nehru to the PCC presidents, in, Jagdish Saran Sharma (ed.), *Indian National Congress: A Descriptive Bibliography of India's Struggle for Freedom* (Delhi: S. Chand, 1959), available at: https://catalog.hathitrust.org/Record/001170533 (last visited 8 November 2018), at p. 43. According to Rohit De, the British army was the largest buyer of beef in India. De, *A People's Constitution*, p. 125. In fact, in a letter to Viceroy Lord Lansdowne written on 8 December 1893, Queen Victoria conveyed the message that the cow protection agitation was actually directed against the British, 'who kill far more cows for our army, etc., than the Muhammadans'. Dharampal and T.M. Mukundan, *The British Origin of Cow-Slaughter in India: With Some British Documents on the Anti-Kine-Killing Movement 1880–1894* (Mussoorie: Society for Integrated Development of Himalayas, 2002), at p. 429. According to these authors, Hindu–Muslim tensions over cow-killing were instigated by the British, who encouraged Muslims to slaughter cows on account of the needs of the British army.

30. 'Hindu–Muslim Tension: Its Cause and Cure', in, *Collected Works*, vol. 28, at p. 59. Groves points out that members of Hindu castes like Ahirs and Gwalas sold their cows for slaughter without compunction until the late nineteenth century. Groves, 'Law, Religion and Public Order in Colonial India', p. 94.

31. 'Speech at Exhibition', *Harijan*, 19 February 1938. *Collected Works*, vol. 72, at p. 461.

32. M.K. Gandhi, 'Speech at Public Meeting, Kadi', 23 July 1929, in, *Collected Works*, vol. 46, at p. 305. See further, M.K. Gandhi, 'The U.P. Tour IX', ibid., vol. 47, at p. 429.

33. M.K. Gandhi, 'Our Cattle Wealth', *Harijan*, 27 February 1937, in, *Collected Works*, vol. 71, at p. 7.

34. Ambedkar, *The Untouchables*, at p. 80.

35. M.K. Gandhi, 'Village Tanning and Its Possibilities', *Harijan*, 7 September 1934, in, *Collected Works*, vol. 64, at p. 408.

36. M.K. Gandhi, 'Speech at Prayer Meeting', 25 April 1947, in, *Collected Works*, vol. 94, at p. 385.

37. M.K. Gandhi, 'Hind Swaraj', in, *Collected Works*, vol. 10, at p. 271.

38. In fact, several cow protection movements in colonial India made economic arguments rather than religious ones. See, C.S. Adcock, 'Sacred Cows and Secular History: Cow Protection Debates in Colonial North India', *Comparative Studies of South Asia, Africa and the Middle East*, vol. 30, no. 2 (2010), pp. 297–311. Gandhi was not the first to make such an argument, and the economic argument in support of the cow was not new. De, *A People's Constitution*, p. 132.

39. M.K. Gandhi, 'Cow Protection', *Navajivan*, 8 August 1920, in, *Collected Works*, vol. 21, at p. 128.

40. M.K. Gandhi, 'Why I Am a Hindu', in, *Collected Works*, vol. 40, at p. 291.

41. M.K. Gandhi, 'Village Tanning and Its Possibilities', *Harijan*, 7 September 1934, in, *Collected Works*, vol. 64, at p. 408.

42. M.K. Gandhi, 'Our Cattle Wealth', *Harijan*, 27 February 1937, in, *Collected Works*, vol. 71, at p. 8.

43. M.K. Gandhi, 'Speech at All-India Goseva Sangh Conference', 1 February 1942, in, *Collected Works*, vol. 81, at p. 481.

44. M.K. Gandhi, 'How to Save the Cow?', *Harijan*, 31 August 1947, in, *Collected Works*, vol. 96, at p. 262.

45. M.K. Gandhi, 'Hindu–Muslim Unity', *Young India*, 18 September 1924, in, *Collected Works*, vol. 29, at p. 144.

46. M.K. Gandhi, 'Cow Protection', *Young India*, 4 August 1920, in, *Collected Works*, vol. 21, at p. 119. Similarly, the Congress in its Amritsar, Nagpur and Calcutta sessions held in 1919, 1920 and 1927 passed resolutions thanking the Muslim League and Muslim associations for passing resolutions against cow slaughter. Jagdish Saran Sharma (ed.), *India's Struggle for Freedom: Select Documents and Sources* (Delhi: S. Chand, 1962), available at: https://catalog.hathitrust.org/Record/001249599 (last visited 8 November 2018), vol. 1, at p. 170.

47. M.K. Gandhi, 'Notes', *Young India*, 12 June 1924, in, *Collected Works*, vol. 28, at p. 146.

48. M.K. Gandhi, 'Presidential Address at Cow-Protection Conference, Belgaum', *Young India*, 29 January 1925, in, *Collected Works*, vol. 30, at p. 21.

49. M.K. Gandhi, 'The Cow in Mysore', *Young India*, 7 July 1927, in, *Collected Works*, vol. 39, at p. 177.

50. M.K. Gandhi, 'Question Box', *Harijan*, 27 April 1940, in, *Collected Works*, vol. 78, at p. 163.

51. See, letter dated 11 July 1944 issued by B. Sahay, deputy secretary to the Government of India, to all provincial governments. Available at: http://dahd.nic.in/hi/related-links/annex-i-1 (last visited 12 November 2018). See further, intervention of Pandit Thakur Dass Bhargava in the Constituent Assembly, Constituent Assembly Debates, Vol. VII, p. 579. During the Second World War, the province of Assam banned the slaughter of milch and draught cattle. Assam used to import most of its draught cattle from Bihar, which was stopped during the war. It was for this reason that the ban was temporarily imposed. See, speech of Syed Muhammad Saadulla in the Constituent Assembly, 24 November 1948, Constituent Assembly Debates, vol. VII, p. 579.

52. Sahay's letter, ibid. According to Robb, though the colonial government pursued a formal policy of neutrality towards religions, its treatment of the cow slaughter issue showed that 'in practice neutrality was a relative and not an absolute concept'. Robb, 'The Challenge of Gau Mata',

p. 303. 'Special precautions' were taken, at Muslim festivals, like troop
deployments to keep the peace. Ibid., pp. 303–04. The government had
to decide what past custom was and then regulate or enforce it. Ibid.,
p. 316. In requiring slaughter-places to be 'secluded and arranged as
far as possible so as to avoid any offence to Hindus', the government
interfered in religious customs. Ibid., p. 316. Muslims were encouraged
to claim new rights of cow slaughter. Ibid., p. 318.

53. See, Sarfraz Manzoor, 'Father to a Nation, Stranger to His Son',
The Guardian, 10 August 2007, available at: https://www.theguardian.
com/film/2007/aug/10/india (last visited 18 May 2019).

54. Letter dated 1 December 1926. S. Gopal (ed.), *Selected Works of
Jawaharlal Nehru* (Delhi: B.R. Publishing Corporation, 1988 reprint),
available at: http://nehruportal.nic.in/writings (last visited 8 November
2018), vol. 2, at p. 253.

55. Letter dated 6 April 1938, in, Sharma (ed.), *India's Struggle for
Freedom*, vol. 3, at p. 1025.

56. George E. Jones, *Tumult in India* (New York: Dodd, Mead, 1948),
available at: https://catalog.hathitrust.org/Record/001868537 (last visited
8 November 2018), at p. 115.

57. M.K. Gandhi, 'Speech at Prayer Meeting', 19 July 1947, in, *Collected
Works*, vol. 96, at p. 86.

58. M.K. Gandhi, 'Speech at Prayer Meeting', 25 July 1947, ibid., at
p. 137.

59. Ibid., at pp. 138–39.

60. M.K. Gandhi, 'Speech at Prayer Meeting', 30 July 1947, ibid., at
p. 180.

61. Letter dated 7 August 1947, in, Valmiki Choudhary (ed.), *Dr Rajendra
Prasad: Correspondence and Select Documents* (New Delhi: Allied
Publishers Pvt. Ltd, 1987), vol. 7, at pp. 91–92.

62. Nehru's letter to Prasad dated 7 August 1947, in, S. Gopal (ed.),
Selected Works of Jawaharlal Nehru: Second Series (New Delhi:
Jawaharlal Nehru Memorial Fund, 1985), vol. 3, pp. 189–92.

63. Smith says that a propaganda campaign had been launched to ban cow
slaughter by Dalmia. Smith, *India as a Secular State*, at p. 484.

64. Bhargava was a lawyer and a congressman from Lahore, who
represented East Punjab in the Constituent Assembly. He was later

a member of the Lok Sabha in 1952–57. See, profile on the Lok Sabha website, available at: http://loksabhaph.nic.in/writereaddata/biodata_1_12/619.htm (last visited 19 May 2019).

65. Das was a member of the Constituent Assembly representing C.P. and Berar. He was later a member of the Lok Sabha in 1952–70. He was awarded the Padma Bhushan in 1961. See, profile on the Lok Sabha website, available at: http://164.100.47.194/loksabha/writereaddata/biodata_1_12/730.htm (last visited 19 May 2019).

66. It is not clear when the word 'useful' was dropped from the draft which eventually became Article 48 of the Constitution.

67. Rao, *The Framing of India's Constitution*, vol. 4, at p. 30. In a speech dated 24 November 1948 in the Constituent Assembly, Bhargava suggested that Ambedkar was also of the view that it could be included in the directive principles instead of the fundamental rights chapter.

68. Constituent Assembly Debates (24 November 1948) (available on SCC Online).

69. Ibid. He also said that there were laws for preventing cow slaughter in every province, but they were not very effective.

70. Sahai was a member of the Constituent Assembly from Madhya Bharat. He was later a member of the Lok Sabha (1952–57, 1957–62). See, profile on the website of the Lok Sabha, available at: http://loksabhaph.nic.in/writereaddata/biodata_1_12/1074.htm (last visited 19 May 2019).

71. Constituent Assembly Debates (24 November 1948) (available on SCC Online).

72. Saksena was a member of the Constituent Assembly from the United Provinces. He was later a member of the Lok Sabha (1954–57, 1957–62 and 1971–77). See, profile on the Lok Sabha website, available at: http://loksabhaph.nic.in/writereaddata/biodata_1_12/987.htm (last visited 19 May 2019).

73. Constituent Assembly Debates (24 November 1948) (available on SCC Online).

74. Vira, who represented C.P. and Berar in the assembly, was subsequently a member of the Rajya Sabha between 1952–56 and 1956–62. See, profile on the Rajya Sabha website, available at: https://rajyasabha.nic.in/rsnew/pre_member/1952_2003/r.pdf (last visited 19 May

2019). Though he started out as a congressman, he later became the president of the Bharatiya Jana Sangh. See, Ashoka Jahnavi Prasad, 'Remembering Raghu Vira', *The Pioneer*, 8 May 2015, available at: https://www.dailypioneer.com/2015/columnists/remembering-raghu-vira.html (last visited 19 May 2019).

75. Constituent Assembly Debates (24 November 1948) (available on SCC Online).

76. Dhulekar was a congressman from the United Provinces. See, profile on the Lok Sabha website, available at: http://loksabhaph.nic.in/writereaddata/biodata_1_12/695.htm (last visited 19 May 2019).

77. Constituent Assembly Debates (24 November 1948) (available on SCC Online).

78. See, 'Famous Pakistanis', available at: http://www.nazariapak.info/Famous-Pakistani/politicians.php (last visited 19 May 2019).

79. Section 144.

80. Constituent Assembly Debates (24 November 1948) (available on SCC Online).

81. Saadulla was a member of the Muslim League and was the prime minister of Assam. See, Dr Syed Ahmed, 'Remembering Sir Syed Muhammad Saadulla, the first Premier of Assam', TwoCircles.net, available at: http://twocircles.net/2011oct10/remembering_sir_syed_muhammad_saadulla_first_premier_assam.html (last visited 19 May 2019).

82. Constituent Assembly Debates (24 November 1948) (available on SCC Online).

83. Ibid.

84. Ibid. On 16 November 1949, the language of the clause changed, and the words 'for improving the breeds of milch and draught cattle including cows and calves and for prohibiting their slaughter' were replaced with the words 'for preserving and improving the breeds and prohibiting the slaughter of cows and calves and other milch and draught cattle'. Constituent Assembly Debates (16 November 1949) (available on SCC Online).

85. Seth Govind Das (17 November 1949); Lakshminarayan Sahu (17 November 1949); Ramnarayan Singh (18 November 1949); Shibban Lal Saksena (19 November 1949); Algu Rai Shastri (21 November 1949). Ramnarayan Singh was from Bihar. See, profile in the Lok

Sabha website, available at: http://loksabhaph.nic.in/writereaddata/
biodata_1_12/945.htm (last visited 19 May 2019). Pandit Algu Rai Shastri
was from the United Provinces. See, profile in the Rajya Sabha website,
available at: https://rajyasabha.nic.in/rsnew/pre_member/1952_2003/s.
pdf (last visited 19 May 2019). The debates of the Constituent Assembly
reveal that Sahu was from Orissa.

86. See, 'The Church of God', website of the Church of God, Meghalaya
& Assam Quallapaty, Shillong, available at: http://www.chogmai.org/
page.php?page=1 (last visited 19 May 2019).

87. November 1949.

88. Ibid.

89. Anthony was an Anglo-Indian who was subsequently nominated to
all the terms of the Lok Sabha from the first term to the tenth term,
from 1950 to 1984, barring the sixth and ninth terms. See, profile
on the Lok Sabha website, available at: http://loksabhaph.nic.in/
writereaddata/biodata_1_12/594.htm (last visited 19 May 2019).

90. November 1949.

91. Bombay Animal Preservation Act, 1948 (enacted on 8 February
1949). Available at: https://archive.org/details/1948MH81/page/n1
(last visited 8 November 2018).

92. Ibid., Section 5, read with Section 2(1) and the Schedule.

93. At fifteen, a cow might have been too old to be useful anyway.

94. In fact, on 23 April 1951, President Rajendra Prasad wrote to the
Central minister for food and agriculture and expressed a hope
that useful cattle would not be slaughtered, and that the unlicensed
slaughter of cattle would be made a cognizable criminal offence.
Choudhary (ed.), *Dr Rajendra Prasad*, vol. 14, at p. 203.

95. Nehru's speech in the Lok Sabha, dated 2 April 1955, at p. 4149.

96. Speech dated 14 July 1951. Gopal (ed.), *Selected Works of Jawaharlal
Nehru: Second Series*, vol. 16 part ii, at pp. 26–27.

97. Nehru's letter to Das dated 5 September 1951. Ibid., at p. 530.

98. Nehru's letter to Bhargava dated 5 September 1951. Ibid., at p. 490.

99. Indian Cattle Preservation Bill. The Bill was introduced on 16 July 1952.
The consideration motion was moved on 27 November 1953. Further
discussion on the consideration motion was resumed on 11 December
1953, 26 February 1954, and 12 March 1954. See, Lok Sabha

Debates, 2 April 1955, at p. 4115. The bill was finally voted down on 2 April 1955.

100. On 1 May 1954. See, Gopal (ed.), *Selected Works of Jawaharlal Nehru: Second Series*, vol. 28, p. 554.

101. Item 15 of List II of the Seventh Schedule to the Constitution contains the following entry: 'Preservation, protection and improvement of stock and prevention of animal diseases; veterinary training and practice.' However, item 17 of List III of the Seventh Schedule to the Constitution contains the following entry: 'Prevention of cruelty to animals.'

102. Lok Sabha Debates, 2 April 1955, at pp. 4148–49.

103. Lok Sabha Debates, 2 April 1955, at p. 4148.

104. Ibid., p. 4149.

105. Ibid., p. 4149.

106. Ibid., p. 4150–51.

107. Ibid.

108. Ibid.

109. Chatterjee, who hailed from West Bengal, had been a judge of the Calcutta High Court and served as president of the All India Hindu Maha Sabha. See, profile on the Lok Sabha website, available at: http:// loksabhaph.nic.in/writereaddata/biodata_1_12/650.htm (last visited 19 May 2019). His son, Somnath, became the Speaker of the Lok Sabha. 'Somnath Chatterjee . . .', *Outlook*, 13 August 2018, available at: https://www.outlookindia.com/website/story/somnath-chatterjee-a-distinguished-parliamentarian-who-wore-many-hats/314940 (last visited 23 May 2019).

110. Chatterjee was a member of the first Lok Sabha on the Hindu Mahasabha ticket. See, 'First Lok Sabha: Party Wise Details', available at: https://loksabha.nic.in/members/partyardetail.aspx?party_code= 48&lsno=1 (last visited 23 May 2019). The fact that he was no longer a judge of the Calcutta High Court by this time is established by the fact that his appearance as an advocate before the Supreme Court was recorded in this case: *Workers of the Industry Colliery v. Management of the Industry Colliery*, AIR 1953 SC 88.

111. Lok Sabha Debates, 2 April 1955, p. 4151.

112. Ibid., at pp. 4153–54.

113. Tandon hailed from Uttar Pradesh. He was a member of the Lok Sabha between 1952 and 1957, and of the Rajya Sabha between 1957 and 1960. See, profile on the Rajya Sabha website, available at: https://rajyasabha.nic.in/rsnew/pre_member/1952_2003/t.pdf (last visited 19 May 2019).

114. Smith, *India as a Secular State*, p. 486. On 4 April 1955, Nehru wrote a letter to Tandon asking the latter not to resign over the question, and explaining his point of view. Gopal (ed.), *Selected Works of Jawaharlal Nehru: Second Series*, vol. 28, pp. 549–59.

115. Letter dated 4 April 1955. Gopal (ed.), *Selected Works of Jawaharlal Nehru: Second Series*, vol. 28, pp. 554–55.

116. AIR 1958 SC 731 (decided by five judges, with Chief Justice S.R. Das writing the judgment for the court) (all paragraph numbers are from the SCC Online version) ('Quareshi-I'). The petitioners were 3000 Muslim men who were members of the Qureshi community. De, *A People's Constitution*, p. 148.

117. The Bihar statute defined a 'bull' as an uncastrated male above the age of three years, a 'bullock' as a castrated male above the age of three years, a 'calf' as a male (castrated or otherwise)/female of three years or less, and a 'cow' as a female above the age of three years. Paragraph 7.

118. Paragraphs 7–9. In the Madhya Pradesh statute, buffaloes could be slaughtered after obtaining a certificate.

119. They also challenged the statutes for violating their right to equality under Article 14 of the Constitution.

120. Paragraph 11.

121. Paragraph 12.

122. Rohit De argues that this argument was of the least importance to the petitioners in the case, who did not merely want the right to slaughter cattle during Bakr Id, but to do so throughout the year, which was their means of livelihood. De, *A People's Constitution*, p. 150.

123. Charles Hamilton, *The Hedaya or Guide: A Commentary on the Mussulman Laws* (Lahore: Premier Book House, 1963 reprint), available at: https://archive.org/details/hedayaorguide029357mbp/page/n5 (last visited 23 May 2019). Hamilton's translation itself has been the subject of some criticism. He referred to the Prophet Mohammed in pejorative terms. See, Ahmed, *Religious Freedom*, p. 39.

124. Hamilton, ibid., p. 592.

125. Ibid.

126. Paragraph 13. The court also found that the law did not violate the right to equality under Article 14. Paragraphs 14–16. See further, *State of W.B. v. Ashutosh Lahiri*, (1995) 1 SCC 189 (paragraph 8).

127. Hamilton, *The Hedaya or Guide*, at p. 594. Upendra Baxi has argued that the court did not apply the same rigorous standards to determine whether cow killing is contrary to Hinduism as it did to determine that cow sacrifice is optional in Islam. Upendra Baxi, '"The Little Done, The Vast Undone"—Some Reflections on Reading Granville Austin's "The Indian Constitution"', *Journal of the Indian Law Institute*, vol. 9, pp. 323–430, 349 (1967).

128. J. Duncan M. Derrett, 'Case Comment', *International and Comparative Law Quarterly*, vol. 8, pp. 221–24, at p. 223 (1959).

129. Paragraph 23.

130. Paragraph 24.

131. Paragraph 42.

132. Paragraph 45. See further, *Hashmattullah v. State of MP*, (1996) 4 SCC 391.

133. Paragraphs 43–44.

134. AIR 1961 SC 448.

135. *Haji Usmanbhai Hasanbhai Qureshi v. State of Gujarat*, (1986) 3 SCC 12 (paragraphs 17, 19).

136. (2005) 8 SCC 534 (decided by seven judges). Justice A.K. Mathur wrote a dissenting judgment.

137. Paragraph 47. The court also took into account provisions of the Constitution which were not in existence when Quareshi-I was decided, viz., Articles 48-A and 51-A(g), paragraph 58.

138. The Gujarat statute did not deal with buffaloes, but the court's reasoning ought to apply to them as well since they are within the category of 'milch and draught cattle'. However, in paragraph 108, the court said that '[t]he controversy in the present case is confined to cow progeny.'

139. Paragraphs 65–68.

140. Paragraph 67.

141. Paragraph 104.

142. Paragraph 81(iv). Referring to the statement of objects and reasons.

143. Paragraph 82.

144. Ibid.

145. Ibid.

146. Paragraphs 122–36.

147. Maharashtra Animal Preservation Act, 1976, as amended by the Maharashtra Animal Preservation (Amendment) Act, 1995 (which received the assent of the President on 4 March 2015).

148. *Shaikh Zahid Mukhtar v. State of Maharashtra*, (2016) SCC Online Bom 2600.

149. Sections 5A–5B.

150. Sections 5C–5D.

151. Section 9B.

152. Paragraphs 143, 149, 192.

153. Paragraph 246.

154. Rule 22(b)(iii), Prevention of Cruelty to Animals (Regulation of Livestock Markets) Rules, 2017, available at, http://www.egazette.nic.in/WriteReadData/2017/176216.pdf (last visited 8 November 2018).

155. Ibid., rule 22(e)(i) and (iii).

156. Ibid., rule 2(e).

157. See, *S. Selvagomathy v. Union of India*, (2017) SCC Online Mad 23867. The Supreme Court applied the stay to the whole country.

158. See, 'States Where Cow Slaughter Is Banned So Far, and States Where It Isn't', News18, 26 May 2017, available at: https://www.news18.com/news/india/states-where-cow-slaughter-is-banned-so-far-and-states-where-it-isnt-1413425.html (last visited 10 November 2018); Saptarishi Dutta, 'Where You Can and Can't Eat Beef in India', *Wall Street Journal*, 6 August 2015, available at: https://blogs.wsj.com/indiarealtime/2015/08/06/where-you-can-and-cant-eat-beef-in-india/ (last visited 10 November 2018); Sen, *Articles of Faith*, p. 129. Between 1949 and 1955, nine out of fourteen states in India enacted laws banning cow slaughter. De, *A People's Constitution*, p. 145.

159. Ian Copland, 'History in Flux: Indira Gandhi and the "Great All-Party Campaign" for the Protection of the Cow, 1966–8', *Journal of Contemporary History*, vol. 49(2), pp. 410–39, at p. 428 (2014).

According to Granville Austin, the ban on cow slaughter was extended to most of India during her tenure as Prime Minister. Granville Austin, *Working a Democratic Constitution: A History of the Indian Experience* (New Delhi: Oxford University Press, 1999), p. 399, note 18. This was done during the Emergency.

160. McLane, *Indian Nationalism and the Early Congress*, p. 275; Copland, ibid., p. 435.

161. See further, Granville Austin, *The Indian Constitution: Cornerstone of a Nation* (New Delhi: Oxford University Press, 2015 reprint), p. 104 (Austin wrote that 'Article 48 shows that Hindu sentiment predominated in the Constituent Assembly'); Shraddha Chigateri, 'Negotiating the "Sacred" Cow: Cow Slaughter and the Regulation of Difference in India', in, Monica Mookherjee (ed.), *Democracy, Religious Pluralism and the Liberal Dilemma of Accommodation* (London: Springer, 2011) pp. 137–59.

162. Of course, one might argue that the Supreme Court was balancing rights in the cow protection cases. Slaughtering a cow during Bakr Id is optional in Islam, but slaughtering cows is against Hinduism. So the court balanced the rights of each group, and held that a ban on cow slaughter was justifiable. However, a similar argument can be made in the temple ban example as well. Visiting temples during Diwali is not mandatory in Hinduism. Worshipping 'false' gods is prohibited in Islam. Accordingly, would a court balance rights and uphold a ban on visiting temples during Diwali?

163. Derrett, 'Case Comment', p. 224, note 8.

164. See further, Kancha Ilaiah, 'Beef, BJP and Food Rights of People', *Economic and Political Weekly*, 15 June 1996, available at: https://www.epw.in/node/149991/pdf (last visited 10 November 2018); De, *A People's Constitution*, p. 166–67.

165. See further, Baxi, 'The Little Done, The Vast Undone', p. 349.

166. 'Contribution of various sectors to GDP', Press Information Bureau, 14 December 2018, available at: http://pib.nic.in/newsite/PrintRelease.aspx?relid=186413 (last visited 19 May 2019). See further, 'Livestock Sector Brief: India', Food and Agriculture Organization of the United Nations, July 2005, available at: http://www.fao.org/ag/againfo/

resources/en/publications/sector_briefs/lsb_IND.pdf (last visited 10 November 2018), p. 1.

167. Ibid., p. 7, 10. In 2002, India produced 29,12,000 metric tonnes of beef and buffalo meat, 7,03,000 metric tonnes of mutton, 487 metric tonnes of pork, and 14,60,000 metric tonnes of poultry. Similarly, in 2002, Indians consumed 26,07,000 metric tonnes of beef and buffalo meat, 6,98,000 metric tonnes of mutton, 6,13,000 metric tonnes of pork, and 14,00,000 metric tonnes of poultry.

168. See, Sushruth Sunder, 'India Economic Survey 2018', *Financial Express*, 29 January 2018, available at: https://www.financialexpress.com/budget/india-economic-survey-2018-for-farmers-agriculture-gdp-msp/1034266/ (last visited 19 May 2019).

Chapter 2: Profess, Practise, but Don't Propagate

1. Section 282, first draft of the Indian Penal Code (1837). *A Copy of the Penal Code, Prepared by the Indian Law Commissioners* (Hertford: S. Austin, 1851), available at: https://catalog.hathitrust.org/Record/011627302 (last visited 12 November 2018), p. 64. This became Section 298 of the Indian Penal Code, 1860, which still stands on the statute books.

2. 'Note J', ibid., p. 155.

3. 'Second Report on the Indian Penal Code', 5 November 1846, Indian Law Commission (composed of C.H. Cameron and D. Eliot), in, *Reports from Commissioners: 1847–1848* (London: ?, 1847–48), vol. 28, available at: https://babel.hathitrust.org/cgi/pt?id=hvd.32044106497787;view=1up;seq=9 (last visited 13 November 2018), p. 52. They wanted the word 'wounding' in the clause to be replaced by the word 'insulting'. The commissioners agreed with this suggestion, p. 54.

4. Ibid., p. 52.

5. Ibid., p. 52. The judge was a man by the name of Mr Giberne.

6. Ibid., p. 54.

7. Ibid., p. 54.

8. Ibid., p. 54.

9. Smith, *India as a Secular State*, p. 196.

10. Lawrence James, *Raj: The Making of British India* (London: Abacus, 1997), p. 224. See further, Stephen Neill, *A History of Christianity in India: 1707–1858* (Cambridge: Cambridge University Press, 1985); Robert Eric Frykenberg, *Christianity in India: From Beginnings to the Present* (Oxford: Oxford University Press, 2008); Ivermee, *Secularism, Islam and Education in India, 1830–1910*, p. 23.

11. 'An Act for extending the principle of Section 9, Regulation VII, 1832, of the Bengal Code, throughout the territories subject to the Government of the East India Company.' Available at: https://babel. hathitrust.org/cgi/pt?id=hvd.hl466g;view=1up;seq=258 (last visited 12 November 2018), p. 200. This Act has now been repealed by the Repealing and Amending (Second) Act, 2017. Available at: http:// legislative.gov.in/sites/default/files/A2018-04.pdf (last visited 11 April 2019).

12. Section 1, ibid. This statute did not apply to the princely states, and in many of them, no comparable law was ever enacted. Smith, *India as a Secular State*, at pp. 176–77.

13. Thakkar's letter dated 31 July 1937 to Prasad. Choudhary (ed.), *Dr Rajendra Prasad*, vol. 1, p. 78. A roll-call of members of criminal tribes was taken by the local magistrate at irregular intervals. See, Tayyab Mahmud, 'Colonialism and Modern Constructions of Race: A Preliminary Inquiry', *University of Miami Law Review*, vol. 53 (1998–99), pp. 1219–46, at p. 1236; Sanjay Nigam, 'Disciplining and Policing the "Criminals By Birth", Part 2: The Development of a Disciplinary System, 1871–1900', *Indian Economic and Social History Review*, vol. 27(3), pp. 257–87 (1990), at p. 259, available at: http:// cscs.res.in/dataarchive/textfiles/textfile.2008-07-22.6206820644/file (last visited 19 May 2019).

14. See, speech of Algu Rai Shastri in the Constituent Assembly, dated 1 May 1947.

15. Sir James Fitzjames Stephen, *A Digest of the Criminal Law* (London: Macmillan and Co., 1887), 4th edition, available at: https://catalog. hathitrust.org/Record/011352797 (last visited 12 November 2018), Article 161, at pp. 110–11. Article 22, page 18, ibid.

16. Courtney Kenny sought to introduce a bill that would have replaced the blasphemy law there with Section 298 of the Indian Penal Code.

Courtney Kenny, 'The Evolution of the Law of Blasphemy', *The Cambridge Law Journal*, vol. 1(2), pp. 127–42 (1922), at p. 138. See further, Ivan Hare, 'Blasphemy and Incitement to Religious Hatred: Free Speech Dogma and Doctrine', in, Ivan Hare and James Weinstein (eds.), *Extreme Speech and Democracy* (Oxford: Oxford University Press, 2011 reprint), p. 296.

17. Kenny, 'The Evolution of the Law of Blasphemy', at p. 127; Mark Hill and Russell Sandberg, 'Blasphemy and Human Rights: An English Experience in a European Context', available at: http://www.deltapublicaciones.com/derechoyreligion/gestor/archivos/07_10_00_355.pdf (last visited 19 May 2019), at p. 149.

18. Section 79, Criminal Justice and Immigration Act, 2008, available at: https://www.legislation.gov.uk/ukpga/2008/4/section/79 (last visited 13 November 2018). See further, Lucinda Maer, 'The Abolition of the Blasphemy Offences', *Library of the House of Commons*, 9 May 2008, available at: researchbriefings.files.parliament.uk/documents/SN04597/SN04597.pdf (last visited 12 November 2018).

19. Kenny, 'The Evolution of the Law of Blasphemy', at pp. 134–35. In the fourth edition of his digest of the criminal law of England, published in 1887, Stephen set out both versions of the definition. Stephen, *A Digest of the Criminal Law*, at pp. 110–11. He wrote that there was 'authority for each of these views', though in 'modern times' no one had been 'convicted of blasphemy . . . for a mere decent expression of disbelief in Christianity'. However, he concluded by stating that he was 'now unable to agree with the milder view of the law'. Ibid., p. 110 (n. 2). In other words, he still maintained that a mere denial of the truth of Christianity constituted blasphemy in England. He expressed this view in greater detail in Sir James Fitzjames Stephen, *A History of the Criminal Law of England* (London: Macmillan and Co., 1883), vol. 2, at p. 474, available at: https://babel.hathitrust.org/cgi/pt?id=hvd.hl57k3;view=1up;seq=490 (last visited 23 May 2019).

20. Kenny, ibid., at pp. 137–38. But see, Stephen, ibid.

21. Ibid., p. 140. The case was *Bowman v. The Secular Society, Ltd*, (1917) A.C. 406.

22. Religious Offences in England and Wales—First Report', 10 April 2003, House of Lords, available at: https://publications.parliament.

uk/pa/ld200203/ldselect/ldrelof/95/9501.htm (last visited 19 May 2019).

23. 'Religious Offences in England and Wales—First Report'.

24. Hill and Sandberg, 'Blasphemy and Human Rights', at p. 148.

25. Kenny, 'The Evolution of the Law of Blasphemy', p. 141. The case was *R v. Gathercole*, (1838) 2 Lew. 237.

26. See, Chandrachud, *Republic of Rhetoric*, pp. 226–30.

27. Laura Dudley Jenkins, 'Legal Limits on Religious Conversion in India', *Law and Contemporary Problems*, vol. 71(109), pp. 109–27, at p. 113 (2008), available at: https://scholarship.law.duke.edu/lcp/vol71/iss2/9/ (last visited 23 May 2019). Upon Independence in 1947, seventeen states had such laws, including Jodhpur, Patna and Udaipur. Smith, *India as a Secular State*, p. 177. See further, Tariq Ahmad, 'State Anti-conversion Laws in India', *The Law Library of Congress*, updated October 2018, available at: https://www.loc.gov/law/help/anti-conversion-laws/india-anti-conversion-laws.pdf (last visited 14 November 2018), p. 2.

28. Section 393A, Compiled Penal Code of Bhopal. Cited in Gandhi's article in Young India, 12 June 1924, *Collected Works*, vol. 28, pp. 146–47.

29. Cited in Gandhi's article in Young India, 10 July 1924, *Collected Works*, vol. 28, p. 274.

30. Ibid.

31. Gandhi referred to the incident as the 'Moplah outbreak'. Gandhi's interview in the *Daily Express*, 15 September 1921, *Collected Works*, vol. 24, p. 232.

32. Article in *Young India*, 26 June 1924, *Collected Works*, vol. 28, at p. 210.

33. M.K. Gandhi, 'Speech at Rawalpindi', 5 February 1925, *Collected Works*, vol. 30, p. 191. The riots took place on 9–10 September 1924. *Collected Works*, vol. 30, p. 160, note 1.

34. 'Mr. Gandhi's Statement', *Young India*, 26 March 1925, ibid., at p. 451.

35. Shuddhi meant 'cleansing' or 'purification'. Smith, *India as a Secular State*, p. 169. See further, C.S. Adcock, *The Limits of Tolerance: Indian Secularism and the Politics of Religious Freedom* (New York: Oxford University Press, 2014).

36. M.K. Gandhi, 'Hindu–Muslim Tension: Its Cause and Cure', *Young India*, 29 May 1924, *Collected Works*, vol. 28, p. 56.

37. M.K. Gandhi, 'Speech at Public Meeting, Ramna', *Young India*, 27 January 1927, *Collected Works*, vol. 38, p. 66.

38. Article in *Young India*, 6 January 1927, *Collected Works*, vol. 38, p. 16.

39. Gandhi, 'Hindu–Muslim Tension', *Collected Works*, vol. 28, at p. 57.

40. Article in *Young India*, 23 April 1931, *Collected Works*, vol. 51, p. 414.

41. Gandhi's letter dated 29 November 1946 to Foss Westcott. *Collected Works*, vol. 93, p. 77.

42. Resolution dated 26 December 1927, *Collected Works*, vol. 41, p. 486–87.

43. See, Nehru to Patel, letter dated 7 November 1946, Durga Das (ed.), *Sardar Patel's Correspondence: 1945–1950* (Ahmedabad: Navajivan Publishing House, 1972), vol. 3, p. 167, at p. 169. H.J. Khandekar made a reference to this episode in his speech in the Constituent Assembly on 21 January 1947.

44. Telegram dated 24 April 1947 from Mehrchand Khanna to Patel. Das (ed.), *Sardar Patel's Correspondence*, vol. 4, p. 231.

45. Munshi was a prominent Bombay lawyer who served as home minister of Bombay state, member of the Constituent Assembly, India's political agent in Hyderabad, India's food minister, and governor of Uttar Pradesh. He was also a prolific Gujarati writer and founded the Bharatiya Vidya Bhavan. See, K.M. Munshi, *India's Constitutional Documents: Pilgrimage to Freedom, 1902–1950* (Mumbai: Bharatiya Vidya Bhavan, 2012), vol. 1, at p. 336 (n1). See further, Abhinav Chandrachud, *Supreme Whispers: Conversations with Judges of the Supreme Court of India, 1980–89* (Gurgaon: Penguin Viking, 2018), at p. 246 (n. 30).

46. Letter dated 23 July 1948. Das (ed.), *Sardar Patel's Correspondence*, vol. 7, p. 192.

47. Letter dated 26/28 June 1948 from Rajendra Prasad to Patel. Das (ed.), *Sardar Patel's Correspondence*, vol. 6, p. 265.

48. Nehru's letter dated 9 July 1950 to Gopichand Bhargava. Gopal (ed.), *Selected Works of Jawaharlal Nehru*, Second Series, vol. 14, part 2, p. 145.

49. Patel's letter dated 6 July 1949 to Gopalaswami Ayyangar, minister for transport at New Delhi. Das (ed.), *Sardar Patel's Correspondence*, vol. 8, pp. 51–52.

50. Nehru to Khan, letter dated 13 March 1950. Gopal (ed.), *Selected Works of Jawaharlal Nehru*, Second Series, vol. 14, part 1, p. 111 at p. 113.

51. See, Nehru's statement in Parliament dated 10 April 1950. Gopal (ed.), *Selected Works of Jawaharlal Nehru*, Second Series, vol. 14, part 2, p. 5 at p. 7. Further, it laid down that any conversion that took place 'during a period of communal disturbance' would be 'deemed to be a forced conversion'. Ibid.

52. Letter dated 14 April 1948, Choudhary (ed.), *Dr Rajendra Prasad*, vol. 9, at pp. 23–24. Prasad had received a representation from Catholics protesting against the law.

53. Nehru's note dated 28 October 1953 to M.O. Mathai. Gopal (ed.), *Selected Works of Jawaharlal Nehru*, Second Series, vol. 24, p. 328. Indeed, since Indian independence, there has been a great deal of violence spurred by religious conversions. Sen, *Articles of Faith*, pp. 108–09.

54. Smith, *India as a Secular State*, p. 181.

55. Rammohun Roy, *An Appeal to the Christian Public in Defence of the 'Precepts of Jesus'* (Calcutta: ?, 1820), available at: https://catalog. hathitrust.org/Record/009716698 (last visited 14 November 2018), pp. 119–20.

56. M.K. Gandhi, 'Speech at Prayer Meeting', *Amrita Bazar Patrika*, 14 January 1947. *Collected Works*, vol. 93, p. 262.

57. M.K. Gandhi, 'Foreign Missionaries', *Young India*, 23 April 1931, *Collected Works*, vol. 51, p. 414.

58. See, report of the local Harijan Sevak Sangh, in *Harijan*, 19 June 1937, *Collected Works*, vol. 71, p. 360.

59. See, Sir J.A. Baines, *Census of India, 1891* (London: Eyre and Spottiswoode, 1893), available at: https://catalog.hathitrust.org/Record/012155673 (last visited 11 November 2018), p. 171.

60. A.P. Joshi et al., 'All Illustrated Presentation on Religious Demography of India', *Center for Policy Studies*, available at: https://www.cpsindia.org/dl/religious/ppt-eng.pdf (last visited 24 May 2019). Joshi's figure for Hindus includes Sikhs, Buddhists and Jains, though Hindus formed 95.5 per cent of the figure. Ibid., at p. 8. See further, J.H. Hutton, *General Report on*

the Census of India, 1931 (Delhi: Manager of Publications, 1933), vol. 1, available at: https://archive.org/details/CensusOfIndia1931 (last visited 11 November 2018), p. 387.

61. Ahmad, 'State Anti-conversion Laws in India', p. 1.

62. Article in *Young India*, 29 May 1924, *Collected Works*, vol. 28, p. 57. Gandhi said that he would consider this to be 'conversion by unlawful inducements'.

63. Parkash Chandra's letter dated 27 March 1948 to Rajendra Prasad. Choudhary (ed.), *Dr Rajendra Prasad*, vol. 8, p. 165.

64. Ruthnaswamy studied at the University of Cambridge and was called to the Bar at Gray's Inn. He had been a member of the Madras Legislative Council (1921–25) and the Central Legislative Assembly (1927). He later served on the Rajya Sabha (1962–74). He received the Padma Bhushan in 1968. See, Rajya Sabha profile, available at: https://rajyasabha.nic.in/rsnew/pre_member/1952_2003/r.pdf   (last visited 19 May 2019).

65. According to Smith, the Christian vice president of the assembly, Dr H.C. Mookerjee, played a role in the insertion of the word 'propagate' into the Constitution. Smith, *India as a Secular State*, p. 181.

66. Rao, *The Framing of India's Constitution*, vol. 2, p. 201.

67. Draft dated 18 April 1947. Rao, *The Framing of India's Constitution*, vol. 2, p. 205.

68. Rao, *The Framing of India's Constitution*, vol. 2, p. 265.

69. Ayyar later served as a member of the Rajya Sabha in 1952–53. See, profile on the website of the Rajya Sabha, available at: https://rajyasabha.nic.in/rsnew/pre_member/1952_2003/a.pdf (last visited 19 May 2019). He was a prominent advocate in Madras. See, V.S. Ravi, 'Legal Luminary', *The Hindu*, 28 September 2003, available at: https://www.thehindu.com/thehindu/mag/2003/09/28/stories/2003092800270400.htm (last visited 19 May 2019).

70. Rao, *The Framing of India's Constitution*, vol. 2, p. 268.

71. Ibid., vol. 2, p. 267.

72. Pant was the premier of the state of UP from 1946–54. He also served as Union home minister. He received the Bharat Ratna in 1957. See, profile on the Rajya Sabha website, available at: https://rajyasabha.nic.in/rsnew/pre_member/1952_2003/p.pdf (last visited 19 May 2019).

73. Rao, *The Framing of India's Constitution*, vol. 2, p. 268.

74. Diwakar was a member of the Constituent Assembly. He was later the Union minister of information and broadcasting (1949–52) and governor of Bihar (1952–57). See, profile on the Rajya Sabha website, available at: https://rajyasabha.nic.in/rsnew/pre_member/1952_2003/d. pdf (last visited 19 May 2019).

75. Rao was a member of the Constituent Assembly. He later served as a member of the Rajya Sabha (1952–62) and deputy chairman of the Rajya Sabha (1952–62). See, profile on the Rajya Sabha website, available at: https://rajyasabha.nic.in/rsnew/pre_member/1952_2003/r.pdf (last visited 19 May 2019).

76. Rao, *The Framing of India's Constitution*, vol. 4, p. 41. B.N. Rau opined that this was a question of policy.

77. Constituent Assembly Debates (available on SCC Online).

78. Husain was subsequently a member of the Rajya Sabha in 1952–62. See, profile on the website of the Rajya Sabha, available at: https://rajyasabha.nic.in/rsnew/pre_member/1952_2003/t.pdf (last visited 19 May 2019).

79. Constituent Assembly Debates. He also opined that as a secular state, India should not have anything to do with religion.

80. T.N. Hajela, *History of Economic Thought* (New Delhi: Ane Books Pvt. Ltd, 2009 reprint) (limited preview available on Google Books), at p. 956. Shah was the general secretary of the National Planning Committee, whose chairman was Nehru. Hajela, ibid. Shah stood against Rajendra Prasad in the 1952 elections for the post of president. See, 'How Rajendra Prasad Became the President of India against Nehru's Wish', *India Today*, 7 July 2017, available at: https://www.indiatoday.in/fyi/story/presidential-elections-rajendra-prasad-president-twice-congress-sarvepally-radhakrishnan-1022967-2017-07-07 (last visited 19 May 2019).

81. December 1948.

82. Misra hailed from Orissa and later served on the Rajya Sabha in 1960–66, 1966–72, and 1972–78. See, profile on the website of the Rajya Sabha, available at: https://rajyasabha.nic.in/rsnew/pre_member/1952_2003/m. pdf (last visited 19 May 2019). Misra also served as governor of Assam, Nagaland and Arunachal Pradesh in 1991–97. His brother, Ranga Nath,

became the chief justice of India. See, Manisha Mondal, 'Lokanath Misra', The Print, 24 November 2018, available at: https://theprint.in/forgotten-founders/lokanath-misra-politician-who-opposed-freedom-to-propagate-religion-as-fundamental-right/153814/ (last visited 19 May 2019). Though originally a member of the Congress, he later joined the Swatantra Party, and served as its vice president in Orissa.

83. Santhanam, a congressman from Madras, later served as Union minister for railways (1949–52), lieutenant governor of Vindhya Pradesh (1952–56), chairman of the Finance Commission (1956–57), and member of the Rajya Sabha (1960–64). See, profile on the website of the Rajya Sabha, available at: https://rajyasabha.nic.in/rsnew/pre_member/1952_2003/s.pdf (last visited 19 May 2019).

84. Krishnamachari hailed from Madras. He later served as minister of commerce and industry (1952–55), minister of commerce and industry and iron and steel (1955–56), minister of finance and iron and steel (1956–57), and minister of finance (1957–58). See, profile on the website of the Lok Sabha, available at: http://loksabhaph.nic.in/writereaddata/biodata_1_12/807.htm (last visited 19 May 2019). He resigned as finance minister after the Mundhra scandal. See, Chandrachud, *Republic of Rhetoric*, at p. 195.

85. Constituent Assembly Debates (6 December 1948).

86. Article VI(6), Munshi's draft dated 17 March 1947. Rao, *The Framing of India's Constitution*, vol. 2, p. 76.

87. Article VI(7), ibid.

88. Article 14, Ambedkar's draft dated 24 March 1947. Ibid., vol. 2, p. 87.

89. On 27 March 1947, the subcommittee on fundamental rights accepted these clauses with minor revisions. Ibid., vol. 2, p. 125. The report of the subcommittee on fundamental rights, dated 16 April 1947, also contained similar provisions (Articles 21–22). Ibid., vol. 2, p. 174.

90. Article 21(a)–(b). 19 April 1947. Ibid., vol. 2, p. 206.

91. Smith, *India as a Secular State*, p. 172.

92. Kaur's note dated 20 April 1947. Rao, *The Framing of India's Constitution*, vol. 2, p. 213.

93. April 1947. Ibid., vol. 2, p. 271 and 291.

94. April 1947. Ibid., vol. 2, p. 271.

95. Ibid., vol. 2, p. 271.
96. Ibid., vol. 2, p. 272.
97. Ibid., vol. 2, p. 272.
98. Frank Anthony and Syama Prasad Mookerjee. Ibid., vol. 2, p. 271.
99. Thus, Article 17 of the draft Constitution in the interim report of the Advisory Committee provided: 'Conversion from one religion to another brought about by coercion or undue influence shall not be recognised by law.' 23 April 1947. Ibid., vol. 2, p. 298.
100. Munshi tried to reintroduce his original first clause (dealing with prohibiting conversion among minors) through an amendment in the Constituent Assembly. His amendment was opposed, among others, by J.J. M. Nichols Roy, who said that he himself was converted at the age of fifteen, when he 'heard the voice of God calling [him]'. Ambedkar opposed the amendment for several reasons, including the fact that orphans would otherwise receive no religious instruction. On the other hand, others like Purushottamdas Tandon supported the amendment and said that minors should not be able to convert.
101. Thakur was called to the bar at Lincoln's Inn in London and practised as an advocate at the high court of Calcutta. He later served as minister of state, tribal welfare department, in the government of West Bengal. See, profile on the website of the Lok Sabha, available at: http://loksabhaph.nic.in/writereaddata/biodata_1_12/2004.htm (last visited 19 May 2019).
102. Constituent Assembly Debates (1 May 1947).
103. Pandit Algu Rai Shastri, a member from the United Provinces, later served in the Rajya Sabha in 1956–58. He wrote a book on the Rig Veda. See, profile in the Rajya Sabha website, available at: https://rajyasabha.nic.in/rsnew/pre_member/1952_2003/s.pdf (last visited 19 May 2019).
104. Constituent Assembly Debates (1 May 1947).
105. Ibid.
106. August 1947. Supplementary Report of the Advisory Committee. Rao, *The Framing of India's Constitution*, vol. 2, p. 305. The Christian members of the assembly, led by H.C. Mookerjee, prepared a memorandum and gave it to Patel, in which they set out their objections to the clause. Smith, *India as a Secular State*, p. 183.

107. Constituent Assembly Debates (30 August 1947).

108. Nehru to Prasad, letter dated 10 August 1953. Gopal (ed.), *Selected Works of Jawaharlal Nehru*, Second Series, vol. 23, at pp. 246–47.

109. Ibid. Prasad, on the other hand, was quite vocal in his statements against Christian missionaries. In February 1954, for instance, he made a speech in which he expressed the hope that missionaries would restrict themselves to preaching and not to 'other kinds of activities'. Prasad's reply to the address of welcome given to him in Tura (Garo Hills, Assam), 18 February 1954, Choudhary (ed.), *Dr Rajendra Prasad*, vol. 17, p. 383.

110. Nehru to K.N. Katju, letter dated 14 September 1953. Gopal (ed.), *Selected Works of Jawaharlal Nehru*, Second Series, vol. 23, pp. 251–52. Katju's profile is available on the Lok Sabha website at: http://loksabhaph. nic.in/writereaddata/biodata_1_12/784.htm (last visited 24 May 2019).

111. Nehru's letter to the Ministry of Home Affairs, dated 25 October 1953. Gopal (ed.), *Selected Works of Jawaharlal Nehru*, Second Series, vol. 24, p. 323.

112. *Ratilal Panachand Gandhi v. State of Bombay*, AIR 1954 SC 388 (SCC online version) (paragraph 10).

113. See, Nehru's letter to Amrit Kaur, 25 October 1953. Gopal (ed.), *Selected Works of Jawaharlal Nehru*, Second Series, vol. 24, p. 326.

114. Ibid., p. 327.

115. Ibid.

116. Ibid.

117. Nehru's letter dated 21 November 1953 to Bishop S.K. Mondol. Gopal (ed.), *Selected Works of Jawaharlal Nehru*, Second Series, vol. 24, p. 333.

118. See, Parvathi Menon, 'An Old Debate in a New Context', *Frontline*, 10–23 April 1999, available at: https://frontline.thehindu.com/static/html/fl1608/16080380.htm (last visited 19 May 2019).

119. Report on the Christian Missionary Activities, Enquiry Committee, Madhya Pradesh, 1956, vol. 1, available at: https://archive.org/details/in.ernet.dli.2015.61734/page/n1?q=%22national+christian+council+review%22 (last visited 12 November 2018), at p. 1.

120. Ibid.

121. Ibid., p. 106.

122. Ibid., p. 110.

123. Ibid., p. 112.

124. Ibid., p. 113.

125. Ibid., p. 113.

126. Ibid., p. 122–23.

127. Ibid., p. 123.

128. Ibid., p. 124.

129. Ibid., p. 131.

130. Ibid., p. 131.

131. Ibid., p. 131.

132. Ibid., p. 132.

133. Smith, *India as a Secular State*, pp. 210–13.

134. It had been moved by Jethalal Joshi. Smith, *India as a Secular State*, p. 184.

135. Smith, ibid., p. 184.

136. Nehru's speech in the Lok Sabha dated 2 December 1955. Gopal (ed.), *Selected Works of Jawaharlal Nehru*, Second Series, vol. 31, p. 135, at pp. 136–37.

137. Smith, *India as a Secular State*, p. 174. Later, the 'Backward Communities (Religious Protection) Bill', a private member bill moved by Prakash Vir Shastri, was rejected by the Lok Sabha. Smith, ibid., pp. 185–86. The Freedom of Religion Bill, 1979, was also rejected. Ahmad, 'State Anti-Conversion Laws in India', p. 2.

138. See further, Smith, *India as a Secular State*, at pp. 186–87.

139. Section 26, Hindu Succession Act, 1956. However, the Bombay High Court has taken the view that this restriction does not apply to the convert. *Balchand Jairamdas Lalwant v. Nazneen Khalid Qureshi*, Appeal from Order No. 1175 of 2014, order dated 6 March 2018.

140. Section 13(1)(ii), Hindu Marriage Act, 1955.

141. Section 6, Hindu Minority and Guardianship Act, 1956.

142. Sections 7–8, Hindu Adoptions and Maintenance Act, 1956.

143. Section 18(2)(f), Hindu Adoptions and Maintenance Act, 1956.

144. Ibid.

145. Constitution (Scheduled Castes) Order, 1950. Available at: http://socialjustice.nic.in/writereaddata/UploadFile/scorders-updated-30062016.pdf (last visited 14 November 2018).

146. This was under Article 341 of the Constitution.

147. Paragraph 3, Constitution (Scheduled Castes) Order, 1950 (as originally issued).

148. In fact, in 1956, B.R. Ambedkar and 3,00,000 of his followers converted from Hinduism to Buddhism for this purpose. Niyogi, the chairman of the Madhya Pradesh committee, was one of the converts, though he was a Brahmin. Smith, *India as a Secular State*, p. 167.

149. In 1950, members of some castes who professed Sikhism were included within the list. See, Constitution (Scheduled Castes) Order, 1950, available at: http://socialjustice.nic.in/writereaddata/UploadFile/ CONSTITUTION%20(SC)%20ORDER%201950%20dated%20 10081950.pdf (last visited 19 May 2019). However, after an amendment in 1956, all Sikhs were included within the list. See, The Scheduled Castes and Scheduled Tribes Orders (Amendment) Act, 1956, available at: http://socialjustice.nic.in/writereaddata/ UploadFile/SC%20ST%20ORDER%20(AMENDMENT)%20 ACT%2019566363598873389305949.pdf (last visited 19 May 2019). See further, Galanter, *Law and Society in Modern India*, p. 119; Sen, *Articles of Faith*, p. 117.

150. In *Soosai v. Union of India*, (1985) Supp SCC 590, the constitutional validity of the list was upheld and it was held that there was no discrimination against Christians. According to Marc Galanter, dissuading lower-caste Hindus from converting to another religion was at least part of the purpose of the 1950 order. Marc Galanter, *Competing Equalities: Law and the Backward Classes in India* (Berkeley: University of California Press, 1984), p. 143. There is now a growing movement to include scheduled caste converts to Christianity and Islam within the list. Sen, *Articles of Faith*, pp. 122–23.

   See further, Galanter, *Law and Society in Modern India*, p. 133. Galanter argues that hostility towards conversion in India is 'neither historically nor philosophically a Hindu notion, but is more consonant with the exclusivist creeds of the West, which require the convert to abjure his previous faith'. Galanter, ibid., p. 134. According to Sen, the 1950 presidential order tends to incentivize reconversion to Hinduism. Sen, *Articles of Faith*, p. 123.

151. A complex jurisprudence has emerged over the questions of whether: (i) a convert from Hinduism to another religion retains his caste; and (ii) upon reconversion to Hinduism, whether he reverts to his original caste. Broadly speaking, the answer to (i) is that it depends on the caste (in some cases, conversion to another religion does not wipe out caste membership), and the answer to (ii) is that the old caste, which was only 'eclipsed' upon conversion to another religion, revives upon reconversion. See, *Chatturbhuj Vithaldas Jasani v. Moreshwar Parashram*, AIR 1954 SC 236; *Ganpat v. Returning Officer*, (1975) 1 SCC 589; *C.M. Arumugam v. S. Rajgopal*, (1976) 1 SCC 863; *Principal, Guntur Medical College, Guntur v. Y. Mohan Rao*, (1976) 3 SCC 411; *Kailash Sonkar v. Maya Devi*, (1984) 2 SCC 91; *S. Anbalagan v. B. Devarajan*, (1984) 2 SCC 112.

152. For example, in Maharashtra, 'Christians converted from Scheduled Castes' are considered to be OBCs. See, Central List of OBCs for the State of Maharashtra. Available at: http://www.bcmbcmw.tn.gov.in/obc/faq/maharashtra.pdf (last visited 14 November 2018). See further, Smith, *India as a Secular State*, p. 324; Galanter, *Law and Society in Modern India*, p. 125.

153. Madhya Pradesh Dharma Swatantrya Adhiniyam, 1968.

154. Section 2(c).

155. Section 2(a).

156. Section 3.

157. Section 4.

158. Section 5. All offences under the Act were made cognizable (section 6), but prosecutions could be launched only with the previous sanction of the district magistrate (or other authorized officer) (Section 7). An amendment proposed in 2006 which would have made a police investigation necessary for conversions was not given assent to by the President because it violated the freedom of religion. Ahmad, 'State Anti-conversion Laws in India', p. 7.

159. Orissa Freedom of Religion Act, 1967. This was similar to the Madhya Pradesh statute.

160. (1977) 1 SCC 677 (decided by five judges).

161. *Yulitha Hyde v. State of Orissa*, AIR 1973 Ori 116 (from SCC Online).

162. *Rev. Stainislaus v. State of Madhya Pradesh*, AIR 1975 MP 163 (SCC Online version) (paragraph 11).
163. Paragraphs 18, 25.
164. Paragraph 16.
165. Paragraph 20. For a criticism of this judgment, see, H.M. Seervai, *Constitutional Law of India: A Critical Commentary* (New Delhi: Universal Law Publishing Co. Pvt. Ltd, 2014 reprint), 4th edition, vol. 2, pp. 1286–90; Rajeev Dhavan, 'Religious Freedom in India', *American Journal of Comparative Law*, vol. 35, p. 209 at p. 229 (1987); Faizan Mustafa and Jagteshwar Singh Sohi, 'Freedom of Religion in India: Current Issues and Supreme Court Acting as Clergy', *Brigham Young University Law Review*, p. 915, at p. 942 (June 2017), available at: https://digitalcommons.law.byu.edu/cgi/viewcontent.cgi?article=3113&context=lawreview (last visited 14 November 2018). The court could, instead, have held that the right to propagate religion does not include the right to manipulative proselytism. See, Farrah Ahmed, 'The Autonomy Rationale for Religious Freedom', *UK Constitutional Law Association*, 5 April 2017, available at: https://ukconstitutionallaw.org/2017/04/05/farah-ahmed-the-autonomy-rationale-for-religious-freedom/ (last visited 6 April 2019).
166. Paragraph 20.
167. Ahmad, 'State Anti-conversion Laws in India', p. 3. According to this paper, they are presently in force in eight out of twenty-nine states: Arunachal Pradesh, Orissa, Madhya Pradesh, Chhattisgarh, Gujarat, Himachal Pradesh, Jharkhand and Uttarakhand. The Himachal Pradesh law was brought into being by a Congress government. Jenkins, 'Legal Limits', p. 122.
168. Ahmad, ibid., p. 21. However, they are not entirely absent. Jenkins, 'Legal Limits', p. 116, 123–24; Meghan G. Fischer, 'Anti-Conversion Laws and the International Response', *Penn State Journal of Law and International Affairs*, vol. 6, no. 1, p. 1, at p. 22 (2018), available at: https://elibrary.law.psu.edu/cgi/viewcontent.cgi?article=1175&context=jlia (last visited 14 November 2018); Robert D. Baird, 'Traditional Values, Governmental Values, and Religious Conflict in Contemporary India', *BYU Law Review*, p. 337 at p. 355 (1998), available at: https://digitalcommons.

law.byu.edu/cgi/viewcontent.cgi?article=2795&context=lawreview (last visited 15 November 2018).

169. Section 5, Gujarat Freedom of Religion Act, 2003. Section 5, Jharkhand Freedom of Religion Act, 2017. According to Ahmad, these are the only states in which prior permission is necessary. Ahmad, ibid., p. 23.

170. See, 'The Incident at Manoharpur Was an Avoidable Tragedy', Justice D.P. Wadhwa Commission of Inquiry, 21 June 1999, available at: https://www.hvk.org/specialreports/wadhwa/main.html (last visited 14 November 2018).

171. (2018) 16 SCC 368 (decided by three judges).

172. See, George Jacob, 'How Akhila Became Hadiya', *The Hindu*, 30 October 2017, available at: https://www.thehindu.com/news/national/how-akhila-became-hadiya/article19951404.ece (last visited 14 November 2018).

173. See, Richa Taneja, 'Hadiya's Story: A Timeline of Kerala "Love Jihad" Case', NDTV, 27 November 2017, available at: https://www.ndtv.com/india-news/hadiya-case-a-timeline-of-kerala-love-jihad-case-1780500 (last visited 14 November 2018); Annie Gowen, 'A Muslim and a Hindu Thought They Could Be a Couple . . .', *The Washington Post*, 26 April 2018, available at: https://www.washingtonpost.com/world/asia_pacific/a-muslim-and-a-hindu-thought-they-could-be-a-couple-then-came-the-love-jihad-hit-list/2018/04/26/257010be-2d1b-11e8-8dc9-3b51e028b845_story.html?noredirect=on&utm_term=.c36f4afda007 (last visited 14 November 2018).

174. See, Charu Gupta, 'Hindu Women, Muslim Men: Love Jihad and Conversions', *Economic and Political Weekly*, vol. 44, no. 51, 19–25, December 2009, pp. 13–15.

175. Ibid., p. 15.

176. *Shafin Jahan case* (supra), paragraph 67.

177. Paragraph 28. It was also held that the doctrine of 'parens patriae', adopted by the high court, could only be used in exceptional cases. Paragraph 45.

178. Paragraph 75 (per Chandrachud J concurring).

179. Paragraph 81 (per Chandrachud J concurring).

180. Paragraph 82 (per Chandrachud J concurring).

181. Paragraph 84 (per Chandrachud J concurring).

Chapter 3: 'I Cannot Vote for Mr Jinnah'

1.   See further, Smith, *India as a Secular State*, p. 87.

2.   There were no separate electorates for Catholics, Jews, or other religious minorities in England. The statutes which liberalized voting rights there were: the Reform Acts of 1832, 1867 and 1884, Representation of the People Act, 1918, and Representation of the People Act, 1928 (which enfranchised men and women above the age of 21). See, Laura E. Nym Mayhall, *The Militant Suffrage Movement: Citizenship and Resistance in Britain, 1860–1930* (New York: Oxford University Press, 2003), at pp. 13–15, 20, 134, 139; Julie V. Gottlieb and Richard Toye (eds.), *The Aftermath of Suffrage: Women, Gender, and Politics in Britain, 1918–1945* (New York: Palgrave Macmillan, 2013), at pp. 1–2; 'The Reform Acts and Representative Democracy', website of the UK Parliament, available at: https://www.parliament.uk/about/living-heritage/evolutionof parliament/houseofcommons/reformacts/overview/ (last visited 31 December 2018); 'Birmingham and the Equal Franchise', website of the UK Parliament, available at: https://www.parliament.uk/about/ living-heritage/transformingsociety/electionsvoting/womenvote/case-study-the-right-to-vote/the-right-to-vote/birmingham-and-the-equal-franchise/ (last visited 31 December 2018).

3.   In particular, under the 'Rules as to the Nomination of Additional Members of Legislative Councils', enacted on 23 June 1893. See, Sir Courtenay Ilbert, *The Government of India* (Oxford: Clarendon Press, 1898), available at: https://babel.hathitrust.org/cgi/pt?id=mdp.39015 008843891;view=1up;seq=381 (last visited 28 December 2018).

4.   Ibid., p. 341. The governor had to 'nominate' these members on the basis of the 'recommendation' of these bodies—a recommendation which was given on the basis of a majority vote in the provincial council.

5.   Ibid., p. 337. Only the non-official members of the provincial legislative councils had the right to vote in such elections.

6.   Ibid., p. 338.

7.   *Report on Indian Constitutional Reforms* (London: H.M. Stationery Office, 1918), available at: https://babel.hathitrust.org/cgi/pt?id=ucl. b3456852;view=1up;seq=195 (last visited 28 December 2018),

p. 186; *Report of the Indian Statutory Commission* (London: H.M. Stationery Office, 1930), vol. 1, available at: https://babel.hathitrust. org/cgi/pt?id=mdp.39015027588329;view=1up;seq=164 (last visited 28 December 2018), p. 183.

8.   See, 'Gilbert John Elliot-Murray-Kynynmound, 4th earl of Minto', *Encyclopaedia Britannica*, available at: https://www.britannica.com/ biography/Gilbert-John-Elliot-Murray-Kynynmound-4th-earl-of-Minto (last visited 28 December 2018).

9.   See, 'John Morley, Viscount Morley', *Encyclopaedia Britannica*, available at: https://www.britannica.com/biography/John-Morley-Viscount-Morley (last visited 28 December 2018). Robinson's monograph suggests that Morley was against separate electorates for Muslims. Robinson, *Separatism among Indian Muslims*, pp. 154–56.

10. Mary, Countess of Minto, *India, Minto and Morley, 1905–1910* (London: Macmillan and Co., 1934), available at: https://catalog. hathitrust.org/Record/001868400 (last visited 28 December 2018), pp. 28–29.

11. Ibid., p. 30. Morley wrote that he did not know how true this warning was.

12. Ibid., at p. 31.

13. B.R. Nanda, *Gokhale: The Indian Moderates and the British Raj* (Princeton: Princeton University Press, 1977), p. 324. In August 1906, a committee of the Viceroy's Executive Council was formed to determine whether Indians should get increased representation in the legislation council. 'Memoranda presented to the Indian Statutory Commission by the Government of India' (London: H.M. Stationery Off, 1930), https://babel.hathitrust.org/cgi/pt?id=mdp.39015027588 527;view=1up;seq=132 (last visited 28 December 2018), at p. 130.

14. Nanda, *Gokhale*, p. 324. For biographical details on Mohsin-ul-Mulk, see, Robinson, *Separatism among Indian Muslims*, p. 397. Interestingly, Mohsin-ul-Mulk had won the first prize in the essay competition organized by a committee established by Sayyid Ahmed Khan to investigate why Muslims had not taken to western education in India, which eventually led to the establishment of the Muhammadan Anglo-Oriental College, Aligarh. Ivermee, *Secularism, Islam and Education in India, 1830–1910*, pp. 88–89, 115.

15. Nanda, ibid.

16. M.N. Das, *India under Morley and Minto: Politics behind Revolution, Repression and Reforms* (London: George Allen and Unwin Ltd, 1964), available at: https://archive.org/details/in.ernet.dli.2015.127030 (last visited 28 December 2018), pp. 164–65.

17. Nanda, *Gokhale*, p. 325.

18. Das, *India under Morley and Minto*, p. 165.

19. Nanda, *Gokhale*, p. 325.

20. Ibid., p. 326.

21. Ibid.

22. Stanley Wolpert, *Jinnah of Pakistan* (Oxford: Oxford University Press, 1984), p. 22; Das, *India under Morley and Minto*, p. 166.

23. Das, *India under Morley and Minto*, p. 166.

24. Nanda, *Gokhale*, p. 326.

25. Das, *India under Morley and Minto*, pp. 167.

26. Archbold had to reassure British officials in the administration that the Muslim deputation would not be disloyal. Nanda, *Gokhale*, p. 332.

27. Jagdish Saran Sharma, *India's Struggle for Freedom* (Delhi: S. Chand, 1962–65), available at: https://catalog.hathitrust. org/Record/001249599 (last visited 28 December 2018), vol. 1, at pp. 211–12. Robinson, who rejects divide and rule, does not mention this exchange in his monograph. Robinson, *Separatism among Indian Muslims*, p. 143.

28. Wolpert, *Jinnah of Pakistan*, p. 22.

29. A draft of the memorial had been prepared by Syed Husain Bilgrami (Imad-ul-Mulk). Nanda, *Gokhale*, p. 327, 335–36. Robinson, who rejects divide and rule, does not take note of the role played by Archbold in the preparation of the memorial. Robinson, *Separatism among Indian Muslims*, pp. 143–44. For a biographical note on Bilgrami, see, Ivermee, *Secularism, Islam and Education in India, 1830–1910*, p. 125.

30. See, Robinson, *Separatism Among Indian Muslims*, pp. 144–46. However, Robinson acknowledges that the demand for Muslim representation in the legislative councils constituted the 'greater part of the memorial'. Ibid., p. 145.

31. Das, *India under Morley and Minto*, p. 171.

32. Nanda, *Gokhale*, p. 329.

33. Minto, *India, Minto and Morley*, at p. 47. However, according to Robinson, Minto only expressed his sympathy with the delegation's demands. Robinson, *Separatism among Indian Muslims*, p. 147.

34. Wolpert, *Jinnah of Pakistan*, p. 24.

35. Minto, *India, Minto and Morley*, at p. 47.

36. Das, *India under Morley and Minto*, p. 171.

37. Smith to Harcourt Butler, letter dated 2 October 1906. Nanda, *Gokhale*, p. 330.

38. Sharma, *India's Struggle for Freedom*, p. 212. See further, Wolpert, *Jinnah of Pakistan*, p. 24. However, Robinson argues that the Muslim League was founded because the younger members of the delegation were dissatisfied with Viceroy Minto's response. Robinson, *Separatism among Indian Muslims*, pp. 147–49.

39. Nanda, *Gokhale*, p. 320.

40. Ibid., p. 350.

41. See, Smith, *India as a Secular State*, p. 85. Robinson, however, disagrees. Robinson, *Separatism among Indian Muslims*, pp. 164, 173.

42. Das, *India under Morley and Minto*, p. 173.

43. Sharma, *India's Struggle for Freedom*, p. 212; Nanda, *Gokhale*, p. 331.

44. 26 May 1949.

45. K.M. Munshi, *Indian Constitutional Documents: Pilgrimage to Freedom* (Mumbai: Bharatiya Vidya Bhavan, 2012), vol. 1, p. 3

46. Nanda, *Gokhale*, p. 331–32.

47. Speech dated 10 May 1957. Gopal (ed.), *Selected Works of Jawaharlal Nehru (Second Series)*, vol. 38, p. 3, at pp. 8–9.

48. 'Memoranda presented to the Indian Statutory Commission by the Government of India', p. 132.

49. 'Memoranda presented to the Indian Statutory Commission by the Government of India', p. 134.

50. This was by virtue of the electoral rules issued under the Indian Councils Act, 1909.

51. Among sixty-nine members (including the governor general), eight were ex-officio members of the Governor General's Executive Council; thirty-five were nominated by the governor general; twenty-five were elected members, of whom twelve were to be indirectly elected by the provincial legislative councils, six by the landholders of Madras,

Bombay, Bengal, Eastern Bengal and Assam, United Provinces, Punjab, and the Central Provinces, five by the Muhammadans of Madras, Bombay, Bengal, Eastern Bengal and Assam, and the United Provinces, and two by the Chambers of Commerce of Calcutta and Bombay. Sir Courtenay Ilbert, *The Government of India* (Oxford: Clarendon Press, 1910), available at: https://babel.hathitrust.org/cgi/pt?id=hvd.32044053443099;view=1up;seq=32 (last visited 28 December 2018), p. 432. This was by virtue of the regulations issued under the Indian Councils Act, 1909.

52. No separate electorates were set up for Muslims in Punjab because Muslims had sufficient numbers in the population there and in the Central Provinces because the number of Muslims was negligible there. 'Memoranda presented to the Indian Statutory Commission by the Government of India', at p. 136.

53. 'Memoranda presented to the Indian Statutory Commission by the Government of India', p. 136. For instance, Madras gave only two seats to Muslims, whereas Bengal gave Muslims 5 seats.

54. The Bombay legislative council was to have a total of forty-nine members. Among these, three were ex-officio members of the executive council. The advocate general was also an ex-officio member. Twenty-one members and two experts were nominated. Among the twenty-one elected members, one was to be elected by the Corporation of Bombay, four by municipalities, four by district boards, one by the university, three by landholders, four by Muslims, and one each by the Bombay Chamber of Commerce, Karachi Chamber of Commerce, Millowners' Associations of Bombay and Ahmedabad, and Indian Commercial Community. Ilbert, *The Government of India* (1907), p. 433.

55. 'Memoranda Presented to the Indian Statutory Commission by the Government of India', p. 136. See further, Robinson, *Separatism among Indian Muslims*, p. 162.

56. *Report of the Indian Statutory Commission*, p. 186.

57. 'Memoranda Presented to the Indian Statutory Commission by the Government of India', p. 137.

58. Wolpert says that Gopal Krishna Gokhale's concession to the Muslim lobby on this point was 'probably the greatest blunder of his political

career'. Stanley A. Wolpert, *Tilak and Gokhale: Revolution and Reform in the Making of Modern India* (Berkeley: University of California Press, 1962) (limited preview available on Google Books), at p. 234.

59. Nanda, *Gokhale*, p. 346.

60. Letter from Gokhale to Sir William Wedderburn. Nanda, *Gokhale*, p. 349.

61. Ibid., p. 350.

62. The Lucknow Pact was an arrangement adopted by nineteen members of the central legislative council, which was accepted by the Congress and the Muslim League. 'Memoranda presented to the Indian Statutory Commission by the Government of India', p. 138.

63. 'Congress–League Scheme' (December 1916), Rao, *The Framing of India's Constitution*, vol. 1, p. 26. Thus, it was agreed that Muslims would get the following proportion of seats in the provincial legislative bodies: 50 per cent in Punjab, 30 per cent in the United Provinces, 40 per cent in Bengal, 25 per cent in Bihar, 15 per cent in the Central Provinces, 15 per cent in Madras, and 33 per cent in Bombay. According to K.M. Munshi, this pact evolved into the 'two-nation theory', though nobody could have predicted this at the time. Munshi, *Indian Constitutional Documents*, vol. 1, p. 8.

64. 'Memoranda Presented to the Indian Statutory Commission by the Government of India', p. 138.

65. Ibid., p. 139.

66. See, 'Montagu–Chelmsford Report', *Encyclopaedia Britannica*, available at: https://www.britannica.com/event/Montagu-Chelmsford-Report (last visited 29 December 2018).

67. *Report on Indian Constitutional Reforms*, p. 185, paragraph 227.

68. Ibid., p. 187.

69. Ibid., p. 187.

70. Ibid., p. 187.

71. Ibid., p. 188.

72. Ibid., p. 189.

73. *East India (Constitutional Reforms): Rules under the Government of India Act* (London: H.M. Stationery Office, 1921), available at: https://catalog.hathitrust.org/Record/010457894 (last visited 29 December 2018).

74. Ibid., p. 46.

75. Ibid., p. 47.

76. Ibid., p. 47.

77. Ibid., pp. 48–51.

78. If the land were owned by a joint family, only the manager of the joint family could vote. Ibid., p. 57.

79. Ibid., pp. 53–55.

80. *Report of the Indian Statutory Commission*, p. 134.

81. Ibid., p. 134.

82. Rule 7 of the electoral rules. *Rules under the Government of India Act*, at p. 7; *Report of the Indian Statutory Commission*, p. 134.

83. *Report of the Indian Statutory Commission*, at p. 134 and p. 137.

84. Only a member of the Senate, an honorary fellow of the university, or a graduate of the university of seven years' standing could vote, provided he satisfied the residence requirement. *Rules under the Government of India Act*, p. 57.

85. Ibid., p. 51. The Bombay Chamber of Commerce had two seats. The rest had one seat each.

86. *Rules under the Government of India Act*, pp. 48–51. These figures have been obtained by the author by adding up the figures in the table provided at this source.

87. See, ibid., pp. 153–60. Muslims had approximately twenty-eight out of ninety-eight elected seats in the central legislative assembly. These figures have been obtained by the author by adding up the figures in the table at this source.

88. Ibid., p. 155. Similarly, Bombay province had six seats in the Council of State, of which three were non-Muslim seats, two were Muslim seats, and one seat was for the Bombay Chamber of Commerce. Ibid., at p. 195.

89. *Report of the Indian Statutory Commission*, vol. 1, p. 146.

90. Ibid.

91. The Simon Commission was boycotted by Indian leaders because it was an all-white commission. Munshi, *Indian Constitutional Documents*, vol. 1, p. 24. It was jointly chaired by the liberal lawyer Sir John Simon and Clement Attlee, a future prime minister. 'Simon Commission', *Encyclopedia Britannica*, available at: https://www.britannica.com/topic/Simon-Commission (last visited 29 December 2018).

92. *Report of the Indian Statutory Commission*, p. 137.

93. Ibid.

94. Ibid., p. 139.

95. Ibid., p. 140.

96. *Report of the Indian Statutory Commission*, vol. 2, p. 56.

97. Ibid., p. 60.

98. Ibid., p. 61.

99. Ibid., p. 65–66.

100. Munshi, *Indian Constitutional Documents*, vol. 1, p. 25.

101. Chaudhary (ed.), *Dr Rajendra Prasad*, vol. 7, p. 469.

102. Munshi, *Indian Constitutional Documents*, vol. 1, p. 34.

103. Munshi, ibid., p. 38; Subhas Chandra Bose, *The Indian Struggle, 1920–1934* (London: Wishart & Co. Ltd, 1935), available at: https://catalog.hathitrust.org/Record/001251915 (last visited 29 December 2018), pp. 276–77; Smith, *India as a Secular State*, p. 303.

104. Munshi, ibid., p. 38.

105. Bose, *The Indian Struggle*, p. 279.

106. See, Saran, *India's Struggle For Freedom*, vol. 1, p. 257; Bose, *The Indian Struggle*, p. 278.

107. Available at: http://www.legislation.gov.uk/ukpga/1935/2/pdfs/ukpga_19350002_en.pdf (last visited 29 December 2018).

108. First Schedule, Government of India Act, 1935. The Council of States had a total of 150 elective seats, of which seventy-five were 'general' seats (six seats were reserved for scheduled castes), four seats were for Sikhs, forty-nine seats were for Muslims, and six seats were for women. The Federal Assembly had a total of 250 seats, of which 105 were 'general' seats (nineteen were reserved for scheduled castes), six were for Sikhs, eighty-two were for Muslims, four were for Anglo-Indians, eight were for Europeans, eight were for Indian Christians, eleven were for representatives of commerce and industry, seven were for landholders, ten were for representatives of labour, and nine were for women.

109. Rule 7, Fifth Schedule, Government of India Act, 1935.

110. These figures have been compiled by the author on the basis of the table of seats in the provincial legislative assemblies under the fifth schedule to the Government of India Act, 1935, available at: http://www.legislation.gov.uk/ukpga/1935/2/pdfs/ukpga_19350002_en.pdf (last visited 19 May 2019), at p. 260 of the pdf document.

111. A member of the scheduled castes could show himself or herself to be literate in the prescribed manner. Even a woman could show herself to be literate in the prescribed manner.

112. Sixth Schedule, Government of India Act, 1935.

113. Minto, *India, Minto and Morley*, p. 20.

114. P.N. Chopra (ed.), *The Collected Works of Sardar Vallabhbhai Patel* (New Delhi: Konark Publishers Pvt. Ltd, 2015 reprint), vol. 8, p. 213.

115. Letter dated 16 December 1946 from Patel to V.K. John. Das (ed.), *Sardar Patel's Correspondence*, vol. 3, p. 51.

116. Chopra (ed.), *Collected Works of Sardar Vallabhbhai Patel*, vol. 6, p. 41.

117. Chopra (ed.), ibid., vol. 6, p. 196.

118. Rao, *The Framing of India's Constitution*, vol. 1, p. 96. Chaudhary (ed.), *Dr Rajendra Prasad*, vol. 4, p. 7.

119. Letter dated 4 August 1939 from Satyamurti to Gandhi. Chaudhary (ed.), ibid., at p. 8.

120. Ibid.

121. Chopra (ed.), *Collected Works of Sardar Vallabhbhai Patel*, vol. 10, p. 88.

122. Letter dated 21 April 1946 from Patel to Shri Nalinaksha Sanyal. Chopra (ed.), ibid., vol. 10, p. 218.

123. Letter dated 6 April 1938. Chaudhary (ed.), *Dr Rajendra Prasad*, vol. 2, p. 264.

124. Rao, *The Framing of India's Constitution*, vol. 1, p. 111. This was reiterated in a resolution passed by the Congress Working Committee at Wardha in December 1939. Ibid., at p. 116.

125. Das (ed.), *Sardar Patel's Correspondence*, vol. 3, p. 52.

126. Letter dated 7 December 1946. Das (ed.), ibid., p. 50.

127. Letter dated 16 December 1946, Patel to V.K. John. Das (ed.), ibid., p. 51.

128. Article II, Section IV, Part I, Clause 1(2)(A)(a)-(b), Ambedkar's memorandum and draft articles on the rights of states and minorities (24 March 1947). Rao, *The Framing of India's Constitution*, vol. 2, p. 84 at p. 93.

129. Ibid., p. 108.

130. Ibid., p. 110.

131. B.R. Ambedkar, *What Congress and Gandhi Have Done to the Untouchables* (Bombay: Thacker & Co., 1945), available at: https://archive.org/details/in.ernet.dli.2015.278459 (last visited 30 December 2018), pp. 270–71.

132. Rao, *The Framing of India's Constitution*, vol. 2, p. 620 and p. 628. Some asked for separate electorates to be abolished, while others, like B.G. Kher, asked for '[j]oint electorates with reservation of seats'.

133. Gopal (ed.), *Selected Works of Jawaharlal Nehru (2nd Series)*, vol. 3, p. 162.

134. Rao, *The Framing of India's Constitution*, vol. 2, p. 392.

135. Ibid., p. 392.

136. Ibid., p. 404.

137. 'Report of the Advisory Committee on the Subject of Minority Rights' (8 August 1947). Ibid., p. 411 at p. 412.

138. Ibid.

139. Ibid.

140. 25 May 1949, Constituent Assembly Debates.

141. See, Begam Aizaz Rasul, *From Purdah to Parliament* (New Delhi: Ajanta Publications, 2001), at p. 121. See further, letter dated 16 January 1948 from Rajendra Prasad to G.B. Pant. Chaudhary (ed.), *Dr Rajendra Prasad*, vol. 8, p. 15. In this letter, Prasad planned to replace Khaliquzzaman in the Constituent Assembly with a nationalist Muslim leader.

142. 26 May 1949. Constituent Assembly Debates.

143. Ayyangar later served as deputy speaker of the first Lok Sabha (1952–56), speaker of the first Lok Sabha (1956–57), and speaker of the second Lok Sabha (1957). See, profile on the website of the Lok Sabha, available at: http://loksabhaph.nic.in/writereaddata/biodata_1_12/596.htm (last visited 19 May 2019).

144. Accordingly, the February 1948 draft of the Constitution provided for joint electorates with reservation for religious minorities. Articles 292 and 294, draft Constitution of February 1948. Rao, *The Framing of India's Constitution*, vol. 3, p. 630.

145. In the meantime, Patel advised members of his party not to field Muslim candidates to contest elections on the basis of separate

electorates, as this would cause embarrassment to the party. See, letter dated 28 September 1948 from Patel to M.Y. Nurie, vice president of the Bombay Provincial Congress Committee. Das (ed.), *Sardar Patel's Correspondence*, vol. 6, p. 194.

Article 325 of the Constitution now says that '[t]here shall be one general electoral roll for every territorial constituency for election to either House of Parliament or to the House or either House of the Legislature of a State and no person shall be ineligible for inclusion in any such roll or claim to be included in any special electoral roll for any such constituency on grounds only of religion, race, caste, sex or any of them.' Later, in *Nain Sukh Das v. State of U.P.*, AIR 1953 SC 384 (from SCC Online) (at paragraphs 3–4), the Supreme Court held that an election conducted on the basis of separate electorates violated Article 15 of the Constitution.

146. Rao, *The Framing of India's Constitution*, vol. 4, p. 600.
147. Ibid.
148. Munshi, *Indian Constitutional Documents*, vol. 1, at p. 207.
149. By now, new Muslim members had been appointed to the Advisory Committee. Included among them were Begum Aizaz Rasul, a member of the Muslim League who had decided not to leave India, and Tajamul Husain. Munshi, ibid., p. 206.
150. Munshi, ibid., p. 207.
151. Munshi, ibid., p. 207.
152. The proceedings of the meeting are best described by K.M. Munshi in Munshi, *Indian Constitutional Documents*, vol. 1, pp. 206–08.
153. Munshi, ibid., p. 207.
154. Rasul later claimed that she had consulted the Muslim members of the UP legislative assembly and council as well as the Muslim members of the Constituent Assembly, who had advised her against reservation of seats. Rasul, *From Purdah to Parliament*, at pp. 125–26.
155. Munshi, Indian Constitutional Documents, vol. 1, at p. 208.
156. Smith, *India as a Secular State*, pp. 407–08.
157. Rao, *The Framing of India's Constitution*, vol. 4, pp. 601–02.
158. Speech of Tajamul Husain in the Constituent Assembly (26 May 1949).
159. Rao, *The Framing of India's Constitution*, vol. 4, p. 946 at p. 949.
160. Letter dated 7 January 1952. Gopal (ed.), *Selected Works of Jawaharlal Nehru*, Second Series, vol. 17, p. 599, at p. 603.

161. Rasul, *From Purdah to Parliament*, at p. 132.

162. Mahmud Husain, 'Mohammed Ali Jinnah', *Encyclopedia Britannica*, 7 September 2019, available at: https://www.britannica.com/biography/Mohammed-Ali-Jinnah (last visited 10 September 2019).

163. Rasul, *From Purdah to Parliament*, at p. 132.

164. Ibid.

165. Ibid.

166. Smith, *India as a Secular State*, p. 419.

167. Ibid.

168. Data available at: http://www.censusindia.gov.in/2011census/Religion_PCA.html (last visited 30 December 2018).

169. Data have been compiled by the author from the following website: http://164.100.47.194/Loksabha/Members/AlphabeticalList.aspx (last visited 30 December 2018).

170. Data have been compiled by the author from the following website: http://loksabhaph.nic.in/Members/AlphabeticalList.aspx (last visited 10 September 2019).

171. Data have been compiled by the author from the following website: http://164.100.47.5/Newmembers/memberlist.aspx (last visited 30 December 2018). See further, Aakar Patel, 'The case against a joint electorate', Livemint, 30 June 2016, available at: https://www.livemint.com/Leisure/UfhhSciDjar5kCAgCt9ezL/The-case-against-a-joint-electorate.html (last visited 30 December 2018).

172. Rukmini S., 'Just the fourth Muslim MLA for BJP', *The Hindu*, 24 December 2018, available at: https://www.thehindu.com/news/national/just-the-fourth-muslim-mla-for-bjp/article6720423.ece (last visited 30 December 2018).

173. See, Rajeev Bhargava, 'On the Persistent Political Under-Representation of Muslims in India', *L. & Ethics. Hum. Rts.* 76–133 (2007), at pp. 115–20. See further, Tarunabh Khaitan, 'Ranked-Choice Voting System Could Deepen Democracy, Prevent Polarisation', *Indian Express*, 8 May 2019, available at: https://indianexpress.com/article/opinion/columns/general-elections-lok-sabha-polls-first-past-the-post-fpp-system-bjp-5715812/ (last visited 19 May 2019).

174. Rao, *The Framing of India's Constitution*, vol. 2, p. 404.

175. 25 May 1949, Constituent Assembly Debates.
176. Many different methods of electoral representation were discussed by Sir B.N. Rau, the Constitutional Adviser to the Constituent Assembly of India, in his book. Sir Benegal Rau, *India's Constitution in the Making* (Madras: Allied Publishers Pvt. Ltd, 1960), p. 315.
177. On 25 May 1949, Naziruddin Ahmad in the Constituent Assembly said that cumulative voting in India would be 'extremely difficult to work' and that it was an example of 'intellectual abstractions'.

Chapter 4: Temple and State

1. However, Peter van der Veer argues that this separation between church and state in colonial India did not lead to secularization, as it gave rise to voluntary Hindu revivalist societies. Peter van der Veer, *Imperial Encounters*, p. 343.
2. Dhavan and Nariman have argued that state governments have almost entirely taken over religious endowments which are now run by bureaucrats instead of believers. Dhavan and Nariman, 'The Supreme Court and Group Life', p. 262.
3. Kenneth O. Morgan (ed.), *The Oxford History of Britain* (Oxford: Oxford University Press, 2010), at p. 283.
4. Michael W. McConnell, 'Establishment and Disestablishment at the Founding, Part I: Establishment of Religion', *William and Mary Law Review*, vol. 44, pp. 2105–208 (2002–03), at p. 2112. See further, Rex Ahdar and Ian Leigh, 'Is Establishment Consistent with Religious Freedom?', *McGill Law Journal*, vol. 49, (2003–04), pp. 635–82, at pp. 638–39.
5. O. Morgan (ed.), *The Oxford History of Britain*, at p. 275.
6. Ibid., at p. 275.
7. 'Archbishop of Canterbury', *Encyclopaedia Britannica*, available at: https://www.britannica.com/topic/archbishop-of-Canterbury (last visited 8 May 2018).
8. McConnell, 'Establishment and Disestablishment at the Founding', at p. 2112; Ahdar and Leigh, 'Is Establishment Consistent with Religious Freedom', at pp. 638–39.
9. McConnell, ibid., at p. 2147.

10. Ahdar and Leigh, 'Is Establishment Consistent with Religious Freedom', at pp. 638–39.

11. 'Lords Spiritual and Temporal', website of the UK Parliament, glossary.

12. Smith, *India as a Secular State*, at pp. 72–73. Arjun Appadurai says that pre-colonial rulers used to be minimally involved in temple administration, though they used to arbitrate disputes themselves. Arjun Appadurai, *Worship and Conflict under Colonial Rule: A South Indian Case* (Cambridge: Cambridge University Press, 1981), at pp. 162–63. See further, *Manohar Ganesh Tambekar v. Lakhmiram Govindram*, ILR 12 Bom 247 (1887), at p. 260.

13. Smith, ibid.

14. Nandini Chatterjee, *The Making of Indian Secularism: Empire, Law and Christianity, 1830–1960* (Hampshire: Palgrave Macmillan, 2011) (Kindle edition), at p. 57.

15. Smith, *India as a Secular State*, at p. 73.

16. Chatterjee, *The Making of Indian Secularism*, at p. 58.

17. Regulation IV of 1806, in *Papers Relating to East India Affairs* (12 May 1813), at p. 41, available on Google Books.

18. Michael J. Altman, 'The Origins of the Juggernaut', *OUP Blog*, 2 August 2017, available at: https://blog.oup.com/2017/08/origins-juggernaut-jagannath/ (last visited 8 May 2018).

19. Rev. Claudius Buchanan, *Christian Researches in Asia* (London: G. Sidney, 1812), fifth edition, available at: https://archive.org/stream/christianresearc00buchrich#page/n5/mode/2up/search/juggernaut (last visited 8 May 2018), at p. 28.

20. Regulation 2, Regulation IV of 1806.

21. The salaries of pundits etc. were fixed by the governor general in council. Regulation 18, ibid.

22. Regulation 6, ibid.

23. Regulation 11, ibid.

24. Regulations 12–13, ibid. The collector had to recommend names and send them to the governor general in council through the Board of Revenue. In doing so, he had to 'consult the opinions of the most respectable Hindoos'.

25. That is, 'so long as they shall continue to conduct themselves with integrity, diligence and propriety'. Regulation 15, ibid.

26. Regulation 15, ibid. They could be removed by the governor general in council.

27. Regulation IV of 1809, *Papers Relating to East India Affairs* (12 May 1813), at p. 81. Available on Google Books.

28. Regulation 2(2), ibid.

29. Regulation 3(1), ibid. They were subject to confirmation by the government.

30. Regulation 5, ibid. The collector exercised his powers subject to the superintendence of the Board of Revenue.

31. Regulation XIX of 1810, *The Regulations and Laws Enacted by the Governor General in Council* (Calcutta: Baptist Mission Press, 1828), vol. 6. Available on Google Books.

32. See, preamble, ibid.

33. Regulation 2, ibid. That is, the Board of Revenue and Board of Commissioners.

34. Regulation 3, ibid.

35. Regulations 8–13. The power had to be exercised through a local agent appointed by the government.

36. Regulation VII of 1817. *The Madras Code* (Madras: Superintendent, Government Press, 1936), vol. 1, fifth edition, at p. 40, available at https://archive.org/details/in.ernet.dli.2015.83944?q=%22Madras+Hindu+Religious+Endowments+Act%22 (last visited 8 May 2018).

37. Regulation XVII of 1827. *Accounts and Papers; Seven Volumes, Relating to East India Company and East Indies* (1829), vol. 23 (available on Google Books), at p. 211.

38. Regulation 38(2)–(4), ibid.

39. See, 'A Late Resident in India', *The Connexion of the East-India Company's Government with the Superstitious and Idolatrous Customs and Rites of the Natives of India, Stated and Explained* (London: Hatchard and Son, 1838), https://babel.hathitrust.org/cgi/pt?id=hvd.32044011616299;view=1up;seq=9 (last visited 8 May 2018), at p. 93.

40. Ibid., at p. 5.

41. Ibid., at p. 14.

42. Ibid., at p. 9.

43. Ibid., at p. 9.

44. Smith, *India as a Secular State*, at p. 73.

45. See, ibid., at p. 244; Chatterjee, *The Making of Indian Secularism*, at pp. 54–55; Peter van der Veer, *Imperial Encounters*, p. 293.
46. Smith, ibid., at p. 76. It was called a despatch.
47. The text of the despatch is in 'A Late Resident in India', *The Connexion of the East-India Company's Government*, p. 44 onwards.
48. Ibid., paragraph 9, p. 46.
49. Ibid., paragraphs 9–10, p. 46.
50. Ibid., paragraph 17, p. 48.
51. Ibid., paragraph 14, p. 47.
52. Ibid., paragraph 62, p. 59.
53. Ibid., paragraph 16, p. 48.
54. Ibid., paragraph 20, p. 49.
55. Ibid., paragraph 23, p. 50.
56. Ibid., paragraph 45, pp. 54–55.
57. Ibid., paragraph 62, p. 59.
58. See further, Chatterjee, *The Making of Indian Secularism*, at pp. 55–56.
59. Smith, *India as a Secular State*, at p. 80.
60. Indian Church Act, 1927 and Indian Church Measure, 1927.
61. Smith, *India as a Secular State*, at pp. 82–83.
62. Ibid.
63. Ibid., at p. 76.
64. Ibid.
65. Chatterjee, *The Making of Indian Secularism*, at p. 60.
66. Smith, *India as a Secular State*, at p. 76.
67. Chatterjee, *The Making of Indian Secularism*, at p. 60; Appadurai, *Worship and Conflict Under Colonial Rule*, at p. 157. Peter van der Veer refers to this as 'corporate Hinduism'. *Imperial Encounters*, p. 299.
68. *The Abstract of the Proceedings of the Council of the Governor-General of India Assembled for the Purpose of Making Laws and Regulations* (Calcutta: Office of the Supt. of Govt. Print., 1863), vol. 1, available at: https://babel.hathitrust.org/cgi/pt?id=hvd.hl2qyr;view=1up;seq=3 (last visited 9 May 2018), p. 23 at p. 26.
69. Ibid., at p. 23, pp. 26–27.
70. Ibid., at p. 57, pp. 63–65.

71. 25 February 1863. Ibid., vol. 2 (1863), pp. 47–48. It became Act
XX of 1863, 'An Act to enable the Government to divest itself of the
management of Religious Endowments.' *The Legislative Acts of the
Governor General of India in Council* (Calcutta: Thacker, Spink &
Co., 1868), vol. 4, at p. 293. Available at: https://archive.org/stream/
in.ernet.dli.2015.501879/2015.501879.The-Legislative#page/n299/
mode/2up/search/escheats (last visited 9 May 2018).

Similarly, a law was enacted in 1863 for Bombay, which watered
down the 1827 regulations. Bombay Act II of 1863, Section 8. *The
Bombay Code* (Calcutta: Office of the Superintendent of Government
Printing, 1880), at p. 180. Available on Google Books.

72. Section 1, Act XX of 1863.

73. Sections 3, 7, 8, ibid. Committee members could not be trustees.
Section 11, ibid.

74. Section 4, ibid.

75. Section 13, ibid.

76. Section 14, ibid.

77. *The Abstract of the Proceedings of the Council of the Governor-General of
India Assembled for the Purpose of Making Laws and Regulations*, vol. 2
(1863), 25 February 1863, at p. 48.

78. See, Smith, *India as a Secular State*, at p. 244.

79. Chatterjee, *The Making of Indian Secularism*, at pp. 63–64.

80. Smith, *India as a Secular State*, at p.77.

81. Appadurai, *Worship and Conflict under Colonial Rule*, p. 174. There
was no provision akin to Section 539 in the Code of Civil Procedure,
1859 (Act VIII of 1859). See, L.P. Delves Broughton, *The Code of
Civil Procedure, being Act VIII of 1859* (Calcutta: Thacker, Spink and
Co., 1871) (available on Google Books); *The Code of Civil Procedure
being Act No. X of 1877* (Madras: Higginbotham and Co., 1877)
(available on Google Books).

82. The English law of trusts applied to religious charities as well. See,
Thomas Lewin, *A Practical Treatise on the Law of Trusts and Trustees*
(London: A. Maxwell & Son, 1842), second edition, available on
Google Books, at p. 98, where the case of *Attorney General v. Pearson*,
[1814–23] All ER Rep 60, involving a religious trust, was discussed.

83. 'An Act to Provide a Summary Remedy in Cases of Abuses of Trusts Created for Charitable Purposes'. Archibald John Stephens, *The Statutes Relating to the Ecclesiastical and Eleemosynary Institutions* (London: John W. Parker, 1845), vol. 1, at p. 1022. Available on Google Books.

84. James J. Fishman, 'Charitable Accountability and Reform in Nineteenth-Century England: The Case of the Charity Commission', *Chicago-Kent Law Review*, vol. 80 (2005), pp. 723–78, at p. 728.

85. Ibid., at p. 744.

86. Section 92, Code of Civil Procedure, 1908. Similarly, the Charitable and Religious Trusts Act, 1920, enabled any person who had an interest in a trust to petition a court to ask for information about the trust (nature, object, value of the trust), and ask for its accounts to be audited. This law also allowed the trustee to ask for an advisory opinion on the management or administration of trust property.

    Likewise, the Mussalman Wakf Act, 1923, available at: https://archive.org/stream/in.ernet.dli.2015.208445/2015.208445.A-Collection#page/n507/mode/2up (last visited 9 May 2018), required *mutwallis*, or trustees of wakfs, to furnish particulars about the wakf to the court, etc. However, it did not contemplate any government takeover of the management and administration of wakfs.

87. *Manohar Ganesh Tambekar v. Lakhmiram Govindram*, ILR 12 Bom 247 (1887). The appeal was against a judgment of the district judge of Ahmedabad, who held against the plaintiffs. See further, Pandit Prannath Saraswati, 'Hindu Law of Endowments', Tagore Law Lectures (1892) (available on SCC Online).

88. The court relied on a treatise on Hindu Law written by West and Bühler. The third edition of Raymond West and Johann Georg Bühler, *A Digest of the Hindu Law of Inheritance, Partition, and Adoption* (Bombay: Education Society's Press, 1884), is available at: https://archive.org/stream/adigesthindulaw00bhgoog#page/n4/mode/2up (last visited 9 May 2018) (vol. 1) and https://archive.org/stream/adigesthindulaw01bhgoog#page/n4/mode/2up (last visited 9 May 2018) (vol. 2).

89. *Tambekar v. Lakhmiram*, at pp. 260–61.

90. Ibid., at p. 261.

91. Ibid., at pp. 263–65.

92. A theory of an 'implied contract' or implied trust was also applied by Lord Chancellor Eldon in the well-known case of *Attorney General v. Pearson*, [1814–23] All ER Rep 60.

93. *Tambekar v. Lakhmiram*, at p. 265.

94. Ibid., at p. 267.

95. *Chotalal Lakhmiram v. Manohar Ganesh Tambekar*, (1899) SCC Online PC 13.

96. Government of India Act, 1915.

97. Section 79(3)(e), ibid. See, Panchanandas Mukherji, *Indian Constitutional Documents* (Calcutta & Simla: Thacker, Spink & Co., 1918), 2nd edition, at pp. xxii–xxiii, available at: https://archive.org/details/indianconstituti02mukh/page/n3 (last visited 28 May 2019).

98. Letter from the Government of Madras to the Government of India, dated 31 December 1918, in *East India (Constitutional Reforms)* (London: H.M. Stationery Off., 1919), https://catalog.hathitrust.org/Record/010457904 (last visited 9 May 2018), paragraph 7, p. 174.

99. Ibid.

100. See, *Sir Sankaran Nair's Minutes of Dissent* (Madras: Ganesh & Co., 1919?), at p. 21, https://babel.hathitrust.org/cgi/pt?id=ucl.a0010615862;view=1up;seq=103 (last visited 9 May 2018); *Memorandum Submitted by the Government of the Central Provinces to the Indian Statutory Commission* (London: H.M. Stationary Office, 1930), at p. 81 (where the minister for education was in charge of 'Religious and Charitable Endowments'), https://babel.hathitrust.org/cgi/pt?id=mdp.39015027587651;view=1up;seq=93 (last visited 9 May 2018).

101. See further, Suhrith Parthasarathy, 'How Hinduism was Nationalized', Livemint, 3 April 2016, available at: https://www.livemint.com/Sundayapp/FU6sreM7t13piRRwkvdKfP/Secularism-and-principled-distance-How-Hinduism-was-nationa.html (last visited 9 May 2018).

102. Act II of 1927. *The Madras Code* (Madras: Superintendent, Government Press, 1936), fifth edition, vol. 4, available at: https://archive.org/stream/in.ernet.dli.2015.211496/2015.211496.The-Madras#page/n137/mode/2up/search/%22Madras+Hindu+Religious+Endowments+Act%22 (last visited 9 May 2018), at p. 1661.

103. Sections 10–15, ibid.
104. Section 52, ibid.
105. Section 59, ibid.
106. Section 67, ibid.
107. Section 57, ibid.
108. Article II, Section 1, Clause 17, Rao, *The Framing of India's Constitution*, vol. 2, at pp. 87–88.
109. Article 16, ibid., at p. 50 (draft dated 23 December 1946).
110. Ibid. (meeting dated 26 March 1947), at p. 122.
111. Ibid., at p. 123.
112. Ibid., at p. 149 (8 April 1947). These provisions were in clauses 17 and 19 in the draft report of the subcommittee on fundamental rights (dated 3 April 1947). Ibid., at p. 140.
113. Panikkar, who was the chief minister of Bikaner State (1944–48), later served as India's ambassador to China (1948–52), Egypt and other Arab countries (1952–54), and France (1955–59). He was also a member of the Rajya Sabha (1959–60, 1960–61). See, profile on the website of the Rajya Sabha, available at: https://rajyasabha.nic.in/rsnew/pre_member/1952_2003/p.pdf (last visited 19 May 2019).
114. Rao, *The Framing of India's Constitution*, vol. 2, at p. 165 (14 April 1947).
115. Ibid., at p. 174 (16 April 1947).
116. Ibid. The deliberations begin at p. 269.
117. In May 1947, Munshi moved an amendment in the Constituent Assembly to make the right to manage one's affairs in matters of religion available not merely to religious denominations but also to a 'section thereof'. In support of this amendment, he only said the following words: 'It was felt that the use of the term 'religious denomination' may prevent a section of a denomination from being protected.' The amendment was adopted with barely any discussion. Constituent Assembly Debates (1 May 1947).
118. The draft is available at: Rao, *The Framing of India's Constitution*, vol. 3, at p. 524.
119. Sitaramayya later served as a member of the Rajya Sabha in 1952. See, profile on the website of the Rajya Sabha, available

at: https://rajyasabha.nic.in/rsnew/pre_member/1952_2003/s.pdf (last visited 19 May 2019).

120. The others were: Shrimati G. Durgabai, Thakurdas Bhargava, B.V. Keskar, T.T. Krishnamachari, M. Ananthasayanam Ayyangar and K. Santhanam. Rao, *The Framing of India's Constitution*, vol. 4, p. 42.

121. Rao, *The Framing of India's Constitution*, vol. 4, p. 42. Sitaramayya and others also wanted to make the right of religious denominations to be 'subject to public order, morality and health'. Rao, *The Framing of India's Constitution*, vol. 4, at p. 42. The drafting committee of the Constitution decided to sponsor this amendment. Ambedkar later moved this amendment in the Constituent Assembly, and said: 'it is not [our] purpose to give absolute rights in these matters relating to religion. The State may reserve to itself the right to regulate all these institutions and their affairs whenever public order, morality or health require it.' Constituent Assembly Debates (7 December 1948).

122. Rao, *The Framing of India's Constitution*, vol. 4, at p. 42.

123. Constituent Assembly Debates (7 December 1948).

124. Kamath later served as a member of the Lok Sabha (1955–57 and 1962–67). He had been a member of the Indian Civil Service. *See*, profile on the website of the Lok Sabha, available at: http://loksabhaph.nic.in/writereaddata/biodata_1_12/776.htm (last visited 19 May 2019).

125. His clause, however, would not 'prevent the State from imparting spiritual training or instruction to the citizens of the Union'. Constituent Assembly Debates (6 December 1948).

126. Ibid.

127. Lakshmi Kanta Maitra, Constituent Assembly Debates (6 December 1948).

128. Constituent Assembly Debates (6 December 1948).

129. Rao, *The Framing of India's Constitution*, vol. 2, at pp. 76 and 140.

130. Section 44(2)1. B.N. Rau said so in his comments on the draft as well, dated 8 April 1947. Rao, *The Framing of India's Constitution*, vol. 2, at p. 149.

131. Meeting of the Advisory Committee dated 21–22 April 1947, ibid., at p. 265.

132. Article VI(1), Munshi's draft of the fundamental rights, dated 17 March 1947. Ibid., at p. 76.

240240240240 Notes

133. Meeting dated 26 March 1947, ibid., at p. 122. The right of Sikhs to wear and carry kirpans was added to the Constitution thanks to an intervention by Harnam Singh on this date in the subcommittee. Ibid., at p. 123.
134. Ibid., at p. 122.
135. Note dated 14 April 1947, ibid., at p. 160.
136. Meeting of the Advisory Committee, 21–22 April 1947, ibid., at p. 266.
137. Meeting of the Advisory Committee dated 22 April 1947, ibid., at pp. 290–91.
138. Constituent Assembly Dates (1 May 1947).
139. Draft Constitution dated 3 November 1949, Rao, *The Framing of India's Constitution*, vol. 4, at p. 758.
140. An early draft of the subcommittee on fundamental rights sought to exclude conscientious objection from the ambit of the fundamental right to freedom of religion. It said that no person could 'refuse the performance of civil obligation or duties on the ground that his religion so requires' it. Clause 16, Explanation III. Draft report of the subcommittee on fundamental rights (3 April 1947). Ibid., vol. 2, at p. 140. However, K.T. Shah objected to this and said that a Jain would be forced, because of this clause, to kill rats during a plague, even though his religion forbade taking life. K.T. Shah's minute of dissent (April 1947), ibid., at p. 194. K.M. Panikkar wrote that Indians would be prevented from taking *sanyasa* and renouncing worldly life if this clause were to stand in the Constitution. K.M. Panikkar's minute of dissent (April 1947), ibid., at pp. 187–88. It was on account of their opinions that the Advisory Committee decided to drop this clause in April 1947. Meeting of the Advisory Committee dated 21–22 April 1947, ibid., at p. 269.

K.T. Shah wanted the government to have the power not merely to 'regulate' or 'restrict' the 'economic, financial, political or other secular activity' associated with religious practice but also to 'prohibit' it. Constituent Assembly Debates (6 December 1948). 'Material possessions, worldly wealth and worldly grandeur', he said, 'are things which have been the doom of many an established Church.' He spoke of 'heads of religions' who, 'in the name of their religion claim exemption from income-tax' and indulged in 'open or illicit trading, speculation, investments, or what not.' He wanted the government to have the power to absolutely prohibit this kind of 'non-religious, non-spiritual activity'. Ibid. However, his suggestion was rejected.

141. Item 28, List III (Concurrent List), 7th Schedule, Constitution of India.

142. The Supreme Court has held that legislation which singles out one temple does not violate the right to equality under Article 14 of the constitution so long as it can be shown that the temple occupies a class by itself on account of its unique position. *Tilkayat Shri Govindlalji Maharaj v. State of Rajasthan*, AIR 1963 SC 1638 (from SCC Online), paragraph 53; *S.P. Mittal v. Union of India*, (1983) 1 SCC 51, paragraphs 149, 156, 161, 164; *Raja Bira Kishore Deb v. State of Orissa*, AIR 1964 SC 1501 (from SCC Online), paragraph 5.

143. They were Assam, Punjab, West Bengal and Uttar Pradesh. Hindu Religious Endowments Commission, 1960—Report, available at: https://archive.org/stream/in.ernet.dli.2015.128903/2015.128903. Committees-And-Commission-In-India-Vol-iv#page/n53/mode/2up/search/%22Madras+Hindu+Religious+and+Charitable+Endowments+Act%22 (last visited 15 May 2018), p. 46.

144. Additionally, Article 25 is also subject to the other provisions of Part III of the Constitution.

145. *Commissioner, Hindu Religious Endowments, Madras v. Sri Lakshmindra Thirtha Swamiar of Sri Shirur Mutt*, AIR 1954 SC 282 (from SCC Online), paragraph 18; *Ratilal Panachand Gandhi v. State of Bombay*, AIR 1954 SC 388 (from SCC Online), paragraphs 10, 12.

146. *Shirur Mutt case*, paragraph 17; *Ratilal case*, paragraph 12.

147. *Shirur Mutt case*, paragraph 17; *Durgah Committee, Ajmer v. Syed Hussain Ali*, AIR 1961 SC 1402 (from SCC Online), paragraph 33; *Dr M. Ismail Faruqui v. Union of India*, (1994) 6 SCC 360 (paragraphs 77–78). See further, *Indian Young Lawyers Association v. State of Kerala*, (2018) SCC Online SC 1690 (paragraphs 206–25). For a criticism of the 'essential practices' test, see, Dhavan and Nariman, 'The Supreme Court and Group Life', p. 259. See further, Ronojoy Sen, 'Secularism and Religious Freedom', in, Choudhry et al. (eds.),

The Oxford Handbook of the Indian Constitution, pp. 885–902. Once a practice is found to be essential to religion, it may still be regulated in the interests of public order, morality or health.

148. Article 25(2)(a) of the Constitution permits the government to regulate or restrict any 'secular activity which may be associated with religious practice', even if the law is not in furtherance of public order, morality, health or the other provisions of Part III of the Constitution.

149. *Indian Young Lawyers Association v. State of Kerala*, (2018) SCC Online SC 1690 (paragraph 209), relying on *Sri Venkataramana Devaru v. State of Mysore*, AIR 1958 SC 255.

150. *Commissioner of Police v. Acharya Jagadishwarananda Avadhuta*, (2004) 12 SCC 770 (paragraph 9). In this case it was held that the Tandava dance of Anand Margis was not essential. This was because the Anand Margi order was founded in 1955 and the Tandava dance was started in 1966. Ibid., paragraph 10.

151. Ibid.

152. *Indian Young Lawyers Association v. State of Kerala*, (2018) SCC Online SC 1690, paragraphs 224–25.

153. *Dr M. Ismail Faruqui v. Union of India*, (1994) 6 SCC 360 (paragraph 82).

154. *Shirur Mutt case*, paragraph 17.

155. *Shirur Mutt case*, paragraph 20.

156. *Shri Jagannath Temple Puri Management Committee v. Chintamani Khuntia*, (1997) 8 SCC 422, paragraph 49.

157. *S.P. Mittal v. Union of India*, (1983) 1 SCC 51, paragraph 121.

158. *Sardar Syedna Taher Saifuddin Saheb v. State of Bombay*, AIR 1962 SC 853 (SCC Online version).

159. See further, *Shirur Mutt case*, paragraph 20; *Ratilal case*, paragraph 13.

160. *Sardar Syedna Taher Saifuddin Saheb v. State of Bombay*, AIR 1962 SC 853 (SCC Online version), at paragraph 33. See further, *Tilkayat Shri Govindlalji Maharaj v. State of Rajasthan*, AIR 1963 SC 1638 (from SCC Online), paragraph 57. However, the views of the religious community are not determinative.

161. *Sardar Syedna Taher Saifuddin Saheb v. State of Bombay*, AIR 1962 SC 853 (SCC Online version), at paragraph 39.

162. Article 25(2)(b). Ibid., at paragraph 43.

163. Article 26(b) has been held to be subject to Article 25(2)(b). *Sri Venkataramana Devaru v. State of Mysore*, AIR 1958 SC 255 (from SCC Online), paragraphs 24–29, followed in *Sardar Syedna Taher Saifuddin Saheb v. State of Bombay*, AIR 1962 SC 853 (from SCC Online), paragraph 40.

164. *Sri Venkataramana Devaru v. State of Mysore*, AIR 1958 SC 255 (from SCC Online), paragraphs 32–33.

165. *M. Siddiq v. Mahant Suresh Das*, Civil Appeal Nos. 10866–10867 of 2010, judgment dated 9 November 2019 (paragraph 77). Earlier, Justice D.Y. Chandrachud, in the Sabarimala judgment, had held that this test required courts to 'don a theological mantle' and needed a 'close look' again 'in an appropriate case in the future'. *Indian Young Lawyers Association v. State of Kerala*, (2018) SCC Online SC 1690 (paragraphs 193, 289).

166. *Kantaru Rajeevaru v. Indian Young Lawyers Association*, Review Petition (Civil) No. 3358 of 2018, majority judgment dated 14 November 2019.

167. *Ratilal case*, paragraph 14.

168. *Shirur Mutt case*, paragraph 26.

169. *Shirur Mutt case*, paragraph 23.

170. *Ratilal case*, paragraph 13.

171. *Shirur Mutt case*, paragraphs 33, 39. See further, *Mahant Moti Das v. S.P. Sahi*, AIR 1959 SC 942 (from SCC Online), paragraph 12, where a similar provision was upheld because the statutory board had to take into account the wishes of the founder, and the mere possibility of abuse was insufficient to strike a law down.

172. *Ratilal case*, paragraph 16.

173. Ibid. *State of Rajasthan v. Shri Sajjanlal Panjawat*, (1974) 1 SCC 500, paragraph 27.

174. *Ratilal case*, paragraph 16. The government official in this case was the charity commissioner.

175. *Ratilal case*, paragraph 15.

176. *Tilkayat case*, paragraph 60. In other words, it is not covered by Articles 25 and 26(b), but it can still be covered by Article 26(d) of the Constitution.

177. *Indian Young Lawyers Association v. State of Kerala*, (2018) SCC Online SC 1690 (per Misra CJI [with Khanwilkar J.] at paragraphs 122–23; Chandrachud J. [paragraph 227]). However, Chandrachud J. held that the essential religious practices test requires a close look in a future case (paragraphs 193, 285, 289). The review petition is pending in the Supreme Court. *Kantaru Rajeevaru v. Indian Young Lawyers Association*, Review Petition (Civil) No. 3358 of 2018, majority judgment dated 14 November 2019.

178. AIR 1964 SC 1501 (from SCC Online).

179. Section 5.

180. Section 6.

181. *Raja Bira case*, paragraph 9.

182. AIR 1954 SC 282 (from SCC Online).

183. *Shirur Mutt case*, paragraph 27.

184. *Ratilal case*, paragraph 17.

185. *Tilkayat case*, paragraph 73.

186. *Seshammal v. State of T.N.*, (1972) 2 SCC 11, paragraph 21; *A.S. Narayana Deekshitulu v. State of A.P.*, (1996) 9 SCC 548, paragraphs 118–19. Though a similar view was taken about hereditary trustees in *Pannalal Bansilal Pitti v. State of AP*, (1996) 2 SCC 498, paragraphs 20, 22–23, 26–29 (the court in this case read down the impugned provision and said that the founder or a member of his family should be a part of the statutory committee), the point has now been referred to a larger bench in *A. Ramaswamy Dikshitulu v. Govt of AP*, (2004) 4 SCC 661, paragraphs 2, 5. In *Adi Saiva Sivachariyargal v. Government of Tamil Nadu*, (2016) 2 SCC 725 (paragraphs 48, 50), it was held that if an Agama (i.e. a treatise 'pertaining to matters like construction of temples, installation of idols and conduct of worship of the deity') of a temple requires *archakas* to belong to a certain sect or denomination in Hinduism, without discrimination on the basis of caste or class, then a government order which overrode the Agama, and said that any Hindu could be appointed an archaka, would violate the Constitution.

187. *N. Adithayan v. Travancore Devaswom Board*, (2002) 8 SCC 106 (paragraph 17).

188. *Shri Jagannath Temple Puri Management Committee v. Chintamani Khuntia*, (1997) 8 SCC 422, paragraphs 3, 21, 27. However, the sevaks were being remunerated for their work, and the government was asked to frame rules regarding payment to be made to them. Ibid., paragraphs 29, 39.

189. Section 53 of the Andhra Pradesh Charitable and Hindu Religious Institutions and Endowments Act, 1987.

190. *Sri Sri Sri Lakshamana Yatendrulu v. State of AP*, (1996) 8 SCC 705, paragraphs 23–24.

191. Ibid. It was held that if the commissioner acted arbitrarily, his action could be challenged.

192. Ibid., paragraphs 28, 32.

193. Ibid., paragraph 32. The court took note of the fact that the commissioner had to obtain the opinions of 'eminent persons in the field of religion, philosophy and [the] Sampradayam to which the math belongs' in order to 'satisfy himself that the nominee possessed the prescribed qualifications', and that he had to give the mahant and nominee a hearing if the nominee was found not to be fit and record reasons for rejecting him.

194. Ibid., paragraphs 21, 25–26. This was under section 51 of the Andhra Pradesh Charitable and Hindu Religious Institutions and Endowments Act, 1987.

195. Durgah Khawaja Saheb Act, 1955. A copy of this statute is available at: http://theindianlawyer.in/statutesnbareacts/acts/d65.html#_Toc39310517 (last visited 15 May 2018).

196. Section 5, ibid.

197. Section 11(f), ibid.

198. Section 11(h), ibid.

199. See, Mohammed Iqbal, 'Flurry of Activity among Khadims', *The Hindu*, 11 July 2001, available at: http://www.thehindu.com/2001/07/11/stories/14112212.htm (last visited 15 May 2018).

200. See, *Faqruddin v. Tajuddin*, (2008) 8 SCC 12.

201. *Durgah Committee, Ajmer v. Syed Hussain Ali*, AIR 1961 SC 1402 (from SCC Online), paragraph 41. The court relied on Section 15 of the statute. The fact that there was a provision for arbitration between

the khadims and the committee also found favour with the court. Ibid., paragraphs 42–43.

202. A Religious Trusts Bill was mooted in the 1960s, but did not materialize. See, Smith, *India as a Secular State*, p. 258.

203. Section 32. A mutawalli is akin to a manager of a waqf. See, *Bibi Saddiqa Fatima v. Saiyed Mohammad Mahmood Hasan*, (1978) 3 SCC 299 (paragraph 16).

204. Section 14.

205. However, the Supreme Court has held that the 'right freely to profess, practice and propagate religion' under Article 25 of the Constitution belongs not to an institution, like a temple, mosque or church, but to individuals. *Shirur Mutt case*, paragraph 14; *Sardar Syedna Taher Saifuddin Saheb v. State of Bombay*, AIR 1962 SC 853 (from SCC Online), paragraph 17; *Sri Sri Sri Lakshamana Yatendrulu v. State of AP*, (1996) 8 SCC 705, paragraph 14. In other words, corporate bodies are not constitutional 'persons' capable of exercising the right to the freedom of religion.

206. *Shirur Mutt case*, paragraph 15.

207. *Nallor Marthandam Vellalar v. Commissioner, Hindu Religious and Charitable Endowments*, (2003) 10 SCC 712, paragraph 7.

208. *Sri Venkataramana Devaru v. State of Mysore*, AIR 1958 SC 255, paragraph 14.

209. *Nallor Marthandam Vellalar v. Commissioner, Hindu Religious and Charitable Endowments*, (2003) 10 SCC 712, paragraph 7.

210. *Sri Adi Visheshwara of Kashi Vishwanath Temple v. State of UP*, (1997) 4 SCC 606, paragraph 33. See further, *N. Adithayan v. Travancore Devaswom Board*, (2002) 8 SCC 106, paragraphs 1, 17, where a Siva temple was held not to be denominational.

211. *Indian Young Lawyers Association v. State of Kerala*, (2018) SCC Online SC 1690 (per Misra CJI [with Khanwilkar J] at paragraphs 95–96; Nariman J. at paragraphs 171–72; Chandrachud J. at paragraph 246).

212. *Sri Venkataramana Devaru v. State of Mysore*, AIR 1958 SC 255 (from SCC Online), paragraph 15.

213. AIR 1954 SC 388 (from SCC Online).

214. Sections 44–47.

215. *Ratilal case*, paragraph 17.

216. AIR 1954 SC 282 (from SCC Online).

217. Ibid., paragraph 35.

218. Ibid.

219. Ibid. The invalidation of Sections 63–69 was upheld on a concession made by the advocate general of Madras. Ibid., paragraph 38.

220. *Subramanian Swamy v. State of Tamil Nadu*, (2014) 5 SCC 75, paragraphs 65–66, 69.

221. *Tilkayat case*, paragraph 70; *Durgah Committee, Ajmer v. Syed Hussain Ali*, AIR 1961 SC 1402 (from SCC Online), paragraph 44; *Sri Digyadarsan Rajendra v. State of AP*, (1969) 1 SCC 844, paragraph 10; *Sri Sri Sri Lakshamana Yatendrulu v. State of AP*, (1996) 8 SCC 705, paragraph 27.

222. Section 55(c) and a portion of section 56.

223. *Ratilal case*, paragraph 19. See further, *Mahant Sri Jagannath Ramanuj Das v. State of Orissa*, AIR 1954 SC 400, paragraph 8; Tilkayat case, paragraph 74.

224. Section 30, Madras Hindu Religious and Charitable Endowments Act, 1951.

225. *Shirur Mutt case*, paragraph 31. See further, *Mahant Sri Jagannath Ramanuj Das v. State of Orissa*, AIR 1954 SC 400, paragraph 8.

226. Section 31.

227. *Shirur Mutt case*, paragraph 32.

228. *Shirur Mutt case*, paragraph 34.

229. *Shri H.H. Sudhindra Thirtha Swamiar v. Commissioner for Hindu Religious and Charitable Endowments*, AIR 1963 SC 966 (from SCC Online), paragraph 14. See further, *Sri Sri Sri Lakshamana Yatendrulu v. State of AP*, (1996) 8 SCC 705, paragraphs 41–44.

230. *Tilkayat case*, paragraphs 43–45.

231. *Shri Jagannath Temple Puri Management Committee v. Chintamani Khuntia*, (1997) 8 SCC 422, paragraphs 30, 35.

232. *Khajamian Wakf Estates v. State of Madras*, (1970) 3 SCC 894, paragraph 12.

233. *Acharya Maharajshri Narendra Prasadji Anandprasadji Maharaj v. State of Gujarat*, (1975) 1 SCC 11, paragraph 26.

234. The Shri Jagannath Temple Act, 1954. An amended version of the statute is available at: http://www.jagannath.nic.in/sites/default/files/notifications/ACT.pdf (last visited 15 May 2018).

235. Sections 19–21, ibid.
236. *Raja Bira case*, paragraph 10.
237. AIR 1963 SC 1638 (from SCC Online).
238. Section 3. An amended version of the statute is available at: http://
     devasthan.rajasthan.gov.in/Files/Nathdwara_Temple_Act%201959_
     Eng.pdf (last visited 15 May 2018).
239. Defined by the statute to mean the occupant of the *gaddi* of Shri
     Tilkayaji Maharaj of Nathdwara.
240. Section 5.
241. Section 7.
242. Section 10.
243. Section 22.
244. Section 36. See further, *Mahant Moti Das v. S.P. Sahi*, AIR 1959 SC
     942 (from SCC Online), paragraph 12. A similar provision was upheld
     in this case especially because the objects of the trust and wishes of the
     founder had to be taken into account.
245. *Tilkayat case*, paragraphs 42, 60–61, 63, 76. See further, *State of
     Rajasthan v. Shri Sajjanlal Panjawat*, (1974) 1 SCC 500, paragraph
     32. But see, *Shri Jagannath Temple Puri Management Committee v.
     Chintamani Khuntia*, (1997) 8 SCC 422, paragraph 49.
246. *Tilkayat case*, paragraph 63.
247. Ibid., paragraph 68.
248. *State of Rajasthan v. Shri Sajjanlal Panjawat*, (1974) 1 SCC 500,
     paragraph 35.
249. Ibid.
250. *Durgah Committee, Ajmer v. Syed Hussain Ali*, AIR 1961 SC 1402
     (from SCC Online).
251. Section 5, Durgah Khawaja Saheb Act, 1955.
252. *Durgah Committee, Ajmer v. Syed Hussain Ali*, AIR 1961 SC 1402
     (from SCC Online), paragraph 37. See further, *State of Rajasthan v.
     Shri Sajjanlal Panjawat*, (1974) 1 SCC 500, paragraph 18.
253. *Shirur Mutt case*, paragraph 36. See further, *Ratilal case*, paragraph 18;
     Mahant Sri Jagannath Ramanuj Das v. State of Orissa, AIR 1954 SC 400
     (from SCC Online), paragraph 7; *Sri Sadasib Prakash Brahmchari v.
     State of Orissa*, AIR 1956 SC 432 (from SCC Online), paragraphs 7–8;

Sri Sri Sri Lakshamana Yatendrulu v. State of AP, (1996) 8 SCC 705, paragraphs 33–34.

254. The prohibition was only against Congress, i.e. the central legislative body, and not the states. Indeed, many states had established churches in the US. However, the established churches of the states were later disestablished, and the first amendment was applied to states as well, through the fourteenth amendment. See, Laurence H. Tribe, *American Constitutional Law* (New York: Foundation Press, 1978), p. 812, 814 (n5).

255. 'Jefferson's Letter to the Danbury Baptists', 1 January 1802, *Library of Congress*, available at: https://www.loc.gov/loc/lcib/9806/danpost.html (last visited 16 May 2018).

256. Steven K. Green, 'Church and State in Nineteenth-Century America', *in*, Derek H. Davis, *The Oxford Handbook of Church and State in the United States* (Oxford: Oxford University Press, 2010), at p. 76.

257. See, Michael Sandel, 'Religious Liberty: Freedom of Choice or Freedom of Conscience', in, Rajeev Bhargava (ed.), *Secularism and its Critics* (New Delhi: Oxford University Press, 1998), at p. 74. Before this case, the US Supreme Court had decided two cases that had a bearing on the free exercise clause of the First Amendment. Ibid., at p. 77. The first of these was *Reynolds v. United States*, 98 US 145 (1878), in which the court held that an anti-polygamy statute did not interfere with the free exercise of religion by Mormons. The second was *Cantwell v. Connecticut*, 310 U.S. 296 (1940), in which the court set aside the conviction of a Jehovah's Witness who had solicited contributions for the religion.

258. 330 US 1 (1947).

259. 403 US 602 (1971).

260. Kathleen M. Sullivan and Gerald Gunther, *First Amendment Law*, third edition (New York: Foundation Press, 2007), at p. 550.

261. 465 US 668 (1984).

262. Smith, *India as a Secular State*, at p. 257.

263. Ibid., at p. 247.

264. Ibid., at p. 247.

Chapter 5: To Divorce Religion from Personal Law

1. Broadly speaking, 'personal law' is the law of the family—marriage, divorce, succession, adoption, maintenance, etc.
2. Differences in the legal systems of say, England and Scotland, are not based on personal laws alone. Cf., 'The Law of Scotland, Wales, and Northern Ireland: Scotland', *Jerome Hall Law Library*, Indiana University, Bloomington, available at: http://law.indiana.libguides. com/c.php?g=19840&p=112546 (last visited 26 May 2018); Sarah Carter, 'A Guide to the UK Legal System', *Globalex*, Hauser Global Law School Program, available at: http://www.nyulawglobal.org/ globalex/United_Kingdom1.html (last visited 26 May 2018).
3. However, Jews and Quakers were exempt from the Clandestine Marriages Act, 1753. Gillian Douglas et al, 'Social Cohesion and Civil Law: Marriage, Divorce and Religious Courts', Report of a Research Study funded by the AHRC, June 2011, Cardiff University, at p. 13; Henry Kha, 'The Reform of English Divorce Law: 1857–1937', DPhil Thesis, University of Queensland, 2017, at p. 19. Parashar says that the distinction, under old English law, between ecclesiastical and temporal laws (ecclesiastical matters were within the jurisdiction of the Bishop's courts) does not adequately explain how religious personal law emerged in India. This is partly because the distinction between ecclesiastical and territorial law had dissolved in England by the time the English had 'assumed judicial powers in India'. Archana Parashar, *Women and Family Law Reform in India: Uniform Civil Code and Gender Equality* (New Delhi: Sage Publications India Pvt. Ltd, 1992, Kindle Edition), p. 1174, 5815 (note 27).
4. Douglas et al., ibid.
5. The text of the Act is available here: https://babel.hathitrust.org/cgi/ pt?id=pst.000057640501;view=1up;seq=7 (last visited 23 May 2018). See further, Stephens, *Governing Islam*, p. 9.
6. See further, Parashar, *Women and Family Law Reform in India*, p. 5815, note 27.
7. Thomas Baty, 'Capacity and Form of Marriage in the Conflict of Laws', *Yale Law Journal*, vol. 26, issue 6, 1917, pp. 444–63, available at http://digitalcommons.law.yale.edu/cgi/viewcontent.

cgi?article=2546&context=ylj (last visited 23 May 2018); David Pearl, 'Muslim Marriages in English Law', *Cambridge Law Journal*, vol. 30, 1972, pp. 120–43.

8. [1904–7] All ER Rep 86.

9. Ibid., p. 92.

10. Ian Edge, 'Islamic Finance, Alternative Dispute Resolution and Family Law: Developments towards Legal Pluralism?', in Robin Griffith-Jones (ed.), *Islam and English Law: Rights, Responsibilities and the Place of Shari'a* (Cambridge: Cambridge University Press, 2013), p. 132.

11. Edge, 'Islamic Finance', at p. 125. See further, Elizabeth Butler-Sloss and Mark Hill, 'Family Law: Current Conflicts and Their Resolution', in Griffith-Jones (ed.), *Islam and English Law*, p. 108.

12. Edge, ibid.

13. Edge, ibid., p. 135 (n. 78).

14. Butler-Sloss and Hill, 'Family law', at p. 109; Douglas et al., 'Social Cohesion and Civil Law', p. 47.

15. P.J. Marshall, 'Warren Hastings', *Encyclopaedia Britannica*, available at: https://www.britannica.com/biography/Warren-Hastings (last visited 23 May 2018).

16. Section 23, 'A Plan for the Administration of Justice, Extracted from the Proceedings of the Committee of Circuit, 15th August, 1772', in G.W. Forrest (ed.), *Selections from the State Papers of the Governors-General of India* (Oxford: B.H. Blackwell, 1910), vol. 2, available at: https://catalog.hathitrust.org/Record/001249598 (last visited 23 May 2018). The Hastings plan was the result of negotiations that took place between Warren Hastings and the advisors of the nawab of Bengal in Murshidabad. Stephens, *Governing Islam*, p. 25. However, the plan applied only to Bengal. Stephens, ibid., p. 30. According to Stephens, it was not the foundation of the personal law system. The term 'personal law', she writes, emerged in the nineteenth century. Ibid., p. 33. It is interesting that the Hastings plan was to apply to Hindus and Muslims, but not to other religious communities like Buddhists, Sikhs, Jains, and Parsis. As Parashar points out, for quite some time, the religious personal laws of Jews, Parsis and Armenians were not recognized in British India. Parashar, *Women and Family Law Reform in India*, p. 1201. Sharafi surmises that this was because the British

believed that these groups had no 'general body of religious law'. Sharafi, *Law and Identity in Colonial South Asia*, pp. 130–32. This was partly on account of the members of some of these communities themselves. Jains, for instance, hid their religious texts from colonial officials because they were afraid that Britons would use saliva to turn pages, thereby polluting the texts. Sharafi, ibid., p. 132.

17. Smith, *India as a Secular State*, at p. 274. This was largely because British officials thought that their Indian intermediaries were corrupt. See, Bijay Kisor Acharyya, *Codification in British India: Tagore Law Lectures, 1912* (Calcutta: S.K. Banerji & Sons, 1914), p. 80; Cohn, *Colonialism and its Forms of Knowledge*, pp. 66–75. However, in doing so, the government gave an inordinate weightage to written texts over customary practices.

18. Acharyya, ibid., at pp. 116–17; Smith, ibid.

19. *Hansard's Parliamentary Debates*, vol. 19 (London: T.C. Hansard, 1833) (available on Google Books), 10 July 1833. Macaulay's speech begins at p. 503, and the relevant portion is at p. 533.

20. Section 53, Charter Act, 1833. *The Law Relating to India, and the East-India Company* (London: Wm. H. Allen & Co., 1842) (available on Google Books), at p. 422.

21. Ivermee writes that even when it came to the colonial government's secular educational policy, 'the Rebellion marked less of an ideological rupture than is often posited.' *Secularism, Islam and Education in India, 1830–1910*, p. 37.

22. Queen Victoria's proclamation dated 1 November 1858. Available at: http://www.csas.ed.ac.uk/mutiny/confpapers/Queen%27sProclamation.pdf (last visited 23 May 2018).

23. Sections 19 and 43, Indian Councils Act, 1861; Section 67(2), Government of India Act, 1915, available at: https://www.scribd.com/document/28828165/Government-of-India-Act-1915 (last visited 23 May 2018). However, there does not appear to have been a comparable provision in the Government of India Act, 1935.

24. Eleanor Newbigin, *The Hindu Family and the Emergence of Modern India: Law, Citizenship and Community* (Cambridge: Cambridge University Press, 2013), p. 118.

25. *A Code of Gentoo Laws, or Ordinations of the Pundits, from a Persian Translation, Made from the Original, Written in the Shanscrit*

Language (London: 1776), available at: https://archive.org/stream/
codeofgentoolaws00halh#page/n5/mode/2up (last visited 23 May
2018). Hastings then sent the code to the Court of Directors in
England. It is not clear how extensively translations/codes like these
were practically used. Stephens, *Governing Islam*, p. 27.

26. Ibid., pp. ix–x.

27. See, Sir Courtenay Ilbert, *The Government of India: Being a Digest of
the Statute Law Relating Thereto* (Oxford: Clarendon Press, 1915),
pp. 367–68.

28. The need to reform gender-biased personal laws was cited by Britons
as a justification for colonial rule in India. Sharafi, *Law and Identity in
Colonial South Asia*, p. 168.

29. Sir William Wilson Hunter (ed.), *Rulers of India: Lord William
Bentinck* (Oxford: Clarendon Press, 1897), p. 85.

30. H.H. Dodwell (ed.), *The Cambridge History of India*, vol. 6
(Cambridge: Cambridge University Press, 1932), p. 133 (available on
Google Books).

31. Ibid. See further, Hunter (ed.), *Rulers of India*, pp. 80–81.

32. Bennie R. Crockett, Jr., '"West Meets East": *Sati* and Universal
Morality', 8 November 2007, William Carey University, available at:
https://www.wmcarey.edu/carey/lectures/sati11-8-07.pdf (last visited
23 May 2018), p. 6 (n. 23).

33. Rev. Thomas Smith, *The History and Origin of the Missionary Societies*
(London: Thomas Kelly & Richard Evans, 1824), vol. 1, at p. 361.

34. F. Deaville Walker, *William Carey: Missionary Pioneer and Statesman*
(London: Church Missionary Society, 1926), available at: https://
babel.hathitrust.org/cgi/pt?id=ucl.$b155665;view=1up;seq=9   (last
visited 23 May 2018), p. 247.

35. 'Richard Colley Wellesley, Marquess Wellesley', *Encyclopaedia
Britannica*, available at: https://www.britannica.com/biography/
Richard-Colley-Wellesley-Marquess-Wellesley (last visited 23 May
2018).

36. Hunter (ed.), *Rulers of India*, p. 81; Parashar, *Women and Family Law
Reform in India*, p. 1307.

37. 'Gilbert Elliot-Murray-Kynynmound, 1st Earl of Minto', *Encyclopaedia
Britannica*,   available   at: https://www.britannica.com/biography/

Gilbert-Elliot-Murray-Kynynmound-1st-Earl-of-Minto (last visited 23 May 2018). He must not be confused with the Minto who served as viceroy in the early twentieth century.

38. Hunter (ed.), *Rulers of India*, at p. 82; Parashar, *Women and Family Law Reform in India*, p. 1307.

39. 'Francis Rawdon-Hastings, 1st Marquess of Hastings', *Encyclopaedia Britannica*, available at: https://www.britannica.com/biography/ Francis-Rawdon-Hastings-1st-Marquess-of-Hastings (last visited 23 May 2018).

40. Hunter (ed.), *Rulers of India*, pp. 84, 106–07; Parashar, *Women and Family Law Reform in India*, p. 1306.

41. See, Smith, *India as a Secular State*, at p. 218.

42. Rev. Claudius Buchanan, *Christian Researches in Asia* (London: G. Sidney, 1812), fifth edition, available at: https://archive.org/stream/ christianresearc00buchrich#page/n5/mode/2up/search/juggernaut (last visited 23 May 2018), at p. 40.

43. Wilberforce was a prominent British politician who was instrumental in the abolition of the slave trade and slavery. See, 'William Wilberforce', *Encyclopaedia Britannica*, available at: https://www.britannica.com/ biography/William-Wilberforce (last visited 18 May 2019).

44. See, *The Evangelical Magazine and Missionary Chronicle (1829)* (London: Frederick Westley and A.H. Davis, 1829?) (available on Google Books), at pp. 24–26.

45. See, e.g., J. Peggs, *The Suttees' Cry to Britain* (London: Seely and Son, 1828?), available at: https://babel.hathitrust.org/cgi/pt?id=wu.8900 1982313;view=1up;seq=18 (last visited 23 May 2018). Peggs was a Christian missionary who had served in Orissa. The fact that this was a publication of the Society is clear on reading *The Evangelical Magazine and Missionary Chronicle (1829)*.

46. Hunter (ed.), *Rulers of India*, at p. 79; Smith, *India as a Secular State*, p. 218.

47. Ram Mohan Roy, 'Modern Encroachments on the Ancient Rights of Hindoo Females', in *The Oriental Herald and Journal of General Literature*, vol. 10, July to September 1826, p. 254 (available on Google Books).

48. Ibid., p. 258.

49. Sharafi, *Law and Identity in Colonial South Asia*, p. 168.

50. He served as such during 1828–33. Philip Mason, 'Lord William Bentinck', *Encyclopaedia Britannica*, available at: https://www. britannica.com/biography/Lord-William-Bentinck (last visited 23 May 2018).

51. Hunter (ed.), *Rulers of India*, p. 96 onwards.

52. This was despite the fact that Ram Mohan Roy had advised a more cautious, gradual approach. Smith, *India as a Secular State*, p. 218.

53. Hunter (ed.), *Rulers of India*, p. 96.

54. Ibid., p. 98.

55. Ibid., p. 99.

56. Ibid., pp. 99–100.

57. Ibid., p. 102.

58. Ibid.

59. Ibid., p. 108.

60. Ibid., p. 111.

61. Regulation XVII of 1829. Available at: https://babel.hathitrust.org/cgi/pt?id=umn.31951000969868b;view=1up;seq=368 (last visited 23 May 2018).

62. Preamble, ibid.

63. Section 5.

64. Hunter (ed.), *Rulers of India*, at p. 91. Regulation I of 1830, abolishing Sati in Madras, is available here: https://babel.hathitrust.org/cgi/pt?id=mdp.39015060556225;view=1up;seq=538 (last visited 23 May 2018).

65. See, 'Anti-Suttee Petition' in *The Asiatic Journal and Monthly Register* (London: Parbury, Allen, and Co., 1831) (available on Google Books), p. 20.

66. Hunter (ed.), *Rulers of India*, at pp. 91–92.

67. Ibid. However, solitary instances of sati occurred even thereafter. Robb, 'The Challenge of Gau Mata', pp. 287–88.

68. Regulation VI of 1802, in *The Regulations and Laws Enacted by the Governor General in Council*, vol. 3 (Calcutta: Baptist Mission Press, 1828) (available on Google Books).

69. See, Abstract of the Proceedings of the Council of the Governor General of India (1870), vol. 9 (Calcutta: Office of the Superintendent

of Government Printing, 1906), at p. 5, available at: https://babel.
hathitrust.org/cgi/pt?id=chi.78206105&view=1up&seq=11 (last visited
1 September 2019). Act No. VIII of 1870 is available here: https://
babel.hathitrust.org/cgi/pt?id=hvd.hl3ep9&view=1up&seq=66   (last
visited 23 May 2018).

70. Section 15, Bengal Regulation XVII of 1817, available here: https://
babel.hathitrust.org/cgi/pt?id=hvd.hl3kn8;view=1up;seq=493 (last visited
23 May 2018). The regulations which had given Banares Brahmins the
exemption were Section 23, Regulation XVI of 1795, and Sections 7
and 9, Regulation XXI of 1795.

71. Code of Manu quoted in *The Oriental Herald and Colonial Review*,
vol. 2 (London: J.M. Richardson, 1824), p. 346 (available on Google
Books).

72. Sharafi writes that opposition to reform usually took the form of
endorsements of the practices that were sought to be reformed and
'resistance to imperial cultural domination generally'. Sharafi, *Law and
Identity in Colonial South Asia*, p. 167.

73. *Proceedings of the Legislative Council of India* (Calcutta: P.M.
Cranenburgh, 1857), vol. 2, at p. 434, available at: https://babel.
hathitrust.org/cgi/pt?id=nyp.33433014358927;view=1up;seq=225
(last visited 23 May 2018).

74. Act XV of 1856, available at: https://babel.hathitrust.org/cgi/pt?id=hvd.
hl446k;view=1up;seq=266 (last visited 23 May 2018).

75. Stanley A. Wolpert, *Tilak and Gokhale: Revolution and Reform in the
Making of Modern India* (Berkeley: University of California Press,
1962), at p. 49. See further, Richard P. Tucker, *Ranade and the
roots of Indian nationalism* (Bombay: Popular Prakashan, 1977), at
pp. 208–30.

76. Scoble served as advocate general of Bombay (1870–77), law member
of the Viceroy's Council and judge of the Privy Council in London.
See, 'Death of Sir A. Scoble: A Great Anglo-Indian Jurist', *The Times
(London)*, 19 January 1916, available at: https://www.findagrave.com/
memorial/126898160/andrew-richard-scoble (last visited 18 May 2019).

77. *Abstract of the Proceedings of the Council of the Governor General of
India (1891)* (Calcutta: Superintendent of Government Printing,
1892), vol. 30, at p. 10 (available on Google Books).

78. Ibid., pp. 12–13.

79. Ibid., p. 27.

80. Brojendra Mitter, *Eminent Indian Judges* (Delhi: Mittal Publications, 1988 reprint) at p. 325.

81. Abstract of the Proceedings of the Council of the Governor General of India (1891), vol. 30, pp. 14–15.

82. Ibid., p. 16.

83. Ibid., p. 17.

84. Ibid., p. 82.

85. Ibid., p. 146.

86. Ibid., p. 146.

87. Ibid., p. 149.

88. Ibid., p. 148.

89. Ibid., p. 153.

90. Ibid., at p. 154. Act X of 1891.

91. Sir Henry Moncrieff-Smith, 'British India', *Journal of Comparative Legislation and International Law*, 1931, pp. 119–25; P.R. Ganapathi Iyer, 'The Child Marriage Restraint Act', *Calcutta Law Journal*, Vol. 51, no. 1, 1930, pp. 1n–8n. This was the Child Marriage Restraint Act, 1929. Now the age is twenty-one for men and eighteen for women. Prohibition of Child Marriage Act, 2006.

92. As Parashar points out, Hindu and Muslim laws were not restricted to the personal sphere alone. Parashar, *Women and Family Law Reform in India*, p. 1175.

93. Sir Thomas Strange, *Elements of Hindu Law* (London: Payne and Foss, 1825), at p. 271 (available on Google Books).

94. John D. Mayne, *A Treatise on Hindu Law and Usage* (London: Stevens and Haynes, 1878), at p. 266.

95. *A Code of Gentoo Laws, or Ordinations of the Pundits, from a Persian Translation, Made from the Original, Written in the Shanscrit Language* (London: 1776), available at: https://archive.org/stream/codeofgentoolaws00halh#page/n5/mode/2up (last visited 23 May 2018), at p. 123.

96. Ibid., p. 124.

97. Ibid., p. 125.

98. Ibid., p. 126.

99. Charles Hamilton, *The Hedaya or Guide: A Commentary on the Mussulman Laws* (Lahore: Premier Book House, 1963), available at: https://archive.org/stream/hedayaorguide029357mbp#page/n361/mode/2up/search/infidel (last visited 23 May 2018), pp. 353–54.

100. James Fitzjames Stephen, 'The Law of Evidence', 31 March 1871, available at: https://babel.hathitrust.org/cgi/pt?id=hvd.32044057460 388;view=1up;seq=253 (last visited 23 May 2018), p. 5.

101. *A Code of Gentoo Laws*, at p. 238. Unless the perpetrator derived a living by killing animals.

102. Ibid., p. 248.

103. Lord Macaulay, *Speeches and Poems: With the Report and Notes on the Indian Penal Code* (New York: Hurd and Houghton, 1867), available at: https://catalog.hathitrust.org/Record/011530235 (last visited 15 August 2016), vol. 2, p. 315.

104. Ibid., p. 316.

105. Ibid.

106. Bombay Regulation XIV of 1827.

107. Macaulay, *Speeches and Poems*, p. 317.

108. Sir Henry Sumner Maine, *Village-Communities in the East and West: Six Lectures Delivered at Oxford* (London: John Murray, 1876), p. 298, available at: https://archive.org/stream/villagecommuniti031891mbp#page/n7/mode/2up (last visited 23 May 2018).

109. Ibid. He made a case for codification and said: 'there are probably half-a-dozen law-libraries at most in all India. The books they contain are written in a foreign language, and the persons able to consult these books and to use them properly are extremely few'. Ibid., pp. 300–01.

110. However, the line between the personal and the public was sometimes difficult to draw. For instance, at the time of the enactment of the Indian Majority Act, 1875, the Muhammadan Literary Society of Calcutta protested and said that majority must be determined not merely by age but by sexual capacity, etc. Stephens, *Governing Islam*, pp. 53–54.

111. See, Thomas R. Metcalfe, *Ideologies of the Raj* (Cambridge: Cambridge University Press, 1995), pp. 10, 132; R.B. Bhagat, 'Census and the Construction of Communalism in India', *Economic and Political*

Weekly, 24 November 2001, available at: http://www.sacw.net/2002/CensusandCommunalism.html (last visited 23 May 2018).

112. Elphinstone's Minute dated 14 May 1858 in *Report of the Commissioners Appointed to Inquire Into the Organization of the Indian Army* (London: Her Majesty's Stationery Office, 1859), available at: https://babel.hathitrust.org/cgi/pt?id=hvd.32044106495658;view=1up;seq=514 (last visited 23 May 2018), p. 145.

113. Ibid., at p. 146.

114. However, Menski argues that the colonial encounter did not alter customary Hindu law. Werner F. Menski, *Hindu Law: Beyond Tradition and Modernity* (New Delhi: Oxford University Press, 2003, Kindle edition), pp. 5176–202.

115. Sharafi, *Law and Identity in Colonial South Asia*, pp. 140–41; Satyajeet A. Desai (ed.), *Mulla Hindu Law* (Gurgaon: LexisNexis, 2016), twenty-second edition, p. 552. According to Sharafi, colonial courts also relaxed Muslim law rules in the Hanafite School to allow more than a third of a Muslim's property to be disposed of through a Will. Sharafi, ibid., pp. 141–42. In the pre-colonial period, Parsis also had limited powers of testamentary disposition which were enhanced with the arrival of the British. Sharafi, ibid., p. 142.

116. *Soorjeemoney Dossee v. Denobundoo Mullick*, (1854–57) 6 Moo IA 526: (1857) SCC Online PC 6. See further, *Mancharji Pestanji v. Na'ra'yan Lakshumanji*, (1863) Bombay High Court Reports 77. Any statutory modification of the law relating to Hindu Wills was not really a modification of Hindu personal law. As such, the Hindu Wills Act, 1870 and the Indian Succession Act, 1925 did not really modify Hindu personal law concerning wills. The former required some Hindu wills to be in writing, while the latter (as amended in 1926) required all Hindu wills to be in writing. Desai (ed.), *Mulla Hindu Law*, at p. 556.

117. This is possibly because colonial officials relied on pundits and maulvis, who were more likely to have relied on text over custom, to understand indigenous law. However, courts in British India applied customary Hindu and Muslim law as well. Parashar, *Women and Family Law Reform in India*, pp. 1382, 1259.

118. Rajeev Dhavan, 'The Supreme Court and Hindu Religious Endowments 1950–1975', *Journal of the Indian Law Institute*, vol. 20(1), pp. 52–102, at p. 60 (1978).

119. See, Parashar, *Women and Family Law Reform in India*, p. 1343.

120. Ahmed, *Religious Freedom*, p. 28–30; Dhavan, 'The Supreme Court and Hindu Religious Endowments', p. 56; Rohit De, 'Personal Laws: A Reality Check', *Frontline*, 6 September 2013, available at: https://frontline.thehindu.com/cover-story/personal-laws-a-reality-check/article5037670.ece (last visited 12 April 2019).

121. Flavia Agnes, 'Politicization of Personal Laws: A Study of Colonial India', in Bharati Ray (ed.), *Women of India: Colonial and Post-Colonial Periods* (New Delhi: Centre for Studies in Civilizations, 2005), at p. 12; Sharafi, *Law and Identity in Colonial South Asia*. Parsis lobbied colonial legislatures to enact statutes that restored Parsi personal laws over English law doctrines like primogeniture and coverture. Sharafi, ibid., p. 128. Thus, for instance, though the Parsi Marriage and Divorce Act, 1865, prohibited polygamy, Parsis hardly practiced it. Polygamy among Parsis occurred when a couple had separated informally and then one of its members took on another spouse. Sharafi, ibid., pp. 172–73. Further, the 1865 Act allowed Parsi men to have sex with prostitutes—their wives could not ask for a divorce from them if they did so. The prostitution exception was only done away with under the Parsi Marriage and Divorce Act, 1936. Sharafi, ibid., pp. 173–74, 177. The 1865 Act also did not prohibit child marriage, which was only done away with by a statute in 1929. Sharafi, ibid., p. 182, p. 187.

122. A copy of the statute, as originally enacted, is in *A Collection of the Acts of the Indian Legislature and of the Governor General for the year 1937* (New Delhi: Manager, Government of India Press, 1938), available at: https://archive.org/stream/in.ernet.dli.2015.208444/2015.208444.A-Collection#page/n81/mode/2up/search/Shariat+application+act (last visited 25 May 2018).

123. Section 2, ibid.

124. Eleanor Newbigin, 'The Codification of Personal Law and Secular Citizenship: Revisiting the History of Law Reform in Late Colonial India', *Indian Economic and Social History Review*, vol. 46(1), pp. 83–104 (2009), at pp. 95–96.

125. Section 3.

126. See, Newbigin, *The Hindu Family*, at p. 119; Eleanor Newbigin, 'Personal Law and Citizenship in India's Transition to Independence', in Taylor C. Sherman et al, *From Subjects to Citizens: Society and the Everyday State in India and Pakistan, 1947–1970* (Delhi: Cambridge University Press, 2014) (partially available on Google Books), at pp. 28–31.

127. 9 September 1937. The text of the debate is available here: https://link.springer.com/content/pdf/bbm%3A978-1-349-26885-6%2F1.pdf (last visited 26 May 2018).

128. Ibid.

129. Ibid.

130. Newbigin, *The Hindu Family*, at p. 118.

131. Ibid., at p. 120.

132. Section 2, Act No. VIII of 1939. Available on archive.org. See further, Rohit De, 'Mumtaz Bibi's Broken Heart: The Many Lives of the Dissolution of Muslim Marriages Act', *Indian Economic and Social History Review*, vol. 46(1), pp. 105–30 (2009).

133. Section 4, Act No. VIII of 1939.

134. Legislative Assembly Debates, 1938, vol. 1, 3 February 1938, at p. 318.

135. Ibid.

136. Ibid., 10 February 1938, at p. 509.

137. Ibid.

138. 'Sir Muhammad Zafrulla Khan', *Encyclopaedia Britannica*, available at: https://www.britannica.com/biography/Muhammad-Zafrulla-Khan (last visited 26 May 2018).

139. Legislative Assembly Debates, vol. 5, 9 September 1938, at p. 1969.

140. Legislative Assembly Debates, 1938, vol. 1, 3 February 1938, p. 319.

141. Ibid., p. 322.

142. Similarly, G.V. Deshmukh introduced the Hindu Women's Rights to Property Bill, which was enacted in 1937. See, Newbigin, *The Hindu Family*, at p. 117; Agnes, 'Politicization of Personal Laws', pp. 18–19. The Hindu Gains of Learning Act, 1930, which ensured that an educated Hindu's earnings would be considered property separate from the property of the joint Hindu family, was piloted by

M.R. Jayakar. P. Ishwara Bhat, 'A Critical Appraisal of the Hindu Gains of Learning Act', *Journal of the Indian Law Institute*, vol. 27(4), pp. 578–93, pp. 583–84 (1985).

143. Legislative Assembly Debates, 10 Feb 1938, at pp. 511–12.

144. Newbigin argues that its non-justiciable character suggested colonial continuity. Newbigin, 'The codification of personal law and secular citizenship', p. 99. However, directive principles generally were 'fundamental to the governance of the country' and were often taken into account by the Supreme Court while interpreting law. See, *Maharao Sahib v. Union of India*, (1981) 1 SCC 166 (paragraph 77).

145. Rao, *The Framing of India's Constitution*, vol. 2, at p. 136. Later, on 18 April 1947, the subcommittee on minorities said that the clause (draft clause 39) affected minorities and required consideration. Ibid., at p. 204. The words 'throughout the territory of India' were added (to draft clause 36) by the Drafting Committee on 3 November 1947. Ibid., vol. 3, at p. 334.

146. Masani was educated at the London School of Economics. He was called to the bar at Lincoln's Inn in London. He served as India's ambassador to Brazil (1948–49). Though he started out as a congressman, he later joined the Swatantra Party. See, profile on the website of the Lok Sabha, available at: http://loksabhaph.nic.in/writereaddata/biodata_1_12/1252.htm (last visited 19 May 2019).

147. Mehta later served as India's delegate to the United Nations Human Rights Commission (1947–48). She is given credit for replacing the word 'men' with the words 'human beings' in Article 1 of the Universal Declaration of Human Rights, which says '[a]ll human beings are born free and equal'. See, Sonakshi Awasthi, 'Hansa Jivraj Mehta', *Indian Express*, 24 January 2018.

148. Rao, *The Framing of India's Constitution*, vol. 2, at p. 162.

149. Ibid., at p. 206.

150. The debates are available on SCC Online.

151. Mohammad Ismail Sahib.

152. Ibid.

153. Naziruddin Ahmad.

154. Mahboob Ali Baig Sahib Bahadur.

155. Ibid.
156. B. Pocker Sahib Bahadur.
157. Ibid.
158. 2 December 1948.
159. Newbigin argues that the 1937 Shariat Act served as the impetus for the Hindu Code. Newbigin, 'The Codification of Personal Law and Secular Citizenship', p. 100. According to Parashar, the process of Hindu law codification began with the Hindu Law Committee in the colonial period. Parashar, *Women and Family Law Reform in India*, p. 1485. The Hindu Code bill dealt with marriage, divorce, intestate succession, minority, guardianship, maintenance, adoption, and mitakshara joint family property. Parashar, ibid., p. 1509. There was no popular demand for a Hindu Code, and nor was reform of Hindu law part of the Congress party's manifesto. Parashar, ibid., p. 1654.
160. His profile is available here: http://governor.mp.gov.in/pataskar.aspx (last visited 2 September 2019).
161. See, Vasant Moon (ed.), *Dr Babasaheb Ambedkar: Writings and Speeches*, vol. 14, (New Delhi: Dr Ambedkar Foundation, 2014 reprint), available at: http://www.mea.gov.in/Images/attach/amb/Volume_14_01.pdf (last visited 25 May 2018), at pp. 606–07.
162. Ibid., p. 606.
163. Ibid., p. 607.
164. Ibid.
165. Ibid., p. 608.
166. He resigned on 27 September 1951. Ambedkar's correspondence with Nehru over his resignation is available in the Lok Sabha debates for 11 October 1951, at pp. 4733–34. The bill was abandoned because President Rajendra Prasad threatened not to give his assent to it even if it were enacted. Parashar, *Women and Family Law Reform in India*, p. 1617.
167. See, Christophe Jaffrelot, 'Nehru and the Hindu Code Bill', *Outlook*, 8 August 2003, available at: https://www.outlookindia.com/website/story/nehru-and-the-hindu-code-bill/221000 (last visited 25 May 2018).
168. Lok Sabha Debates, vol. 4, 1955 (29 April 1955), p. 6836.
169. Ibid. (7 May 1955), pp. 8129–30.

170. Lok Sabha Debates, vol. 4, 1955 (2 May 1955), pp. 7437–38.
171. Parashar, *Women and Family Law Reform in India*, pp. 1885–1903. This author argues that by recognizing various customary exceptions to the general law, the Hindu Code 'consistently proclaimed but only partially achieved' the aim of uniformity. Ibid., pp. 2066–85. She also argues that the Hindu Code did not bring about equality for women. Ibid., p. 2123. Before the Hindu Code, Hindu women were worse off than Muslim women under their respective personal law systems. However, it was only after 2005 that Hindu men and women were placed on an equal footing under their inheritance law. De, 'Personal laws'. Until then, a woman could be the prime minister of India but not the *karta* of a joint Hindu family. Rajeev Dhavan, 'Codifying personal laws', *The Hindu*, 1 August 2003. In the colonial period, Muslim women were in some respects even better off than their English counterparts, because Muslim personal law recognized the separate property rights of women, which was not so under English law until the Married Women's Property Act, 1882. Stephens, *Governing Islam*, p. 57.
172. Desai (ed.), *Mulla Hindu Law*, p. 821–22; Ahmed, *Religious Freedom*, p. 30. However, as De points out, more Hindus have bigamous marriages than Muslims. Further, the second Hindu wife enjoys fewer rights than the second Muslim wife since the former is not recognized. De, 'Personal laws'. Earlier, under section 494 of the Indian Penal Code, bigamy was a crime for all but Hindu and Muslim males. Sharafi, *Law and Identity in Colonial South Asia*, p. 171. This was because the section applied only when a person married again 'in any case in which such marriage is void by reason of its taking place during the life of such husband or wife'. Angelo J. Lewis, *The Indian Penal Code* (London: Wm. H. Allen, 1870), p. 146. It was also not applicable to Parsis until the Parsi Marriage and Divorce Act, 1865, barred polygamy among them. Sharafi, ibid., p. 171.
173. Ahmed, *Religious Freedom*, p. 32; Newbigin, 'The Codification of Personal Law and Secular Citizenship', p. 100.
174. Section 2(1)(b), Hindu Marriage Act, 1955; Section 2(1)(b), Hindu Succession Act, 1956; Section 3(1)(b), Hindu Minority and

Guardianship Act, 1956; Section 2(1)(b), Hindu Adoptions and Maintenance Act, 1956.

175. Section 2(1)(c), Hindu Marriage Act, 1955; Section 2(1)(c), Hindu Succession Act, 1956; Section 3(1)(c), Hindu Minority and Guardianship Act, 1956; Section 2(1)(c), Hindu Adoptions and Maintenance Act, 1956. The onus would be on such persons to show that Hindu law would not apply to them.

176. In fact, Jewish personal law in India is entirely uncodified. Ahmed, *Religious Freedom*, p. 28. This is except to the extent that secular statutes like the Code of Criminal Procedure 1973 and the Juvenile Justice (Care and Protection of Children) Act, 2015 apply to the community.

177. However, Flavia Agnes argues that since the Hindu Marriage Act, 1955 recognizes both unregistered marriages (s. 8) and customary divorces (s. 29[2]), some Hindus need not approach the state either to solemnize a marriage or dissolve it, which makes the Hindu law of marriage resemble Muslim personal law. Agnes, 'Personal Laws', in, Choudhry et al. (eds.), *The Oxford Handbook of the Indian Constitution*, at p. 915.

178. See, Indira Jaising, 'The Ghost of Narasu Appa Mali Is Stalking the Supreme Court of India', *The Leaflet*, 28 May 2018. Cited in *Indian Young Lawyers Association v. State of Kerala*, (2018) SCC Online SC 1690 (paragraph 268).

179. De, 'Personal Laws'; Werner Menski, 'The Uniform Civil Code Debate in Indian Law: New Developments and Changing Agenda', *German Law Journal*, vol. 9(3), pp. 211–50, at p. 234.

180. See, Sharafi, 'The Semi-Autonomous Judge in Colonial India'.

181. AIR 1952 Bom 84 :: (1951) SCC Online Bom 72 (per Chief Justice M.C. Chagla and Justice P.B. Gajendragadkar).

182. Ibid., paragraph 14.

183. Article 13(1) of the Constitution says that all 'laws in force' in India before the commencement of the Constitution are void to the extent that they are inconsistent with Part III of the Constitution. Article 13(3)(b) defines 'laws in force' as including 'laws passed or made by a Legislature or other competent authority . . .'. Article 13(2) says that the State cannot make any 'law' which takes away or abridges

any of the rights conferred by Part III of the Constitution. Article 13(3)(a) defines 'law' as including 'custom or usage having in the territory of India the force of law'. Article 372 of the Constitution also uses the term 'law in force' (it provides that laws in force in India before the Constitution will continue to operate thereafter), which has a comparable definition in that provision. However, Article 372(2) permits the President to make adaptations/modifications of such laws.

In Narasu Appa Mali's case, Chief Justice Chagla held that personal laws were not 'laws in force' in India within the meaning of Article 13(1) because a similar phrase was used in Article 372 and the President had the power to modify/adapt 'laws in force'. Since it could not be held that the President had the power to modify/adapt personal laws, it was clear that personal laws were not included within the meaning of the phrase 'laws in force' (paragraph 16) (Justice Gajendragadkar agreed with this at paragraph 23). He also held that personal law was not a 'custom or usage' and therefore it was not 'law' within the meaning of Article 13(2) (Paragraph 15) (Gajendragadkar agreed at paragraph 26). In arriving at this view, he relied on Section 112 of the Government of India Act, 1915, in which the words 'personal law' and 'custom' were used separately, indicating that the legislature considered these to be distinct (paragraph 16) (Gajendragadkar agreed at paragraph 29). Chief Justice Chagla also held that the scheme of the Constitution indicated that personal law was not to be a part of Article 13 because: (i) if this were not so, Articles 17 (Gajendragadkar also invoked the example of Article 17 at paragraph 26) and 25(2)(b) of the Constitution would have been redundant (paragraph 16); (ii) the words 'personal law' are specifically used in entry 5 of the Concurrent List in the Seventh Schedule to the Constitution, and Article 44 speaks specifically of a uniform civil code (paragraph 16) (Gajendragadkar agreed at paragraphs 27/29). The implication being that the absence of the words 'personal law' in Article 13 was therefore a conscious decision of the Constituent Assembly to save personal laws from judicial scrutiny.

Additionally, Justice Gajendragadkar held that personal law could not be considered 'law in force' under Article 13(1) since that phrase only applied to 'what may compendiously be described as statutory laws' (paragraph 23), whereas personal laws derive their authority from 'their respective scriptural texts' (paragraph 24).

Chief Justice Chagla and Justice Gajendragadkar disagreed over whether the definition of 'law' under Article 13(3)(a) was to apply to the phrase 'laws in force' under Article 13(1). Chief Justice Chagla held that it ought to do so because 'law' was defined under Article 13(3) (a) as including a 'custom or usage' and the State cannot make any custom or usage under Article 13(2) (paragraph 15). However, Justice Gajendragadkar disagreed and held that the State would only make prospective laws under Article 13(2) on the basis of a custom or usage (paragraph 26). Subsequently, Justice Gajendragadkar's reasoning on this point was found to be 'unsustainable both doctrinally and from the perspective of the precedent of this Court' by Justice D.Y. Chandrachud in *Indian Young Lawyers Association v. State of Kerala*, (2018) SCC Online SC 1690 (paragraph 272). He also held in that case that the judges in Narasu Appa Mali's case did not pay sufficient attention to the fact that the definitions of 'laws in force' and 'law' are inclusive (paragraphs 273–74).

184. *Shri Krishna Singh v. Mathura Ahir*, (1981) 3 SCC 689 (paragraph 17) (though Narasu's case was not specifically referred to). See further, *Javed v. State of Haryana*, (2003) 8 SCC 369 (paragraph 52); *Ahmedabad Women Action Group v. Union of India*, (1997) 3 SCC 573.

185. Dhavan, 'Codifying personal laws'. Relying on *Mary Roy v. State of Kerala*, (1986) 2 SCC 209.

186. (1985) 2 SCC 556 (decided by five judges). According to Dhavan and Nariman, the Supreme Court in Shah Bano's case 'merely affirmed' previous Supreme Court judgments. Dhavan and Nariman, 'The Supreme Court and Group Life', p. 286, note 122.

187. Ibid., paragraph 9.

188. This provision was inserted into the code because of a delegation led by Sheikh Abdullah and other Muslim leaders who met Indira Gandhi and asked her to exempt Muslims. A.G. Noorani, 'Zeal and poor scholarship', *Frontline*, 11 December 2015, available at: http://www.frontline.in/the-nation/zeal-and-poor-scholarship/article7912018.ece (last visited 27 May 2018). Noorani criticized

Chief Justice Chandrachud's judgment in the case, especially the opening paragraph, in which Chandrachud had cited Edward William Lane, who had said that the 'fatal point in Islam is the degradation of women'. However, in the same paragraph, Chandrachud had also cited Manu, the Hindu lawgiver, as having said: 'The woman does not deserve independence'. The point being made in that paragraph was that antiquated religious dogmas had to give way to a modern, uniform civil code.

189. (1985) 2 SCC 556, paragraph 7.

190. Ibid., paragraph 14.

191. Ibid., paragraphs 15, 22.

192. Ibid., paragraphs 23–24.

193. Ibid., paragraph 31.

194. Ibid., paragraph 32.

195. Ibid.

196. A text of this statute is available here: http://legislative.gov.in/sites/ default/files/A1986-25_1.pdf (last visited 2 September 2019).

197. Or if the woman is bearing a child, the period between the divorce and the date on which the child is delivered or the pregnancy is terminated.

198. Section 3.

199. That is unless, on the first date of hearing, both the husband and wife agree to be bound by Sections 125–28 of the code. Section 5.

200. Section 4.

201. (2001) 7 SCC 740 (paragraphs 28, 29, 31, 32, 33, 34, 36(1)–(2)).

202. However, De argues that this process did not occur overnight in Latifi's case, and took place over decades. De, 'Personal laws'.

203. (1985) 3 SCC 62.

204. Ibid., paragraph 7.

205. (1995) 3 SCC 635.

206. Ibid., paragraph 1.

207. Ibid., paragraph 35.

208. Ibid., paragraph 33.

209. Ibid.

210. Ibid.

211. Ibid., paragraphs 37–38.

212. Ibid., paragraph 44. Seervai believed that Justice Sahai's judgment (particularly the words contained in paragraph 44) indicated that he had dissented from the view taken by Justice Kuldip Singh on the question of the uniform civil code. See, Noorani, 'Zeal and poor scholarship'. In *Ahmedabad Women Action Group v. Union of India*, (1997) 3 SCC 573 (paragraph 12), the Supreme Court took the view that 'the question regarding the desirability of enacting a Uniform Civil Code did not directly arise in that case'.

213. Sarla Mudgal's case, ibid., paragraphs 46–47.

214. (2003) 6 SCC 611 (paragraph 44).

215. (2000) 6 SCC 224.

216. Ibid., at paragraphs 40 and 68. See further, *Maharshi Avadesh v. Union of India*, (1994) Supp (1) SCC 713.

217. (1996) 2 SCC 498.

218. Ibid., paragraph 12.

219. (1996) 8 SCC 525 (three judges).

220. Ibid., paragraph 15. See further, paragraph 26.

221. (2017) 9 SCC 1 (decided by five judges). See further, *Shamim Ara v. State of U.P.*, (2002) 7 SCC 518. Earlier, in *Ahmedabad Women Action Group v. Union of India*, (1997) 3 SCC 573 (paragraph 11), the Supreme Court had taken the view that such matters were 'to be dealt with by the legislature'.

222. Paragraph 51.

223. Paragraphs 338–39. They refrained from determining whether Narasu Appa Mali's case was validly decided because of a concession made by the Attorney General that Narasu Appa Mali's case had been followed by two Constitution Bench decisions, in the cases of Shah Bano Begum and Danial Latifi.

224. Anthropological research has suggested, however, that this form of divorce was rarely exercised. See, De, 'Personal laws'.

225. (2017) 9 SCC 1, paragraph 104.

226. Paragraph 47. See further, paragraphs 48 and 50 of their judgment.

227. Ibid., paragraph 12. Noorani also took the view that the practices of triple divorce and polygamy were un-Islamic. Noorani, 'Zeal and poor scholarship'.

228. Paragraph 5.

229. Paragraph 12.
230. Paragraphs 54–55. They held that it was therefore not protected by Article 25 of the Constitution.
231. A copy of the original ordinance is available here: https://bombayhighcourt. nic.in/libweb/ordinc/2018/2018.07.pdf (last visited 2 September 2019). A copy of the re-promulgated ordinance is available here: https:// bombayhighcourt.nic.in/libweb/ordinc/2019/2019.01.pdf (last visited 2 September 2019).
232. Section 7(a). This is only if the complaint is filed by the wife or any person related to her by blood or marriage. This means that a police officer may investigate the case and arrest the accused without a warrant or order from a magistrate.
233. Section 7(c). This means that bail can be granted to the accused by a magistrate at his discretion.
234. 'Talaq' was defined by Section 2(b) of the ordinance as '*talaq-e-biddat* or any other similar form of *talaq* having the effect of instantaneous and irrevocable divorce pronounced by a Muslim husband'.
235. Section 4.
236. Muslim Women (Protection of Rights on Marriage) Act, 2019. A copy is available here: http://egazette.nic.in/WriteReadData/2019/209473. pdf (last visited 2 September 2019).
237. *Indian Young Lawyers Association v. State of Kerala*, (2018) SCC Online SC 1690.
238. Paragraph 278.
239. Ibid.
240. Paragraph 276.
241. Hindus, Jains, Buddhists, and Sikhs are governed by the Hindu Marriage Act, 1955 (marriage and divorce), the Hindu Succession Act, 1956 (intestate succession), the Indian Succession Act, 1925 (testamentary succession) (to the extent of some provisions as per Section 57). Christians are governed by the Indian Christian Marriage Act, 1872 (marriage), Indian Divorce Act, 1869 (divorce), and Indian Succession Act, 1925 (intestate and testamentary succession as per sections 29 and 58). According to De, when Christian personal law statutes were reformed through legislation, there were hardly any protests because the community had been extensively consulted. De, 'Personal Laws'. Parsis

are governed by the Parsi Marriage and Divorce Act, 1936 (marriage and divorce) and the Indian Succession Act, 1925 (intestate and testamentary succession as per sections 29 and 58). Menski argues that many of these laws, though separate, are becoming uniform. Menski, 'The Uniform Civil Code Debate in Indian Law', p. 244–45.

242. The Dissolution of Muslim Marriages Act, 1939 applies to Muslim divorces.

243. See further, Ahmed, *Religious Freedom*, pp. 22–23.

244. De calls this 'a voluntary UCC'. De, 'Personal laws'. This statute was originally a part of the Hindu Code. Parashar, *Women and Family Law Reform in India*, p. 1617. It was preceded by the Special Marriage Act, 1872, a copy of which is available here: https://babel.hathitrust.org/cgi/pt?id=osu.32437122279728;view=1up;seq=80;size=150 (last visited 17 April 2019), which was for marriages between couples neither of whom were Christian, Jewish, Hindu, Muslim, Parsi, Buddhist, Sikh or Jain.

245. Section 21-A, Special Marriage Act, 1954. This was inserted by an amendment in 1976.

246. Section 21, Special Marriage Act, 1954.

247. Section 19, Special Marriage Act, 1954.

248. Section 5, Special Marriage Act, 1954.

249. Ahmed, *Religious Freedom*, p. 22.

250. Section 488, Code of Criminal Procedure, 1898.

251. Explanation (b), Section 125, Code of Criminal Procedure, 1973.

252. This was the Juvenile Justice (Care and Protection of Children) Act, 2000, sections 40–41. It was substantially amended in 2006.

253. (2014) 4 SCC 1 (paragraph 13).

254. Iqbal Ali Khan (ed.), *Mulla Principles of Mahomedan Law* (Gurgaon: LexisNexis, 2017), twenty-second edition, p. 442.

255. *Laxmidas Morarji v. Jehangir Bamji*, (1998) SCC Online Bom 75.

256. *Raj Kumar Mohan Singh v. Raj Kumar*, AIR 1969 SC 135 (SCC Online version) (paragraph 20).

257. Section 41(2).

258. Section 56(2), Juvenile Justice (Care and Protection of Children) Act, 2015, permits adoption from a relative by another relative, regardless of religion.

259. Sections 56–73, Juvenile Justice (Care and Protection of Children) Act, 2015. Section 56(3), says that it does not apply to adoptions covered by the Hindu Adoptions and Maintenance Act, 1956, i.e. to Hindus, Jains, Buddhists and Sikhs.
260. Section 3, Explanation I (iv).
261. Section 17.
262. See, Menski, 'The Uniform Civil Code Debate in Indian Law', p. 214, 242. Menski speaks of the Prohibition of Child Marriage Act, 2006, the Maintenance and Welfare of Parents and Senior Citizens Act, 2007, and the Code of Criminal Procedure (Amendment) Act, 2001.
263. *Seema v. Ashwani Kumar*, (2006) 2 SCC 578. Until then, only a few states provided for the mandatory registration of marriages.
264. Ahmed, *Religious Freedom*, p. 7.
265. Newbigin, 'The Codification of Personal Law and Secular Citizenship', p. 84; Dhavan and Nariman, 'The Supreme Court and Group Life', p. 273.
266. Ahmed, *Religious Freedom*, p. 7.
267. See, De, 'Personal Laws'; Dhavan, 'Codifying Personal Laws'; Menski, 'The Uniform Civil Code Debate in Indian Law'.

Chapter 6: Secularly Swearing

1. See, 'Eucharist', *Encyclopaedia Britannica*, available at: https://www.britannica.com/topic/Eucharist (last visited 16 May 2018); 'Transubstantiation', *Encyclopaedia Britannica*, available at: https://www.britannica.com/topic/transubstantiation (last visited 16 May 2018).
2. Available at: http://www.britainexpress.com/History/tudor/supremacy-text.htm (last visited 2 January 2018). See further, Yossi Nehushtan, 'The Case for a General Constitutional Right to be Granted Conscientious Exemption', *Oxford Journal of Law and Religion*, vol. 5(2), (2016), pp. 230–54.
3. Frederick B. Jonassen, 'So Help Me?: Religious Expression and Artifacts in the Oath of Office and the Courtroom Oath', 12 *Cardozo Public Law Policy and Ethics Journal* 303 (2014), pp. 303–73, at pp. 323–24.

4. The four holy evangelists were Matthew, Mark, Luke and John, whose 'gospels' or biblical narratives form a part of the New Testament, in which the Christians believe. See, 'Gospel', *Encyclopedia Britannica*, available at: https://www.britannica.com/topic/Gospel-New-Testament (last visited 2 January 2018).

5. Enid Campbell, 'Oaths and Affirmations of Public Office under English Law: An Historical Retrospect', *Journal of Legal History*, vol. 21 (2000), pp. 1–32, at pp. 9–10.

6. Campbell, id., at p. 10; Luke Beck, 'The Constitutional Prohibition on Religious Tests', *Melbourne University Law Review*, vol. 35, pp. 323–52 (2011), at p. 325; Michael A. Rutz, 'The Problems of Church and State: Dissenting Politics and the London Missionary Society in 1830s Britain', *Journal of Church and State*, vol. 48, pp. 379–98 (2006), at p. 379 (n. 1). Under the Parliamentary Test Act, 1678, similar requirements were imposed on members of Parliament. Campbell, id., at p. 11.

7. Campbell, id., at p. 14; Laura Zwicker, 'The Politics of Toleration: The Establishment Clause and the Act of Toleration Examined', *Indiana Law Journal*, vol. 66, pp. 773–800 (1990–91), at p. 781.

8. Campbell, id., p. 17.

9. Id., p. 17.

10. See, 'Blackstone's Commentaries on the Laws of England', *The Avalon Project*, Yale Law School, available at: http://avalon.law.yale.edu/subject_menus/blackstone.asp (last visited 2 January 2018).

11. Ibid., Book 4, Chapter 4.

12. Campbell, 'Oaths and Affirmations of Public Office under English Law', p. 18. Jonassen, 'So Help Me?'.

13. Campbell, id., p. 19. See further, 'Comment', *Quis Custodiet?*, vol. 29 (1970), pp. 178–80, at pp. 178–79.

14. Id., p. 20.

15. Id., p. 21.

16. Id., p. 21; Jonassen, 'So Help Me?'.

17. Robert Norman et al, 'Benjamin Disraeli', *Encyclopedia Britannica*, available at: https://www.britannica.com/biography/Benjamin-Disraeli (last visited 2 January 2018).

18. Text available at: https://www.legislation.gov.uk/ukpga/Vict/31-32/72/contents (last visited 2 January 2018).

19. Text available at: https://www.legislation.gov.uk/ukpga/Vict/29-30/19/contents/enacted (last visited 2 January 2018). See further, Chris Sear, 'The Parliamentary Oath', Research Paper 01/116 (2001).

20. Ivermee, *Secularism, Islam and Education in India, 1830–1910*, p. 34. The full text of the Universities Tests Act is available at: http://www.legislation.gov.uk/ukpga/1871/26/pdfs/ukpga_18710026_en.pdf (last visited 12 May 2019).

21. Text available at: https://archive.org/stream/righttoaffirmins31brad #page/n1/mode/2up (last visited 2 January 2018). The Oaths Act, 1888, applied to all oaths, not merely judicial oaths. Sidney L. Phipson (ed.), *The Principles of the Law of Evidence* (London: Sweet & Maxwell, Ltd, 1922), available at: https://babel.hathitrust.org/cgi/pt?id=umn.31951d005500810;view=1up;seq=197 (last visited 1 January 2018), at p. 158.

22. 'Charles Bradlaugh', *Encyclopedia Britannica*, available at: https://www.britannica.com/biography/Charles-Bradlaugh (last visited 2 January 2018); 'Celebrating the first atheist MP Charles Bradlaugh', *BBC News*, 14 November 2016, available at: http://www.bbc.com/news/av/uk-politics-37976044/celebrating-the-first-atheist-mp-charles-bradlaugh (last visited 2 January 2018); 'Bust of Charles Bradlaugh MP unveiled in Portcullis House', 2 November 2016, available at: https://www.parliament.uk/about/art-in-parliament/news/2016/november/bradlaugh-bust-unveiled/ (last visited 6 September 2019).

23. Campbell, 'Oaths and Affirmations of Public Office under English Law', p. 27.

24. Ibid., at p. 28.

25. Third Schedule, Constitution of Pakistan. Available at: http://na.gov.pk/uploads/documents/1333523681_951.pdf (last visited 2 January 2018). However, the Constitution of Pakistan does not seem to offer any option to other oath-takers to make an affirmation instead of swearing an oath.

26. Text available at: https://archive.org/details/letterspatentes00walegoog (last visited 2 January 2018).

27. Ibid., at p. 36.

28. Section 37, 'An Act for improving the Administration of Criminal Justice in the East Indies' (available on Google Books).

29. However, under the 1833 Charter Act, members of the 'Secret Committee' appointed by the Court of Directors of the East India Company had to take an oath which ended with the line 'So help me God'.

30. Section 87, Charter Act, 1833.

31. 'An Act for the more extensive employment of Uncovenanted Agency in the Judicial Department'. Act XV of 1843. (Available on Google Books).

32. Act No. XII of 1856. Available at: https://archive.org/details/dli. bengal.10689.19441/page/n319 (last visited 6 September 2019).

33. Civil court amins were like today's court commissioners.

34. Act IV of 1866, available at: https://babel.hathitrust.org/cgi/pt?id=hvd. hl466h&view=1up&seq=729 (last visited 6 September 2019).

35. Act II of 1869, available at: https://babel.hathitrust.org/cgi/pt?id=hvd. hl47mc&view=1up&seq=78 (last visited 6 September 2019).

36. Acts IV and VI of 1871, available at: https://babel.hathitrust.org/ cgi/pt?id=hvd.hl466u&view=1up&seq=23 (last visited 6 September 2019).

37. Section 3, Act VI of 1872, available at: https://babel.hathitrust.org/ cgi/pt?id=hvd.hl466t&view=1up&seq=202 (last visited 6 September 2019).

38. Section 16, Indian Oaths Act, 1873. Available at: https://babel. hathitrust.org/cgi/pt?id=mdp.35112204357356&view=1up&seq=95 (last visited 2 January 2018).

39. Available at: http://www.legislation.gov.uk/ukpga/1935/2/pdfs/ ukpga_19350002_en.pdf (last visited 6 September 2019).

40. Earlier, on 23 July 1947, D.B. Chandrasekharaiya had made a speech requesting that the President take an oath, noting that the Irish Constitution required an oath to be taken '[i]n the presence of Almighty God', and that it ended with the line '[m]ay God direct and sustain me.'

41. The October 1947 draft of the Constitution, in the Third Schedule, contained oaths of office which ended with the line 'So help me God'. However, the February 1948 draft of the Constitution, in the Third Schedule, contained no such line, and the word 'God' did not find a place in the oath of office. B. Shiva Rao (ed.), *The Framing of India's Constitution: Select Documents* (Delhi: Universal Law Publishing Co. Pvt. Ltd, 2012 reprint), vol. 3, p. 106.

42. Tyagi hailed from the United Provinces. He was later a three-term member of the Lok Sabha (1952–57, 1957–62, 1962–67), and a member of the Rajya Sabha (1970–76). He served as Union minister of finance, defence and rehabilitation (1953–66). See, profile on the website of the Rajya Sabha, available at: https://rajyasabha.nic.in/rsnew/pre_member/1952_2003/t.pdf (last visited 19 May 2019).

43. Speech of Mahavir Tyagi in the Constituent Assembly (27 December 1948).

44. Abraham Vazhayil Thomas, *Christians in Secular India* (Cranbury: Associated University Presses, 1974) (available on Google Books), p. 62.

45. The Hindi text was available at: http://lawmin.nic.in/olwing/coi/coi-hindi/coi-indexhindi.pdf (last visited 3 January 2018).

46. *Madhu Parumala v. Speaker, Kerala Legislative Assembly*, (2006) SCC OnLine Ker 230 (DB) (paragraph 8). The court disagreed with a view taken by it earlier, in *Haridasan Palayil v. Speaker,* (2003) SCC OnLine Ker 97 (DB), where an oath in the name of 'Sree Narayana Guru' was held to be illegal, and where it was held that an oath had to be taken in the name of 'God' alone and none else.

47. *Kamal Nayan Prabhakar v. Union of India*, (2011) SCC Online Jhar 946. The Special Leave Petition [SLP (C) 033099 of 2011] was dismissed on 12 December 2011 through a speaking order. See further, 'SC: Oath in Allah's Name Not against Constitution', *Times of India*, 13 December 2011, available at: https://timesofindia.indiatimes.com/india/SC-Oath-in-Allahamp39s-name-not-against-Constitution/articleshow/11088858.cms (last visited 3 January 2018).

48. Ambedkar tried to make the affirmation the first option, while the oath in the name of God the second option. Amendments were introduced to reverse the order.

49. Speech of Sardar Bhopinder Singh Man in the Constituent Assembly (26 August 1949).

50. Prasad later served two terms as a member of the Lok Sabha (1952–57, 1957–62). See, profile on the website of the Lok Sabha, available at: http://loksabhaph.nic.in/writereaddata/biodata_1_12/638.htm (last visited 19 May 2019).

51. Third Schedule, Constitution of India.

52. Speech delivered on 14 August 1947.

53. Speech delivered on 26 May 1949.

54. Bharati was an advocate and legislator. See, T. Saravanan, 'The staircase to freedom', *The Hindu*, 22 December 2011, available at: https://www.thehindu.com/features/metroplus/the-staircase-to-freedom/article2738371.ece (last visited 19 May 2019).

55. Speech delivered on 6 December 1948.

56. Speeches of Jerome D'Souza on 21 January 1947 (complaining that the word 'God' found no mention in the Objectives Resolution); Lala Raj Kanwar on 6 November 1948; Pandit Govind Malaviya on 8 November 1948; and K.M. Munshi on 27 December 1948.

57. Rao, who hailed from Andhra Pradesh, later served two terms in the Lok Sabha (1957–62 and 1962–67), served as deputy minister of food and agriculture in the central government (1950–52) and as lieutenant governor of Vindhya Pradesh (1956). See, profile on the website of the Lok Sabha, available at: http://loksabhaph.nic.in/writereaddata/biodata_1_12/1333.htm (last visited 19 May 2019).

58. See, 'Chief Ministers since 1957', Official Web Portal, Government of Kerala, available at: https://kerala.gov.in/chief-ministers-since-1957 (last visited 19 May 2019).

59. Dr Hriday Nath Kunzru hailed from the United Provinces. He later served two terms in the Rajya Sabha (1952–56 and 1956–62). See, profile on the website of the Rajya Sabha, available at: https://rajyasabha.nic.in/rsnew/pre_member/1952_2003/k.pdf (last visited 19 May 2019).

60. A similar amendment moved by Shibban Lal Saksena was withdrawn.

61. (1994) 3 SCC 1 (Para 184).

62. James E. Pfander, 'So Help Me God: Religion and Presidential Oath-Taking', *Constitutional Commentary*, Volume 16 (1999), pp. 549–53, p. 550.

63. Jonassen, 'So Help Me?', at p. 368.

64. This provision was introduced by Charles Pinckney of South Carolina. Id., p. 331.

65. Id., p. 327.

66. Id.

67. John Murdoch (ed.), *The Indian Missionary Manual: or, Hints to Young Missionaries in India* (Madras: United Scottish Press, 1864), at p. 80; Thomas Babington Macaulay, *Critical and Historical Essays, Contributed to the Edinburgh Review*, fifth edition, vol. 3 (London: Longman, Brown, Green, and Longmans, 1848) (available on Google Books), at pp. 345–46.

68. These apart, a witness may be inclined to tell the truth due to indolence (i.e. it is easier to tell the truth than to tell a lie), and fear of disgrace. Eugene R. Milhizer, 'So Help Me Allah: An Historical and Prudential Analysis of Oaths as Applied to the Current Controversy of the Bible and Quran in Oath Practices in America', *Ohio State Law Journal*, vol. 70, pp. 1–71, at p. 5 (2009). *See further*, Binyamin A. Blum, 'Evidence Rules of Colonial Difference: Identity, Legitimacy and Power in the Law of Mandate Palestine, 1917–1939' (Doctoral Dissertation, Stanford Law School, December 2011).

69. Schedule, Oaths Act, 1969.

70. Jonassen calls this the 'testamentary or assertatory oath'. 'So Help Me?', at p. 310. He calls the official oath the 'promissory or loyalty oath', 'of which the oath of office and the oath of allegiance are types'.

71. Thomas Starkie Esq., *A Practical Treatise of the Law of Evidence* (Philadelphia: T. & J.W. Johnson & Co., 1860), available at: https://babel.hathitrust.org/cgi/pt?id=uc1.b4234623;view=1up;seq=82 (last visited 1 January 2018), p. 26.

72. That is not to say, however, that the testimony of 'native' witnesses was considered to have high probative value in British India. As we will see in this chapter, colonial officials believed that Indian 'native' witnesses often lied.

73. Andrew D.E. Lewis, et al., 'Common Law', *Encyclopedia Britannica*, available at: https://www.britannica.com/topic/common-law#ref465717 (last visited 1 January 2018). Coke, however, died in 1634. 'Sir Edward Coke', *Encyclopedia Britannica*, infra.

74. Coke served as the chief justice of the Court of Common Pleas since 1606. In 1613, he was made the chief justice of the Court of King's Bench. He served as a member of the Privy Council and judge of the Court of Star Chamber. Gareth H. Jones, 'Sir Edward Coke', *Encyclopedia Britannica*, available at: https://www.britannica.com/biography/Edward-Coke (last visited 1 January 2018).

75. Edward Coke, *The Third Part of the Institutes of the Laws of England* (London: E. and R. Brooke, 1797), at p. 164. Available on Google Books. I have modernized spellings while reproducing extracts from this treatise.
76. Id.
77. 'Henry de Bracton', *Encyclopedia Britannica*, available at: https://www.britannica.com/biography/Henry-de-Bracton (last visited 1 January 2018).
78. Coke, *Institutes*, fourth part, available at: https://archive.org/details/fourthpartofinst04coke (last visited 1 January 2018), p. 279.
79. Thomas Peake, *A Compendium of the Law of Evidence* (Philadelphia: P. Byrne, 1806), available at: https://babel.hathitrust.org/cgi/pt?id=nyp.33433008477287;view=1up;seq=163 (last visited 1 January 2018), p. 141.
80. Id., pp. 140–41.
81. Arthur Mitchell Fraas, '"They Have Travailed Into A Wrong Latitude:" The Laws of England, Indian Settlements, and the British Imperial Constitution, 1726–1773', Department of History, Duke University, Doctoral Dissertation 2011, at p. 159.
82. Id., p. 100.
83. Id., p. 252.
84. *First Report of Her Majesty's Commissioners* (London: George Edward Eyre and William Spottiswoode, 1856), available at: https://babel.hathitrust.org/cgi/pt?id=hvd.hl4sid&view=1up&seq=59 (last visited 8 September 2019), at p. 53; Elizabeth Kolsky, *Colonial Justice in British India: White Violence and the Rule of Law* (Cambridge: Cambridge University Press, 2011 edition), pp. 112–113.
85. Kolsky, id., p. 112.
86. See, *The Circular Orders of the Court of Sudder Dewanny Adawlut for the North Western Provinces, from 1795 to 1855 inclusive* (Agra: Secundra Orphan Press, 1856), available at: https://babel.hathitrust.org/cgi/pt?id=hvd.hl3egi;view=1up;seq=288 (last visited 1 January 2018), containing an order dated 15 May 1840.
87. Fraas, 'They Have Travailed Into a Wrong Latitude', p. 252.
88. 1 Atk. 22.
89. *See*, Fraas, 'They Have Travailed into a Wrong Latitude', at pp. 192–93, 322 (note 72).
90. Fraas, 'They Have Travailed Into a Wrong Latitude', p. 321.

91. However, there is some doubt about whether this passage was accurately reported in the Atkins report. See, Thomas Raeburn White, 'Oaths in Judicial Proceedings and Their Effect upon the Competency of Witnesses', 51 *American Law Register* 373 (1903), p. 391.

92. The Letters Patent establishing the Supreme Court is available here: https://archive.org/details/letterspatentes00walegoog (last visited 1 January 2018), p. 13.

93. The Society of Friends was founded by George Fox (1624–91). See, Henry J. Cadbury, 'George Fox', *Encyclopedia Britannica*, available at: https://www.britannica.com/biography/George-Fox (last visited 2 January 2018).

94. Richard T. Vann, 'Society of Friends', *Encyclopedia Britannica*, available at: https://www.britannica.com/topic/Society-of-Friends (last visited 2 January 2018).

95. 'Quakers', *BBC*, last updated 7 March 2009, available at: http://www.bbc.co.uk/religion/religions/christianity/subdivisions/quakers_1.shtml (last visited 2 January 2018).

96. Jeremy Bentham, *Swear Not At All* (London: R. Hunter, 1817), at pp. 26-27. See further, 'A Reconsideration of the Sworn Testimony Requirement: Securing Truth in the Twentieth Century', vol. 75 *Michigan Law Review*, pp. 1681–707, at p. 1691 (note 53) (1977). *See further*, Andrea Seabrook, 'Oath of Office: To Swear or to Affirm', *NPR*, 18 January 2009.

97. Katherine Steiner, 'Quakers and the Law', *The Law Bod Blog*, 7 January 2013, available at: http://blogs.bodleian.ox.ac.uk/lawbod/2013/01/07/quakers-and-the-law/ (last visited 1 January 2018).

98. Id.

99. The Act was entitled: 'An Act that the solemn Affirmation and Declaration of the People called Quakers, shall be accepted instead of an Oath in the usual Form'. It is available on Google Books. It was referred to as the 'Quaker Affirmation Act'. It only applied to civil cases (not criminal cases), and did not allow Quakers to serve on juries or hold public office. It was a temporary law, but it was extended in 1702 and made permanent in 1714. Campbell, 'Oaths and Affirmations of Public Office under English Law', at pp. 20–21.

100. White, 'Oaths in Judicial Proceedings', at p. 421; Jonassen, 'So Help Me?', p. 319; Campbell, 'Oaths and Affirmations of Public Office under English Law', at p. 21.

101. 'A Reconsideration of the Sworn Testimony Requirement', at p. 1691 (note 55). The colonial Pennsylvania law was repealed by the British Parliament in 1693. White, 'Oaths in Judicial Proceedings', at p. 422; Jonassen, 'So Help Me?', at p. 320.

102. See: 'An Act to allow Quakers and Moravians to make Affirmation in all cases where an Oath is or shall be required' (1833) (available on Google Books); 'An Act to allow the People called Separatists to make a solemn Affirmation and Declaration instead of an Oath' (1833) (available on Google Books); Jonassen, 'So Help Me?', p. 319.

103. Bipin Chandra Pal, *Memories of My Life and Times* (Calcutta: Modern Book Agency, 1932), at pp. 144–45. Available at: https://archive.org/stream/in.ernet.dli.2015.31015/2015.31015. Memories-Of-My-Life-And-Times#page/n9/mode/2up (last visited 1 January 2018).

104. S.P., 'Repugnance of the Hindoos to an Oath', *The Asiatic Journal and Monthly Register for British India and Its Dependencies* (London: Kingsbury, Parbury, & Allen, 1825) (available on Google Books).

105. Fraas, 'They Have Travailed Into a Wrong Latitude', pp. 349–54. On the refusal of Hindus to take the oath, *see further*, Kolsky, *Colonial Justice in British India*. According to Kolsky, Hindu witnesses objected to taking the oath because of the 'social equality implied in the taking of an oath'. Id., p. 113.

106. Regulation IV of 1793. Described in *First Report of Her Majesty's Commissioners*, p. 53. See further, Regulation L of 1803, available at: https://babel.hathitrust.org/cgi/pt?id=hvd.hl3kmz;view=1up;seq=886 (last visited 1 January 2018).

107. 'An Act for improving the Administration of Criminal Justice in the East Indies'. Available on Google Books.

108. Section 36.

109. For the distinction between 'crown courts' and 'company courts', see, M.P. Jain, *Outlines of Indian legal history*, third edition (Bombay: N.M. Tripathi, 1972).

110. Act No. V of 1840: 'An Act concerning the Oaths and Declarations of Hindoos and Mahometans'. Available on Google Books. The Law Commission's notes on this statute are available in James C. Melvill, *Copies of the Special Reports of the Indian Law Commissioners* (1842), at pp. 256–65 (available on Google Books).

111. Legislative debate on the Indian Oaths Act, 1873, held on 4 February 1873. *Abstract of the Proceedings of the Council of the Governor General of India, Assembled for the Purpose of Making Laws and Regulations. 1873.* (Calcutta: Office of the Superintendent of Government Printing, 1874), available at: https://babel.hathitrust. org/cgi/pt?id=chi.78206287;view=1up;seq=141 (last visited 1 January 2018), p. 115.

112. Section 3, Act VI of 1872: 'An Act to amend the Law relating to Oaths and Affirmations'. Available at: https://archive.org/details/ lawindiavolume00lyongoog/page/n892 (last visited 8 September 2019).

113. Act No. XVIII of 1863: 'An Act to make provision for the speedy and efficient disposal of the business now pending . . .', available at: https:// archive.org/details/in.ernet.dli.2015.501879/page/n277 (last visited 8 September 2019).

114. John Locke, *A Letter Concerning Toleration* (1689), available at: http://www.constitution.org/jl/tolerati.htm (last visited 2 January 2018).

115. *See*, John Pitt Taylor, *A Treatise on the Law of Evidence* (London: William Maxwell & Son, 1878), vol. 2 (available on Google Books), p. 1161; Phipson (ed.), *The Principles of the Law of Evidence*.

116. Evidence Further Amendment Act.

117. Phipson (ed.), *The Principles of the Law of Evidence*, p. 157.

118. Act VI of 1872 and the Indian Oaths Act, 1873.

119. Section 6, Indian Oaths Act, 1873, available at: https://babel. hathitrust.org/cgi/pt?id=mdp.35112204357356&view=1up&seq=98 (last visited 8 September 2019). However, a witness had the option of taking an oath 'in any form common amongst, or held binding by, persons of the race or persuasion to which he belongs, and not repugnant to justice or decency, and not purporting to affect any third person'. Section 8.

120. Law Commission of India, 28th Report, on the Indian Oaths Act, 1873 (May 1965), p. 10, available at: http://lawcommissionofindia. nic.in/1-50/Report28.pdf (last visited 1 January 2018).

121. H.W. Fowler and F.G. Fowler (eds.), *The Concise Oxford Dictionary of Current English* (Oxford: Clarendon Press, 1919), available at: https://babel.hathitrust.org/cgi/pt?id=uc1.b4089277;view=1up;seq=5 (last visited 1 January 2018), p. 354.

122. See, Section 4, Act VI of 1872; Section 8, Indian Oaths Act, 1873.

123. Sir Jamshedji Byramjee Kanga, 'Reminiscences', *in*, *High Court at Bombay: 1862 to 1962* (Bombay: Government Central Press, 1962), pp. 63–91, p. 79, available at: https://bombayhighcourt.nic.in/libweb/ ebooks/BHC1862-1962.PDF (last visited 8 September 2019).

124. White, 'Oaths in Judicial Proceedings', p. 420.

125. Section 5, Act VI of 1872; Section 13, Indian Oaths Act, 1873.

126. James Oldham, 'Truth-Telling in the Eighteenth-Century English Courtroom', *Law and History Review*, vol. 12(1), pp. 95–121, at p. 103 (1994). Similarly, in the US, one author opines that the judicial oath had become 'a ritual without substance'. See, 'A Reconsideration of the Sworn Testimony Requirement', p. 1681.

127. White, 'Oaths in Judicial Proceedings', p. 427.

128. *First Report of Her Majesty's Commissioners*, p. 53.

129. Law Commission of India, 28th Report, p. 7 (paragraph 17).

130. Oaths Act, 1969.

131. Section 5.

132. Section 6.

133. Section 7.

134. Murdoch (ed.), *The Indian Missionary Manual*, p. 49.

135. Id., pp. 194–95.

136. Section 118, Indian Evidence Act, 1872.

137. Available at: http://www.lawsofpakistan.com/wp-content/uploads/ 2014/07/qanun-e-ShahadatOrder1984.pdf (last visited 1 January 2018). However, according to one author, this law made little de facto difference to the British common law which had been enacted in 1872. Aarij S. Wasti, 'The *Hudood* Laws of Pakistan: A Social and Legal Misfit in Today's Society', *Dalhousie Journal of Legal Studies*, Vol. 12, p. 63–96, p. 77 (2003).

138. See, Moeen H. Cheema, 'Beyond Beliefs: Deconstructing the Dominant Narratives of the Islamization of Pakistan's Law', *American Journal of Comparative Law,* Vol. 60, pp. 875–917, p. 886 (2012). However, this author says that the evidentiary requirement of four Muslim male witnesses was never met in any case, that the judgments were based on ordinary evidence, and that the discrimination between Muslims and non-Muslims was therefore 'symbolic'. Id., at p. 887.

139. Smith, *India as a Secular State*, p. 272.